IS HIP HOP DEAD?

IS HIP HOP DEAD?

THE PAST, PRESENT, AND FUTURE OF AMERICA'S MOST WANTED MUSIC

Mickey Hess

PRAEGER

Westport, Connecticut
London

Library of Congress Cataloging-in-Publication Data

Hess, Mickey, 1975-
 Is hip hop dead? : the past, present, and future of America's most wanted music /
Mickey Hess.
  p. cm.
 Includes bibliographical references and index.
 ISBN-13: 978-0-275-99461-7 (alk. paper)
 1. Rap (Music)—History and criticism. I. Title.
 ML3531H47 2007
 782.421649—dc22   2007020658

British Library Cataloguing in Publication Data is available.

Library of Congress Catalog Card Number: 2007020658
ISBN-13: 978-0-275-99461-7
ISBN-10: 0-275-99461-9

First published in 2007

Praeger Publishers, 88 Post Road West, Westport, CT 06881
An imprint of Greenwood Publishing Group, Inc.
www.praeger.com

Printed in the United States of America

∞™

The paper used in this book complies with the
Permanent Paper Standard issued by the National
Information Standards Organization (Z39.48–1984).

10 9 8 7 6 5 4 3 2 1

CONTENTS

ACKNOWLEDGMENTS

The support of a Rider University Summer Fellowship helped me complete this book. I want to thank my colleagues in the Rider University English Department for their support of my work. Also, thanks to all the great students at Rider University, Indiana University Southeast, and the University of Louisville, especially Izzy Marrero at Rider, Stephanie Smith and Eli Lossner at IUS, and Brad Caudill at U of L.

Thanks to my mom, Wanda Hess, for ignoring the parental advisory stickers and buying me so much rap when I was a kid, and thanks to everyone who listened to me talk about hip hop—my friends, family, and professors—a lot of the ideas in this book came from conversations with you: Danielle Hess, Joe Meno, Todd Dills, Susannah Felts, Sean Carswell, Todd Taylor, Mindy Hess, Magan Atwood, Jason Jordan, Mike Smith, Andrew Walker, Oriana Lee, Count Bass D, Bronwyn Williams, Karen Kopelson, Karen Chandler, David Owen, Dennis Hall, Debra Journet, Pam Takayoshi, and Cindy Selfe.

I thank my editor at Praeger, Dan Harmon, for all his work on this book and our next project, *The Greenwood Guide to American Regional Hip Hop,* and my Greenwood editor, Kristi Ward, for her work on *Icons of Hip Hop: An Encyclopedia of the Movement, Music, and Culture.* Earlier versions of chapters in this book appeared in the following journals in different forms: Chapter two in *Mosaic: A Journal for the Interdisciplinary Study of Literature*; Chapter five in *Critical Studies in Media Communication*; and Chapter three in *Popular Music and Society.* I gratefully acknowledge the editors and peer reviewers of these journals for their help in shaping the essays in earlier stages.

Finally, I have to thank some of the artists who provided me with hours of listening that I can call research: Lil Wayne, MF DOOM, Ol' Dirty Bastard, Ghostface, Wu-Tang Clan, Count Bass D, Masta Ace, Redman, Lootpack, Tha Alkaholiks, Beastie Boys, De La Soul, Black Moon, and A Tribe Called Quest.

INTRODUCTION

In December 2006, Nas released his eighth album, *Hip Hop is Dead*. The Queens rapper's provocative album title caused controversy among rap artists and listeners, and led to complaints from Ludacris, Young Jeezy, and Lil Wayne, who claim that hip hop is alive and well in the South. In fact, Ludacris responded to Nas by wearing and marketing a T-shirt that read, "Hip Hop Ain't Dead. It Lives in the South." On December 7, 2006, Southern rapper Young Jeezy got into an on-air confrontation with old-school MC Monie Love, on her radio program on Philadelphia's WPHI-FM: Jeezy argued that hip hop has changed, not died; but Monie sided with Nas, and blamed the content of today's hip hop for killing the culture. She complained that the MCs of today rhyme only about "struggles, street hustling, and coming up." Yet these stories of struggling and hustling along the path to stardom are central to hip hop's appeal, and connect to an important history of success stories in American autobiographies. They show artists actively engaging with the reality that hip hop has become big business, and that its stars often get rich selling stories of their struggle to make it in hip hop. Hip hop is no less political today than in Monie Love's heyday, and its topics are no less complex.

Nas and Monie Love are certainly not the first rappers to lament the death of hip hop. Saul Williams's song, "Telegram" (2004), for example, finds hip hop lying in a ditch, "dead to itself." Williams proceeds to offer hip hop culture a litany of advice on how to revive itself by abandoning consumer-driven rhymes about cars and jewelry, and returning to its roots. Even Southern rap pioneers OutKast declared hip hop dead. On 2001's "Funkin' Around," Dre claims "I'm out here knowin' hip hop is dead," and complains that the average listener can't comprehend this statement. But for Nas to pronounce hip hop dead at the height of its sales and popularity—and at the pinnacle of Southern hip hop's success—points to a number of contradictions, and the new breed of Southern rapper at the top of the charts found the proclamation insulting. For Nas to name his album *Hip Hop is Dead* is a marketing scheme, of course, but commercialism, insincerity, and marketing to the mainstream are exactly what the album attacks.

According to Nas's lyrics, hip hop died because it strayed too far from its origins. Of course, if hip hop today looked and sounded exactly like it did when it began in the early seventies, it surely would not have survived. Although Nas never specifically calls out Southern artists for killing off hip hop, the implication is that hip hop was at its best and most vital when it was contained to the New York City neighborhoods where it began. *Hip Hop is Dead*, like many other nostalgic recordings ranging from Common Sense's "I Used to Love H.E.R." (1994) to Missy Elliott's "Back in the Day (2003)," promotes the myth of a pure, unadulterated form of hip hop that sought to promote hope and celebrate life rather than make money. In one view, this culture never truly existed; and if it did, Nas would have been too young to participate. In another view, this culture still exists today, just as it did in the seventies, in small neighborhood clubs, kids' basements, and city parks. In 2007, the music and culture has expanded beyond New York City; hip hop exists worldwide in local scenes as much as it does on MTV. In fact, the wealth of hip hop scenes and start-up independent rap labels across the globe would indicate that many more people are involved in making hip hop outside the mainstream than possibly could have been involved in the 1970s. Make no mistake; thousands of people today still rhyme for free and out of love for hip hop. If anything, hip hop is more alive today than it ever was.

Nas is the latest in a series of hip hop doomsday prophets, who for three decades have declared that the music and culture is on its last legs. Because hip hop emerged during the waning days of disco, critics originally saw it as a passing fad. On July 12, 1979, Chicago disco jockeys Steve Dahl and Garry Meier held "Disco Demolition Night" at Chicago's Comiskey Park. In response to his having been fired when WDAI changed to an all-disco format, Dahl called for fellow disco haters to come together at Comiskey and demolish disco records. About 50,000 people attended to watch disco LPs destroyed. That date often is referred to as "The Day Disco Died." Three months later, Sugarhill Gang released "Rapper's Delight," recognized as the first hip hop single to reach nationwide radio.

The death of disco is itself debatable, because disco's influence was heard in the 1980s in American dance music and in the emerging European club sound. Disco even influenced hip hop: the bassline of "Rapper's Delight" was adapted from a segment of the song "Good Times" (1979), by the disco band Chic. But disco as a style, a movement, and a genre did not survive into the eighties. Hip hop, unlike disco, was more than dance music. It incorporated dance music; the feel-good vibes of 1970s funk, soul, and R&B; and the politics of Gil Scott-Heron and The Last Poets. Critics targeted hip hop's digital sampling much in the same way they had attacked disco's electronic production styles. Sampling's critics, though, took the complaint further to argue that hip hop—because it incorporated segments of existing songs—was unoriginal and inartistic. Despite such criticisms, hip hop prospered. "Rapper's Delight" became a worldwide hit, and as record labels rushed to sign rap artists like Kurtis Blow and Grandmaster Flash & the Furious Five, the music quickly diversified into different subgenres with their own production styles, aesthetics, and politics. The emergence of Def Jam Records group Run DMC in 1983 gave hip hop a hard rock sound that set the stage for the sonic assault of Public Enemy and the gangsta politics of N.W.A. in the mid-to-late eighties.

Hip hop survived comparisons to disco and assertions that it was, in fact, not music. Hip hop developed a culture and a music all its own, with shows like *Yo! MTV Raps*, which debuted in 1988, bringing hip hop to new audiences across the world. As hip hop entered the nineties, however, certain artists, fans, and critics began to argue that it had strayed too far from its origins (an argument that Nas furthers in *Hip Hop is Dead*). Although some criticism was directed at pop crossovers like MC Hammer and Young MC, the particular target of this attack was Vanilla Ice, the white rapper who invented a streetwise biography for himself and outsold any black rapper before him. Ice reminded critics of the way in which white stars like Elvis Presley had taken over rock and roll in the 1950s. Again, hip hop survived. MCs killed the threat of the white rapper by addressing Vanilla Ice in their lyrics and in interviews. As hip hop became a mainstream music form, artists began to devote songs to explaining the distinctions between real hip hop and pop rap, and to target those artists they perceived as fake, or only in it for the money.

Hip hop has faced several threats to its culture in its thirty-five year history. Rap artists responded to the initial idea that rap music was a passing fad by continually reinventing the music with more complex rhyme flows and rhythms that moved away from the borrowed disco beats of 1970s hip hop acts like Sugarhill Gang to the jazz-influenced sounds of Eric B. & Rakim in the 1980s. With this reinvention came variation in sound and style. The late eighties and early nineties saw the jazzier, Afrocentric styles of New York artists such as De La Soul, Queen Latifah, and A Tribe Called Quest meet with the West Coast gangsta funk of N.W.A. Hip hop expanded from Los Angeles and New York to include regional acts like Miami's 2 Live Crew, Houston's Geto Boys, and Seattle's Sir Mix-a-Lot, among many others. With this dissemination came more variation, and the development of regional sounds, styles, and slang.

With this history of variation in mind, it is easy to look at hip hop's story as one of evolution. But what is most interesting about hip hop is the emphasis its artists place on knowing and maintaining connections to hip hop's origins. Many MCs devote lyrics to defining their unique musical styles, criticizing biters who steal lyrics or rip off rhyme styles, giving credit to those artists who came before them, and calling out artists whom they perceive as fake. Yet even as rappers call out those artists who are in it only for the money, they also brag about how much money they make from their own music, which they claim stays truer to hip hop's original aesthetic. As hip hop evolved, new artists consistently sought to invent their own new style while calling attention to their roots in the old school. This balance between old and new is at the heart of debates about what constitutes real hip hop, and it is at the heart of the debates between Nas and Lil Wayne, and Young Jeezy and Monie Love.

Hip hop has been America's most wanted music, both in terms of sales and as the target of censorship. With its simultaneous focus on invention and tradition, hip hop has survived sampling lawsuits, FBI boycotts, Supreme Court obscenity hearings, mixtape raids, parody of the culture, pop crossovers, and the threat of white rappers taking over the music. How has hip hop continued to survive and thrive? By attending to these issues in lyrics. Hip hop lyrics tell the story of hip hop, from reporting shady dealings with record labels to reminding us of the music's pioneers, like Nas does on "Where Are They Now?" (2006) and Edan does on "Fumbling over Words that Rhyme" (2005). MCs use their lyrics to hold each other accountable to the ideal of hip hop culture as an art form, whether done for love or for money. Disputes rage on between major label rappers and independent or underground hip hop artists about what constitutes *real* hip hop, and this debate keeps hip hop alive.

Nas's *Hip Hop is Dead* is important because it furthers this debate, but his critique of hip hop falls short in taking any action to correct the problems he identifies. On "Where Are They Now?," Nas provides a litany of forgotten rappers, and laments the fact that they are missing from today's limelight. Yet none of these old-schoolers appear on Nas's album. Instead, his guest stars are Kanye West, Snoop Dogg, and The Game, three of the music's most visible, best-selling stars. Rather than simply complain that listeners have forgotten classic talents like MC Shan and MC Ren, Nas is in the position to offer these MCs a hand up by bringing them back into the studio and having them guest on what promises to be a top-selling album. Kanye West helped revitalize the career of Twista, a Chicago MC whose sales had faltered since the early 1990s, by having him guest on 2004's "Slow Jamz." Dr. Dre helped boost the career of Los Angeles rap pioneer King Tee by signing him to his Aftermath label and having him guest on his album *Chronic 2001* (1999). Such efforts are a much more genuine way to honor hip hop's history and call new attention to those MCs who paved the way for Nas, Dre, and Kanye. Yet even Nas's small effort does introduce his listeners to earlier rap artists, which is crucial to keeping hip hop alive. The importance that many rappers place on paying respect to hip hop's originators and making younger listeners aware of the music's history is one thing that keeps hip hop alive. Artists hold themselves accountable to tradition, and give credit where credit is due, but Nas is in a position to do more than complain about forgotten rappers by offering them guest spots on his album.

In another contradiction, *Hip Hop is Dead* draws a line between real hip hop and commercialism, yet Nas's debut album, 1994's *Illmatic*, was released on Columbia Records, a major label, and so were his seven subsequent albums, including *Hip Hop is Dead*. Although Nas has recorded music independently, via unofficial releases like *Stillmatic Freestyle* (2001) that he circulates directly to radio stations and hip hop clubs, there is no question that Nas is a commercial recording artist. Still, Nas places hip hop's contradictions between culture and commerce at the heart of his death pronouncement. On the title track, "Hip Hop is Dead," Nas embodies these same contradictions: first, he complains that today's rappers all sound alike and have standardized rap in order to sell more records, then, on the same song, he boasts that his face was plastered on Sony's trucks to promote his album, and brags about making millions of dollars for Sony. In these contradictions, Nas's assessment of present-day hip hop pines for a "good old days" that never existed, and ignores a grassroots, independent, underground hip hop scene that exists as much today as it ever did.

Hip hop always embodied contradictions between making music and making money. Sugarhill Gang's "Rapper's Delight" is blamed for taking rap music out of New York City communities and selling it to the masses, but six years earlier—in 1973, the year that marks the invention of hip hop—Kool Herc, the culture's founding father, envisioned hip hop as a way to corner the market on block parties. Herc took music out of Manhattan disco clubs and brought it to Bronx neighborhoods, plugging his sound system into city lampposts and hosting block parties. Yet for all his desire to use music to bring people together, Herc did charge admission to his parties. Unable to make enough money as a club DJ, Herc wanted to own his sound system and not lose a cut of his money to club owners and concert promoters. Instead, the proceeds from his block parties went directly into his pockets, and he used it to improve his sound system, ensuring that Kool Herc's block parties remained better attended than those of his competitors.

Hip hop began with Herc's intent to make money while taking control of his music, and these values of profit and control still exist in the music today. Where today's Southern rappers differ from Kool Herc is that they state their financial agendas directly, and make them a topic in their lyrics, a development that Monie Love has criticized. Lil Wayne, for example, and his label Cash Money Records, make no qualms about their intent to get rich, but to get rich outside the corporate ladder system of the middle-class. Instead, they want to own their master recordings, own their record label, and control the production and promotion of their music.

The hip hop work ethic is best exemplified in the hustlin' and grindin' mentality of artists from New Orleans's Cash Money Records and Houston's Swisha House label. The hustle grows out of using street smarts to find ways to make money outside the system. Hustling has been a part of hip hop's vocabulary from the beginning, as early DJs and MCs were influenced by the 1973 album *Hustler's Convention*, recorded by Last Poets member Jalal Nuriddin under the pseudonym Lightnin' Rod. *Hustler's Convention* influenced hip hop's content and style of storytelling, as it combined poetry, jazz, funk, and toasts to narrate the adventures of fictional hustlers Spoon and Sport. Toasting is a close predecessor to rap vocals; a form of rhythmic storytelling, toasts trace their roots back to African bad man legends, Jamaican selectors and DJs, and prison culture, in which inmates trade boastful stories about their own exploits. Spoon and Sport influenced hip hop pioneers like Kool Herc, who tied his own image to a different kind of hustle: Taking music out of seventies disco clubs and into the streets, where he could control the record selection, the style of the party, and the proceeds. More recently, records like Cormega's *Legal Hustle* (2004) and The Lost Boyz's *Legal Drug Money* (1996), as I'll discuss in chapter two, promote making rap music as a legal way to make a living as an outlaw.

Grindin', the other half of the expression "hustlin' and grindin'," grows out of older expressions like "the daily grind" and "nose to the grindstone," which connote hard work. In lyrics, rap is presented as a renegade endeavor, but to make the hustle productive, you have to learn the rules of the music industry in order to outsmart the corporate executives and manipulate the system to your advantage. Rap artists rhyme about their work to make sure that they are fairly compensated and not signed to unfair contracts like those of several rappers in the eighties, and black R&B stars, rock artists, and studio musicians in earlier decades. Hustlin' and grindin', then, is developing a blend of street smarts and business savvy that allows rap artists to maintain control of their music and make a living as musicians, while maintaining the outlaw identity that makes hip hop so appealing to listeners.

In the end, Nas's message—that we killed hip hop by commercializing it instead of preserving it—and Lil Wayne's agenda—to make music and money on his own terms—are not that far apart. Wayne and Birdman of Cash Money Records exhibit the same individualist, entrepreneurial spirit with which Kool Herc created hip hop. Similar self-styled success stories exist throughout American history, and are closely tied to concepts of the American Dream. The essential structure of this success story can be traced back to Benjamin Franklin's 1791 *Autobiography*. In hip hop lyrics, Benjamin Franklin's name is used mostly in association with the hundred dollar bills that bear his portrait. Puff Daddy's "It's All About the Benjamins" (1997) popularized the slang term in hip hop, and more recently Lil Wayne claims, "Only history I know is Benjamin Franklin," on his 2005 song "Fly Out." When rappers use Franklin's name to signify currency, their songs about making and stacking Benjamins also become an extension of the American self-made man narrative that Franklin laid out in his autobiography, a narrative that extends to the autobiographies of American businessmen such as Henry Ford and Lee Iacocca, and to rap albums like E-40's *Charlie Hustle: Blueprint of a Self-Made Millionaire* (1999).

Franklin laid the foundation for American Dream stories, emphasizing self-examination, the development of virtue, and adherence to a work ethic. His values of thrift, prudence, and diligence established a value system that came to be associated with the American middle class. Yet hip hop, even with all its success, is not a middle-class music. Franklin's prudence and thrift in dicta such as "a penny saved is a penny earned" and "early to bed, early to rise" seem out of place in a genre in which expensive cars and jewelry are status symbols, and late nights in clubs are the standard. Rap artists tend to go for the immediate payoff rather than the long-term investment, but they do rhyme about their career aspirations and business strategies. Hard work is not foreign to hip hop, and artists describe this hard work in their lyrics as they talk about the ingenuity and diligence it took to bring them to the top of the charts.

Slim Thug, Paul Wall, and Mike Jones (who named his 2007 album *The American Dream*) devote song lyrics to describing the hard work that brought them to the top. When Mike Jones tells his listeners to "Work hard, pray and grind, and keep God up on your mind," his advice isn't that far away from Ben Franklin's, but is even closer to the self-made businessperson story of Madam C. J. Walker and the survivalist mentality espoused by Malcolm X. The importance of Malcolm X to shaping hip hop's value system is evident in the numerous references to Malcolm in lyrics from artists such as Ice Cube and Ghostface Killah, and Malcolm's mentality is echoed in the lyrics of Mike Jones above. To hustle and grind is to work hard every day to achieve one's goals, even if that work includes armed robbery and drug trafficking along with practicing the craft of rap. Malcolm's autobiography creates its own version of the American dream, and Malcolm's involvement with crime and drugs along his path to success is similar to the stories heard in some hip hop lyrics. Malcolm's keen sense of his own mortality also is present in hip hop, particularly in the lyrics of Tupac and The Notorious B.I.G., two MCs who—like Malcolm in the end of his autobiography—imagined their own deaths in songs and videos before they were murdered.

Hip hop is distinctly American, and the stories told in its lyrics fit into larger traditions of American success stories like those of the historical figures described above, as well as more recent figures like Oprah Winfrey. In hip hop's version of rags-to-riches, rappers get rich selling stories of their poverty.[1] Even with hip hop's emphasis on getting rich, evidence of social struggle is crucial to establishing credibility. Rap artists must show that their struggle gave them the skills necessary for surviving in the streets and for navigating the music industry without being exploited by record labels. Because hip hop is African-American music and a primary cultural export, its stories become conflated with African-American experience.

Hip hop's representations of racial identity are very much tied to social class. Of course drug abuse, fatherless homes, street gangs, and welfare and housing projects are not strictly African-American problems, nor are they part of the experience of many black Americans. Hip hop's very development, though, has been attributed to the social conditions its pioneers faced in the South Bronx in the 1970s. Rappers often promote their class struggle as key to their legitimacy, and they go so far as to expose the middle-class backgrounds of other artists who claim to have grown up in poverty. The message is that growing up black means growing up poor. The pervading notion is that social disadvantage gives MCs an inimitable quality, and a voice to tell their stories.[2] To develop a hip hop career, artists have to authenticate themselves through stories of social struggle, and MCs get rich selling these stories in their lyrics. Stories of social struggle and the dream of getting rich and famous through rap music are central features of albums from rap artists such as The Game, The Notorious B.I.G., and Jay-Z. The struggle for wealth is central to hip hop success stories, and the artists frame it as black American experience.

In response to this African-American model of the authentic, white artists like Eminem and Nonphixion emphasize their own experiences with poverty and crime as a way to authenticate themselves to black rap artists, and thus gain acceptance with listeners. These white artists argue that poverty, crime, and violence are not exclusive to black experience, and of course they aren't. Ishmael Reed's essay "Airing Dirty Laundry" (Reed 2000) explores the reality of these same social problems in white suburbs, and contrasts this reality with 1990s media representations of black people as part of the political war on drugs, which he calls "a war against black neighborhoods." Reed criticizes black figures who have made their names by exposing black problems, who air blacks' dirty laundry "as if that laundry was unaired" by whites.[3] While the black figures Reed criticizes speak from outside the social conditions they expose, rappers position themselves as representatives of the communities where they grew up. In lyrics, MCs assert that they represent Staten Island, or Linden Boulevard, or the Stapleton Housing Projects. In making themselves avatars for these specific communities, rap artists promote their childhood disadvantage not as dirty laundry, but as an experience that gave them the strength to pursue rap careers and to pull themselves and their families out of those same neighborhoods. Thus, many of the stories told in rap lyrics today are stories of how the MC came to his or her rap career.

My study of hip hop's past, present, and future begins with chapter one, "The Rap Career," which identifies several songs and albums in which hip hop artists trace their paths "from bricks to billboards," "from staircase to stage," or "from Staten Island to the Cayman Islands." These rags-to-riches stories reinforce credibility by reminding listeners that the MCs overcame social disadvantage to achieve their success in the music business. Because hip hop artists use these autobiographical stories of social struggle to establish themselves as "real," I examine the use of the terms "real," "fake," and "phony" in lyrics, and trace the roots of hip hop's emphasis on authenticity.

In chapter two, "The Rap Life," I look at the ways that hip hop career stories redefine rappers' roles in the music industry. I use autobiography studies and African-American literary history to explore hip hop's autobiographical stories and the fictional personae created in the music. I identify two key counterstories ("criminal-to-artist" and "music-as-drug") in which artists use autobiography to justify or celebrate their commercial success by framing it in terms of survival through crime and entrepreneurialism. These narratives counter the history of black musicians exploited by white record executives, as the artists assert their active roles in the production and distribution of their own music.

Chapter three, "The Rap Persona," examines hip hop artists such as Digital Underground and MF DOOM, who complicate hip hop's basis in autobiography as they perform in persona. They split their identities to perform as two or more distinct personalities, using masks, costumes, and different vocal styles to distinguish between the artist and the alter ego. These rappers use their personae to critique the hip hop industry and its focus on marketing the image of the self, often presenting themselves as super villains sent to take revenge on the music industry.

Building from this look at personae, which rappers often borrow from Italian mafia figures, martial arts films, and comic book super villains, chapter four, "Sampling and Stealing," examines the way hip hop identity is constructed through digital sampling. Hip hop artists cut and paste pieces of audio from cartoons, movies, political speeches, and other songs to create different contexts for their own vocals, and to rely on the cultural awareness of their listeners. Chapter four extends chapter two's look at criminal narratives, as it studies the ways lawsuits over digital sampling have led hip hop artists to describe making hip hop music as a Robin Hood story in which rappers steal sounds from the same record companies who refused to grant legal ownership to the black R&B groups that wrote and performed the music. I argue that today's hip hop artists have become very business savvy—they know how to find ways around record industry regulations that prohibit the use of existing material, and this business savvy translates into interesting marketing tactics, such as Dr. Dre's vouching for Eminem as a white rapper who is accepted and respected by his black peers.

Chapter five, "White Rappers," studies the problem white rappers face of framing their biographies within a model of hip hop realness based on the career narratives of black artists. When Vanilla Ice's official artist bio falsely claimed he had come from a ghetto background similar to many of his black hip hop contemporaries, he initiated a backlash against white rappers. More recent white rappers have to contend with the discrediting of Vanilla Ice by addressing their white skin in their music. Eminem, for example, claims that being white made it harder for him to gain acceptance as a hip hop artist, even as it made it easier for him to sell records to white listeners.

Finally, chapter six, "Hip Hop, Whiteness, and Parody," examines the ways that hip hop parodies confront racial stereotypes related to social privilege. The white rapper MC Paul Barman adopts a self-effacing stance in his music to address issues of minstrelsy and whites' attempts to gain hip hop credibility. The white rock group Dynamite Hack addressed concepts of white privilege in the video for their acoustic rock cover of N.W.A.'s gangsta rap classic "Boyz-N-the-Hood." N.W.A.'s involvement with the parodic cover complicates their career as the self-proclaimed "world's most dangerous group."

Each of these chapters takes on a different aspect of hip hop music and culture, but the book as a whole studies the story of what it means to make rap music, and the ways rappers tell this story in their lyrics. Hip hop's metaphors of rap music as a drug promote the idea of making rap music as an outlaw act: It offers opportunities to make money outside the systems of wage labor that put low-income African-Americans at a disadvantage. At the same time, drug metaphors also respresent street-smart entrepreneurialism because rap capitalizes on stories of this disadvantage. The criminal images of rap music often get attributed to shock value and to the marketability of violence, but although images of crime and drugs do sell, rap's criminality goes deeper to critique the processes of making and selling rap music. As MCs write songs about their careers and tell stories of self-styled success, they extend the knowledge they gained in the streets to their interaction with the record industry.[4] In response to that industry's history of taking over African-American music such as blues and rock and roll, rappers promote the very production and distribution of their records as a criminal act that corrects an imbalance in power.

Hip hop's attention to these issues keeps the music and culture very much alive, even as rap sales drop. According to Nielsen Soundscan, rap sales dropped 20.7% from 2005–2006, compared to a 0.5% decrease for country, a 4.5% decrease for metal, and a 9.2% decrease for alternative rock. These numbers do not take into account Internet downloads and file-sharing, ringtone sales, bootleg CDs sold on the street, or the recent revitalization of unofficial mixtapes recorded by major-label artists outside their recording contracts with a label. Mixtapes have become a big business—DJ Drama's mixtapes, featuring major-label artists such as Lil Wayne, Young Jeezy, Rich Boy, and T.I., sell so well that in January 2007 the police, working with the Recording Industry Association of America, raided his office and confiscated four vehicles and 81,000 discs. Still, even with these alternative avenues for circulating hip hop music, the Soundscan records likely reflect some decline in sales.

Yet while this large decline in rap sales has led members of the news media to celebrate the impending death of the music, Nas is making a different argument, and one that accuses the high sales of hip hop albums of killing the music, rather than keeping it alive. If commercialism has killed the original spirit of the music, can declining sales help steer hip hop back to its roots in the underground? In the conclusion, I will return to this question of hip hop's future, and the question of how such a loss in market share will effect hip hop music in the years to come.

THE RAP CAREER

From Scarface's "Money and the Power" (1995) to 50 Cent's *Get Rich or Die Tryin'* (2003), making money is a legitimate goal for rappers, and one that is stated outright in lyrics. This motivation to make money separates hip hop music culture from other forms like punk or indie rock, where monetary success is equated with selling out. In hip hop, money equals power, and making money is celebrated as long as it happens on the artist's own terms. Mike Jones and Slim Thug brag about selling hundreds of thousands of records before they ever signed with a major label. Wu-Tang Clan and Jay-Z boast about maintaining control of their music even as they sign with corporate record companies. Hip hop is big business, and these rappers are entrepreneurs who seek to maintain control of their product, both in financial and artistic terms, using street smarts to negotiate contracts that allow them more control than was granted to earlier black rock and roll and blues musicians. Because of this emphasis on street smarts, hip hop is hostile to rappers who came from privileged backgrounds and didn't have to struggle for their success. Even the wealthiest hip hop artists have established credibility through rags-to-riches stories of the socioeconomic disadvantage they experienced during their rise to fame. In telling these rags-to-riches stories, rappers often juxtapose their childhood poverty with displays of the money they have made through rap music. Rap videos feature tenements and mansions, street corners and penthouse suites, bicycles and limousines. Images of wealth are contrasted with an earlier poverty that authenticates the artist's struggle for success.

This struggle is tied to overcoming a system of racial disadvantage that placed these rappers in ghettos and housing projects. The heroes of songs like RZA's "Grits" (2003) and Naughty by Nature's "Ghetto Bastard" (1991) are born into poverty and struggle to survive by traditional means before turning to crime. Naughty by Nature's Treach says that he started robbing people because, "I couldn't get a job, nappy hair was not allowed."

Masta Killa, in a guest verse on RZA's "Grits," tells listeners "I'm too young, no jobs would hire me legit" before he robs a grocery store to get food. When presented with a lack of educational and occupational opportunities, these rappers forge their own paths by turning this disadvantage into entertainment. They write and sell songs about poverty, street life, and crime. Hip hop developed in some of the poorest sections of the United States, and its lyrics have long reflected the social conditions from which it came: Artists authenticate themselves through their experience of social struggle, and stories of disadvantage give MCs the credibility they need to appear "real" to their listeners. In lyrics, rappers assert that the very qualities of self-reliance and ingenuity they gained growing up poor have helped them forge careers in the music business without leaving behind the ghetto mentality and street smarts that were the impetus for their success. Because this negotiation of race, wealth, and social class is so important to establishing credibility, many MCs devote song lyrics to describing their own career paths.

Lyrics from artists like Jay-Z and The Notorious B.I.G. present achieving a career in rap music as a story of hard work and ingenuity. These artists justify their wealth, success, and celebrity by presenting their careers as a rise from poverty, while Kanye West, who comes from a more middle-class background, devotes "Last Call," the final track on his debut album, *College Dropout* (2004), to telling the story of how he struggled to get the album produced. Here and elsewhere on the album, West tells us he was initially dismissed by Roc-A-Fella Records because of his relatively middle-class background, saw a record deal fall through with Capitol, and nearly died in a car crash along his path to getting his record signed to Roc-A-Fella. Although the types of struggles may vary, each of these stories plays on an archetypal American story of perseverance in achieving one's goals. Rap music becomes a vehicle for self-advancement, but at the same time artists must prove their dedication to preserving hip hop's original culture, rather than selling it out to the mainstream. Through narratives of the hip hop career, artists assert their commitment to an ongoing body of musical work and link their work to agendas of survival, wealth, and philanthropy, which find roots within a larger body of African-American literature. Hip hop lyrics show a unique focus on the artist's role in production and circulation, areas from which popular musicians have traditionally distanced themselves. It is rare to hear a rock or pop star sing about how she secured her record deal. This lyrical attention is framed in response to the threat of appropriation by the music industry. In making their business roles visible, artists reclaim such work as creative and frame themselves as hip hop emissaries to the corporate world. They claim to have maintained the integrity of hip hop culture while at the same time producing a marketable product. Their songs tell the stories of how they came to their careers.

The term "rap career" has entered the hip hop vocabulary recently, but it is used interchangeably with "rap game," a term used in lyrics for more than a decade to describe the hip hop career. Hip hop artists since at least the mid-1980s have highlighted their music's commercial potential in lyrics, album titles, and names of artists and record labels. In rock music, the Mothers of Invention's *We're Only in It for the Money* (1968) and Supergrass's *In It for the Money* (1997) are ironic album titles, yet hip hop artists like EPMD (Erick and Parrish Makin' Dollars) and Too $hort more straightforwardly embrace a financial agenda, and 50 Cent's album *Get Rich or Die Tryin'* portrays making money as essential to survival. The emphasis on wealth and consumerism in commercial rap has overshadowed hip hop's existence as a creative form, and has sparked nostalgia in critics, who long for a purer moment in hip hop as though this focus on material- ism were a new development. Scholarship on hip hop has shifted from reading the music and culture as an expressive community that resisted co- optation, to understanding it as a commercially dominant culture and industry.[1] Earlier scholars theorized hip hop as a resistant art form, yet the music's rise to become the biggest-selling form in the United States has caused more recent scholars to question if an industry as economically dominant as rap music still can be considered resistant.[2] This shift toward skepticism reflects a popular reaction to mainstream rap's heightened focus on materialism since the late 1990s. After all, Cash Money Records is one of the more visible labels of the era, and songs like Puff Daddy's "It's All About the Benjamins" (1997) and B.G.'s "Bling Bling" (1999) would appear to confirm that rap artists are in it only for the money.

Hip hop has drawn criticism from journalists for its artists' focus on wealth and excess. For example, in a 2004 *Atlanta Journal-Constitution* arti- cle, Phil Kloer wrote that "hip hop has gone from a vibrant music that embraced many aspects of life and challenged the world to a narrow, one- way street where popular rappers care only about having the pimpest car, the best intoxicants, the sexiest hotties and money to burn."[3] Yet when critics complain about hip hop's excess, they ignore the fact that many types of artists confront these same issues in their lyrics. Hip hop is unique among popular music forms in the extent to which its artists confront the commercial nature of their music. This critique often takes place within the music *itself.* This attention to the commercial is one of the most vital aspects of hip hop, and though artists cannot escape hip hop's commercial nature (and many in fact embrace it), they critique its position through their unprecedented artistic attention to the stories of their careers.[4]

Hip hop artists authenticate themselves to listeners by describing how they came to their careers, and how their lives intersect with their music. The question of hip hop authenticity relates to both musical style and performer identity. Proponents of "real" hip hop oppose integrating the music with pop styles to sell more records, and "real" MCs must speak as themselves and not take on affectations to enhance marketability. Obviously, though, MCs are in the business of selling records. This shared focus on business and autobiography positions the MC to narrate not only a life, but also a professional agenda that is accountable to the experiences of that life. Hip hop extends black rhetorical traditions that value self-knowledge and knowledge gained from lived experience, as well as traditions of resistance to what R.A.T. Judy calls a history of "dehumanizing commodification" that began with the American slave trade and extends to exploitive systems of wage labor that exist today.[5] Rappers claim that growing up in the streets taught them skills necessary for survival. Hip hop positions the MC as experienced knower, as in Ice Cube's claim "I'm from the street, so I know what's up" on the N.W.A. song "I Ain't Tha One" (1988). N.W.A.'s breakthrough album *Straight Outta Compton* (1988) begins with the spoken disclaimer, "You are now about to witness the strength of street knowledge."

This focus on street knowledge was complicated by the platinum sales of albums such as MC Hammer's *Please Hammer Don't Hurt 'Em* (1990), which spent twenty-one weeks as the number one album in the U.S. Other artists accused Hammer of selling out hip hop because the style of his music and performance were so geared toward pop success. White rapper MC Serch screamed, "Hammer, shut the fuck up!" on 3rd Bass's debut single, "The Gas Face" (1989). A Tribe Called Quest criticized Hammer on "Check the Rhime" (1991), where they call out Hammer by name and state, "Rap is not pop. If you call it that, then stop." Yet even such a pop-oriented album as Hammer's included the track "Crime Story," which served to authenticate him to listeners through stories of his experience in the ghetto.

After hip hop's backlash against MC Hammer and Vanilla Ice (whose racial implications I will discuss further in chapter four), rap artists found it necessary to assert that their own stories of the ghetto were not far removed from their experience or their musical performance. Rap performance shifted from Hammer's colorful costumes, high-energy choreography, and videos set in mansions, to Dr. Dre's denim jackets, weapon-brandishing, and videos set in Compton neighborhood house parties with refrigerators full of forty-ounce bottles of malt liquor. In telling stories of their careers, gangsta rappers assert that they remain criminals even as stars, and maintain the streetwise qualities that make their music so compelling and marketable. When rap performance shifted back to an emphasis on mansions and choreography with the advent of Puff Daddy and Bad Boy Records, these new performances were framed within a distinct gangsta agenda of getting rich. Stars brandished nine-millimeter pistols while sitting in hot tubs, and the message was clear: Rap's street criminals had become its moguls.

This integration of street knowledge with record industry success was inevitable. As hip hop climbed toward its position in 2003 as the biggest selling music in the U.S., artists refused to cede control of the music to industry executives. Several hip hop artists used their songs to warn aspiring rappers of unfair industry practices. On "Check the Rhime," for example, A Tribe Called Quest invokes "Industry rule number 4080 – record company people are shady." Tribe's song "Show Business" (1991) extends their critique of industry practices to specific labels. Wu-Tang's GZA, who found himself signed to an unfair contract early in his career, recorded "Labels" (1995), a song that opens with RZA's spoken introduction: "You gotta read the label. If you don't read the label you might get poisoned." This critique of the music business is a central feature of hip hop lyrics. Though rap artists want to make money, they don't want to achieve sales at the cost of culture and community, or at the cost of their artistic control over the music. GZA's group Wu-Tang Clan, and other artists such as Master P, laid groundwork in the 1990s for unprecedented artist control in recording and distribution contracts with major record labels. Wu-Tang Clan's lyrics tell stories of the group's struggles to maintain artistic individualism in the face of industry conformity, and describe their work to achieve new levels of artist control. GZA's "Shadow Boxing" (1995) points out the ineffectiveness of the traditional process of new artists shopping their publicity headshots and demo tapes to record execs, and urges new artists to follow his example by taking charge of their careers: "You must break through, like the Wu, unexpectedly." Rather than market themselves to record companies with publicity photos and demo tapes, Wu-Tang built an audience through touring and selling independently-produced CDs "out the trunk" at their shows, and then used their established fan base to negotiate more artist control in their contract with a corporate record label. Wu-Tang members RZA and GZA, who had earlier record deals as solo artists Prince Rakeem and Genius, claim that those earlier experiences helped them study the industry's annexation of hip hop, and that now they understand ways to manipulate a pliable music industry, and to maintain more control of production. Selling records and selling out become two very different concepts as Wu-Tang celebrates entrepreneurship and the manipulation of industry business practices to the artist's advantage.

A more skeptical reading finds that the freedom Wu-Tang enjoys is an illusion, and that record companies allow rap artists a modicum of control, or the illusion of control, in order to keep them happy and ultimately make more money from their work.[6] This skepticism is not limited to critics from outside hip hop. In 2004, Mos Def parodied Jay-Z's "The Takeover" (2001) a song that claims that "we runnin' this rap shit." Jay lists himself and his Roc-A-Fella labelmates Freeway and Memphis Bleek, as those in charge of hip hop, but Mos Def's parody "The Rape Over" (2004) instead lists major corporations like Viacom (the parent company of MTV) and AOL/Time Warner as those who run rap. In Mos Def's view, rappers rush to sell themselves out to these corporations. Yet the true power of Mos Def's parody is that he, himself, is a major-label recording artist. In fact, his label, Geffen, was started with funding from Warner Brothers Records, which is now a part of AOL/Time Warner, one corporation he mentions by name in the song. Warner Brothers Records had a history of artists, who, unhappy with how the label treated their contracts, staged public battles with Warner (Frank Zappa in the 1970s, and Prince in the 1990s). Not to exclude his own career from scrutiny, Mos Def preserves the first-person plural "we" from Jay-Z's original song, and thereby includes himself in his criticism of rap stars who sell their souls to multinational media conglomerates, rather than take them over.

Stories of shady record executives have existed in hip hop since the late 1980s, with songs like 3rd Bass's "The Gas Face" (1989) and A Tribe Called Quest's "Check the Rhime" and "Show Business" (1991), which expose industry practices and warn rappers to watch their backs. Since the late 1990s, however, artists like Wu-Tang Clan, Slim Thug, MF DOOM, and Jay-Z have taken this critique further to claim to have beaten the record execs at their own games. On "I Ain't Heard of That," (2005) Slim Thug, who claims he sold a hundred thousand records recording for Houston's independent Swisha House label, describes demanding a bigger advance for his first major-label album. Slim says he secured more money for his advance than most rappers make from sales, and that he made Geffen and Interscope Records "pay for all the days I was livin' in hell." Masta Ace takes this concept of rappers strong-arming record executives to a physical level in his song "The Ways" (2004), where Ace claims to know rappers who got signed to record labels by threatening the staff with weapons. The song is a revenge fantasy in which rappers menace label executives, but Ace connects the fantasy to the real-life examples of Keith Murray, Diddy, and Suge Knight, members of the rap community who have been charged with assault and battery. In 1995, Murray was sentenced to a five-year prison term for his assault on show promoters at a Connecticut nightclub. In 1997, Diddy was arrested for assaulting Interscope Records executive Steve Stoute, after he refused to shelve a music video with which Diddy was unhappy. Suge Knight is rumored to have used violent threats to coerce Vanilla Ice into signing over his publishing rights to his hit "Ice, Ice Baby" (1990) and to coerce Eazy-E into releasing Dr. Dre from his contract with Ruthless Records. Ace contextualizes these violent acts within America's history of violence and intimidation: "Just ask the Indians or the African slaves," he says, and he urges rappers to use violence to counter the record industry's role in this history of exploiting minorities.

The power struggle between rap artists and record executives is a topic of several hip hop songs, and the question of whether rap is a "take over" or a "rape over" remains. The different perspectives on who controls hip hop music speak to a larger issue of how theories of industry exploitation may ignore the work black artists and businesspeople have done to make hip hop the commercial force that it has become. This question is complicated by the fact that hip hop artists often present themselves as entrepreneurs who engage with a record industry that was built, at least in part, by white rock and roll covers of songs by black R&B groups in the 1950s (Mos Def's most revealing line in "The Rape Over," in fact, is "all white men are runnin this rap shit," which touches on a subject of white-black interaction that I will explore further in chapters 5 and 6). This history of white record executives annexing black sounds contextualizes hip hop's resistance to industry appropriation, and artist-entrepreneurs often use their lyrics to convince listeners that they have maintained their integrity while making money from their music. The reality of who controls rap is impossible to determine, but skeptical readings that see rappers as victims of exploitation rob hip hop of the credit it deserves for its lyrical critique of the individual's interaction with the music industry, and for the ways artists like Wu-Tang Clan have gone beyond critique, and negotiated contracts that offer greater levels of artist control over production and distribution. Whether an artist like Jay-Z believes he has taken control of his music, or an artist like Mos Def believes he is selling himself out to

Warner Brothers, what these artists share is an interest in using their lyrics to critique the way the record industry works.

Hip hop critiques corporate entertainment, and presents hip hop artists both as outlaws and savvy participants in the business of producing commercial music. Hip hop artists want to change the record industry by taking it over. Several artists have become label CEOs: Dr. Dre with Aftermath Records, Jay-Z with Roc-A-Fella and Def Jam, Master P with No Limit Records, and Scarface with Def Jam South. These new roles are explored in lyrics. Dr. Dre rhymes about scouting and signing new talent on *Chronic 2001*. Jay-Z's *The Black Album* (2003) asserts his active role in selling his own music, and connects his business agenda to his creativity and to financial survival and philanthropy. Throughout *The Black Album*, Jay-Z reminds listeners that it was not just musical skill, but also his business savvy that helped him reach his position in the industry, and he critiques the industry's marketing practices in lines like "Rap mags try and use my black ass so advertisers can give 'em more cash for ads" ("99 Problems," 2003). Essentially, Jay-Z justifies his platinum sales through his own role in marketing and distribution, arguing that his control over the business side of his music confirms his extension of street knowledge to his position as label CEO.[7]

The opposing concepts of music industry success and fidelity to hip hop culture can create a doubleness for the performer who finds himself accountable to both realms. To maintain his credibility, Jay-Z must be careful in lyrics to narrate his industry position through its accountability to hip hop's origins *outside* the industry. Key dimensions of real hip hop center on remaining true to concepts of a culture that existed before 1979, when Sugarhill Gang's "Rapper's Delight" became a crossover pop hit and sold platinum worldwide.[8] This precommercial culture of hip hop is characterized as African-American, poor, and urban, and focused on musical skills in live performance rather than recordings. Hip hop realness is negotiated through connections to hip hop's origins, whether via geographic proximity to the New York boroughs where the culture originated, through connections to artists who were important players in the creation of the culture, or through emphasis on skills in performing live rather than selling records. Commercial artists, though, have to maintain sales in order to keep their record contracts, and at the same time connect their performance to this conception of hip hop culture.

A theory of hip hop's conflicting concerns of creativity and commerce, or skills and sales, reframes W. E. B. Du Bois's concept of double-consciousness in commercial terms, as artists work to produce marketable music for mainstream listeners, yet at the same time to maintain a necessary level of accountability to the music's cultural origins. While Du Bois described the self-perception versus societal perception of the American Negro at the turn of the century, hip hop double-consciousness finds the rap artist caught between the personal and the commercial: rappers are expected to present a sincere and verifiable self on commercial recordings. Speaking to this double-consciousness, Paul Gilroy situates rap music as one of a series of modern black cultural forms that draw special power from "a doubleness" through artists' understanding of their practice as "autonomous domain," and of "their own position relative to the racial group and of the role of art in mediating individual creativity with social dynamics."[9] Christopher Holmes Smith, illustrating a further doubleness for rap music, positions the ghetto as both crucial signifier of authenticity and a marketable aspect of self, arguing that the ghetto becomes "simultaneously commodity and safe-haven" as MCs market themselves through narratives of their place as other within mainstream culture.[10] I would extend these readings to argue that MCs also address their place within the music industry through career narratives that plot the individual's movement between the worlds of the ghetto and music industry. In lyrics, top-selling MCs often narrate their own struggles from two perspectives, pre- and post-stardom. They claim that socioeconomic hardships helped shape their creativity, but they also represent their interaction with the music industry as a different kind of social dynamic, one that Wu-Tang Clan and Jay-Z claim to understand so well that they can negotiate greater control over their artistic production.

The debate over hip hop's industry position takes place not only in scholarship, but in lyrics. Hip hop artists critique and revise the work of their contemporaries, and hold them accountable to hip hop's origins. Rap artists write lyrics that justify their relationship with the industry and criticize others for selling out. Both Basu and Mark Anthony Neal argue that hip hop functions as part of the black public sphere, and Neal claims that groups like De La Soul, Common, and Jeru the Damaja have served as "critical vanguards" against the same excesses critics attack: "Arguably, no popular genre of music has been as self-consciously critical of itself as hip hop."[11] Through this self-criticism, hip hop extends the black rhetorical tradition of "Signifying," or responding to a text through critique, imitation, or parody.[12] In revising rap's emphasis on wealth and excess, artists like De La Soul move to create or reclaim a space for their own work as they criticize the commercial spectacle of hip hop. From their first MTV video, "Me, Myself, and I" (1989), a song that "ironized earlier rap posturings by counterposing the popular b-boy stance to 'being one's self,'"[13] De La Soul has challenged commercial representations of the MC, parodying rap's fashion, tough-guy posturing, and conformity to a standardized image of the rapper.

De La Soul's parody works to create a space for the different image they project in their music, and they assert that this different image speaks for their originality and integrity because they do not follow trends. De La Soul is not the lone voice of dissent among rap artists. MF DOOM criticizes the shirtless posturing (and emphasis of visuals over vocals) in recent videos from artists like Lil Wayne and 50 Cent: "Yuck, is they rhymers or stripper males?" ("Beef Rap," 2004). DOOM attacks the commercial spectacle of hip hop as untrue to the art form, and claims that he is concerned more with rhyme skills than publicity, while more commercially successful acts are known less for their vocal performance than for the theatrics that keep them in the public eye. Such criticisms of rap music's commercial spectacle separate hip hop into two camps: the fake and the real. The rhetoric of "real" hip hop developed in response to the threat of industry appropriation, and became prevalent in lyrics as hip hop on the radio and on MTV began to move away from the hip hop aesthetic that artists like DOOM and De La Soul claim to preserve. I use the term aesthetic because these groups do not seek to preserve a specific sound or image they label as hip hop. Instead, these artists promote themselves as musical innovators, who preserve hip hop music by keeping it vibrant and evolving. Real hip hop, then, does not have a certain sound, but instead is an aesthetic by which the artist interacts with the music and the industry. Hip hop's career narratives illustrate this aesthetic and justify this interaction through stories of how the artist became a star.

WHAT IS REAL HIP HOP?

The use of terms like "real," "fake," and "phony" in hip hop lyrics illustrate hip hop's ongoing concern with the real, which necessitates that artists stay true to the notions of hip hop as a culture by establishing autobiographical truth, personal sincerity, and integrity of their performance. The dialogue between "mainstream" and "underground" hip hop artists reveals an ongoing lyrical debate over industry structure, the rap career, and notions of "real hip hop" and "real MCs." There is even a commercial tension between the terms "hip hop" and "rap." Hip hop can refer to a culture that extends beyond music to include graffiti art and b-boying (breakdancing), and can even refer to a lifestyle (as in KRS-One's statement that rap is something you do, but hip hop is something you live), but MCs also use the term "hip hop music," or say "hip hop," instead of "rap," to refer specifically to music. In lyrics, "rap" can be used to mean commercial music, and "hip hop" can be used to mean authentic music, as when Defari warns his listener "Don't mistake this for no pop rap, Pop, but that raw deal feel, that real hip hop" ("Focused Daily," (1998)). Other vocalists make the distinction between calling themselves rappers versus MCs, or *real* MCs. Defari's fellow San Francisco Bay area group, The Lootpack, claims that before listeners can appreciate their CD, they "have to know the difference from a fake MC to a real MC" (*The Anthem*, 1999). dead prez claim to perform *real* hip hop. Other artists use this phrase in lyrics and song titles, such as Das EFX's "The Real Hip Hop" (1995) or KRS-ONE's "Represent the Real Hip Hop" (1995). The term extends to performer identity. N.W.A., Nelly and The St. Lunatics, Jay-Z and Too $hort, The Diplomats, B.G., and Redman all have recorded songs titled "Real Niggaz." Nas claims to be "the last real nigga alive." Eminem reminds listeners that he's "the real Slim Shady."

Concepts of the real and the authentic have long and complex philosophical histories.[14] Scholars have theorized that popular music's concern with authenticity is a strategy to preserve an original culture. Philip Auslander views the 1990 Milli Vanilli lip-synching scandal as a reaction to increasing simulation of the live performance that had been central to rock authenticity. Kembrew McLeod reads hip hop's emphasis on the real as a strategy to preserve the culture as it had existed outside the mainstream. This attempt at preservation created a model of "real" hip hop based on performer identity as well as musical style. For hip hop music, realness centers on avoiding pop structures and the mixing of hip hop with dance, rock, or R&B to reach wider audiences. For the performer, realness centers on the proximity of his or her experience to a model of hip hop as black-created, urban music. Edward G. Armstrong identifies three "initially evident" forms of hip hop authenticity that are argued through being true to oneself, claiming "local allegiances and territorial identities," and establishing a connection to hip hop origins—to "an original source of rap"— through locale, style, or links to an established artist.[15] McLeod maps six semantic dimensions of claims to realness as they respond to the threat of assimilation. Through an extensive study of lyrics, hip hop media, and a series of interviews with artists, McLeod developed an outline of the different terms through which realness is argued. The "deeply intertwined" dimensions he defines are: social-psychological (staying true to yourself vs. following trends), racial, political-economic, gender-sexual, social locational, and cultural.[16] Both McLeod and Armstrong include the concept of being true to yourself as a central dimension of realness, and I argue that it is the dimension most called into question by the artist's interaction with the music industry.

Certain artists have parodied hip hop's representations of black identity, and argue that other rappers' performances of black masculinity are adopted to fit a model of hip hop blackness. In establishing their individuality as a key component of what makes them real, rap artists often use their lyrics to reject a more standardized rap image. In fact, artists often assert their individuality by the very fact that they don't fit in. The Atlanta-based group OutKast was booed by fans from New York and Los Angeles when they won "best new artist" at the 1996 Source Awards, because they made their music distinctly Southern. Their vocals emphasize a Southern drawl and they titled their albums *Southernplayalisticcadillacmusik,* and *ATLiens* (which combines "Atlanta" (the ATL) with "aliens" to comment on their initial lack of acceptance because of their Southern locale and style). Also, in an example I'll explore much further in chapter four, Eminem inverts a racial struggle narrative to show the trials he has faced as a white minority in hip hop. While Eminem emphasizes the poverty of his youth, his lyrics employ a strategy of anticipation as they address the ways that Eminem's identity does not meet traditional concepts of hip hop realness through blackness. Like Eminem's career narrative, the biographies of rural artists like Kentucky's Nappy Roots and white redneck rappers like Tennessee's Haystak and Georgia's Bubba Sparxxx are framed in response to notions of real hip hop as a black, urban form, and these artists emphasize their authentication through McLeod's social-psychological dimension, arguing that they stay true to their own lived experiences rather than following trends by imitating a black, urban identity that lies outside their experience. Through making their white or Southern identities visible, these artists assert that they are staying true to themselves.

The importance of staying true to oneself is evident in many rap narratives. While hip hop is a collaborative and dialogic form, artists cannot represent their geographical community, racial heritage, or the culture of hip hop unless they first establish themselves as unique individuals. The importance of basing lyrics in autobiography is supported by Krims's theory that the hip hop performer must symbolically be collapsed onto the artist, so that when O'Shea Jackson performs as Ice Cube, the experiences Ice Cube reports are accepted as Jackson "speaking from authentic experience."[17] In a broader study of popular music forms, Simon Frith explains the listener's judgment of authenticity as "a perceived quality of sincerity and commitment. It's as if people expect music to mean what it says."[18] Rappers' assertions of their personal sincerity in lyrics are tied to concepts of hip hop as a creative, expressive form that opposes the co-optation of its culture for record sales. KRS-ONE, for example, in "Represent the Real Hip Hop" (1995) claims that his career longevity and his role within hip hop's formative years establish his authority to judge the performance of another artist.

In "Represent the Real Hip Hop," KRS lists creativity, as well as skill in composing and performing, as markers of rap quality. To him, platinum sales prove nothing but marketability; the MC's skills must be proven in live performance. Jay-Z, on the other hand, claims that his marketability is an extension of his creativity as he describes building his label, Roc-A-Fella, into a rap dynasty using the street knowledge he developed growing up in New York City's Marcy housing projects. KRS-ONE focuses on the artistic innovation he considers crucial to hip hop, while Jay-Z includes his skill in *selling* music as part of his innovation as an artist and CEO. As hip hop innovation can take these two forms, Frith's idea of a "perceived quality of sincerity" may be lost, or alternatively enhanced, when an artist articulates his intent to make marketable music. Both KRS-ONE and Jay-Z emphasize their accountability to the communities and culture that created hip hop: KRS-ONE through fidelity to its expressive practices, and Jay-Z through an extension of street mentality to the industry. Both artists assert their realness through the lived experiences that demonstrate their connection to the cultures where hip hop developed. In negotiating their realness with listeners, they narrate careers in which they maintain control of their individual expression even while producing music for industry labels.

As rap artists narrate their interaction with the music industry, many artists currently identify their music as "underground" hip hop to indicate a musical aesthetic that differs from mainstream pop rap. The term "underground" can designate artists who record for independent—rather than corporate—labels, yet even those artists who do record for major labels can align themselves with underground styles, and these artists are able to speak within multiple genres. Redman, a commercially successful artist who maintains underground credibility, distinguishes his fashion style from that of other artists on the pop charts (specifically the metallic suits worn in videos by Bad Boy artists Puff Daddy and Ma$e) when he says "I'm too underground to dance with that shiny shit on" ("Can You Dig It?", 1998). De La Soul, on "Oooh" (2000) also target "shiny suit rappers." As usage of an earlier term, "hardcore," shifted from its original usage (hip hop that stayed true to its musical origins and was not

integrated with pop music) to indicate a harder gangsta style, the term
underground replaced it. As the hardness that had distinguished MCs from
the pop styles of crossover rap had itself become a style that sold platinum
for groups like N.W.A. in the early 1990s, "hardcore" came to represent a
musical subgenre rather than an antimainstream aesthetic. Usage of
"underground" was popularized in the mid-1990s, as a new wave of artist-
run independent labels like Rawkus Records, Stones Throw, Definitive
Jux, Quannum Projects, and Hieroglyphics Imperium began to release
influential albums and define new sounds.

Black entrepreneurs played a key role in the development of the hip
hop industry, yet early black-owned labels like Sugarhill Records and Def
Jam were not artist-run, and by the 1990s, many of hip hop's first wave of
independent labels were annexed by larger corporate labels. During the
1990s, the emergence of new independents like Hieroglyphics and Stones
Throw proved an important moment for hip hop's self-identity, for its
artistic innovation, and for more artist control of production and distribution. The independent labels in this second wave tend to operate not as
smaller versions of the corporate model, but as artist collectives, with in-
house production and hands-on distribution at live shows, and through
mail-order and online sales. This aesthetic of the underground finds precedent in other music forms, like punk and indie, where small independents
have fought for control of their own production and distribution. David
Hesmondhalgh identifies the labeling of an "indie" genre of rock music as
the first moment industry structure had dictated musical style, as independent record labels like Britain's Ten Little Indians created an indie
sound in opposition to the pop charts. This sound has developed in different directions and into various subgenres, and "indie" today has come to
describe a sound that corporate labels also produce. The term now can
stand for either musical style *or* industry structure. This history is similar
to 1990s alternative rock, where a genre that was named for its oppositionality to the mainstream came to so influence that same mainstream that
"alternative" came to designate a subgenre of the mainstream. Yet although
indie and underground styles of music—as well as many of the labels that
create them—ultimately are bought up by the industry, it is inevitable that
new independents rise up to take the place of the old, and to challenge the
mainstream with new sounds that ultimately will influence and change the
shape of that mainstream.

Underground hip hop has challenged and changed not only the sound
of mainstream hip hop, but the role of the artist in producing the music.
In his study of rock music, Jon Stratton argues that popular musicians

historically have distanced themselves from the business side of their careers, leaving their repertoire and marketing to the record executives. Stratton sees the production of popular music flowing in one direction: From artist to A&R (artist and repertoire) man—whose job is to recruit and develop new talent—to company, and then out to press and radio, then to consumers. He cites a tension between creativity and commercialism that leads popular music artists to form oppositional personae even as they produce music for the industry:

> The artist, the innovator, tends to see him/herself in opposition to the industry as a commercial enterprise which appears to be continually pressuring the artist to produce new marketable products. In this situation the artist protects him/herself by mystifying the creative process which is experienced as being distinct from the commercial, capitalist side of the industry which would prefer rational, analysable standardisation.[19]

Stratton's article was published in 1982, before rap had reached its current commercial dominance. Throughout rap music's history of commercial success, artists have taken on active roles in marketing and distributing their music. In addressing these roles in their lyrics, rap artists narrate careers in which they work to recast these commercial roles as creative, and to claim the artist's control over the processes traditionally handled by corporate executives—production, distribution, and marketing. In asserting their active roles in these processes, rap artists reclaim an individual sincerity believed to be lost when record companies disconnect them from the steps between the artist's recording the music and listeners' hearing it. Rather than mystifying the creative process as distinct from the commercial, Jay-Z and other rappers synthesize these processes and make them visible in lyrics.

In his influential essay "The Work of Art in an Age of Mechanical Reproduction," Walter Benjamin theorizes the ways that the artist's role in production affects the audience's reaction to, and relationship with, a work of art. Benjamin argues that mechanical reproductions lack the artist's aura, which can be perceived only in a one-of-a-kind original. Benjamin wrote about the perceived loss of authenticity that comes as art objects are mass produced, and he links authenticity to the existence of the original work from which copies are made. Popular music listeners may be less concerned with the existence of a master recording than they are with their perceptions of the authenticity of the recording artist. As Stratton shows that artists often are removed from the processes of production and marketing, he indicates that popular musicians have lost their control of these processes to corporate executives, and the effects of mass production extend to the creation of the recording, not only to its reproduction. Hip hop's new business models challenge this loss of control as artists move between corporate and independent labels.

A hip hop artist's contract with a major or independent label can play an important role in the way listeners categorize his or her music as "mainstream" or "underground," or even as "rap" or "hip hop." Yet perhaps because of hip hop's emphasis on history and tradition, the hip hop career has proven to be a lengthy one, and an artist may shift between major label and independent. Although indie and alternative rock artists tend to follow a career trajectory that takes them from independent to major labels as their fan bases increase, MCs like MF DOOM, Del the Funky Homosapien, or Count Bass D all recorded their first albums on major labels, and then lost their contracts. Yet each remains active and popular recording for independent labels. As the hardcore or gangsta image became hip hop's best-selling subgenre in the 1990s, MCs performing in other subgenres began to lose their record deals. Count Bass D's live instrumentation and Del's bohemian image and non-violent lyrics no longer found a place in corporate labels' marketing of rap music.

When Del and Count Bass D moved outside corporate recording, they were put in a unique position to critique the business practices of that industry as they took control over the production and distribution of their own recordings. After Sony did not renew his contract for a second album, Count Bass D titled the first CD release from his own Countbassd.com label, *Art for Sale* (1997). The title track's chorus repeats "My record company is jerking me." Since leaving Sony, Count Bass D has released six full-length albums. Though none of his independent albums has received the level of coverage the mainstream press gave his Sony release, he continues to tour internationally and to produce songs and record guest vocals for other underground artists such as MF DOOM and Jon Doe. He also recorded a remix of a Beastie Boys song for their 2003 *Criterion Collection* DVD. When asked in an interview if he'd consider a return to a major label, Count Bass D said "I would love to sign with a major and get dropped again just like the first time. That way, they pay to put my name out there and I just give them one album. I'm still living off of the reputation that experience gave me. Hell yeah I'd do it again!"[20]

Count Bass D offers a counterstory in which artists manipulate the marketing structures of the music industry to their own advantage. Count's career trajectory is similar in this way to Del the Funky Homosapien, who was publicized by his label as the bohemian cousin of gangsta rapper Ice Cube. As gangsta increased its grip on the charts, Del's bohemian style became more difficult to sell. After Elektra released Del's second album, *No Need for Alarm*, in 1993, the label dropped Del from their roster. When Del's fellow San Francisco Bay-area artists Casual and Souls of Mischief also lost their major label contracts around that same time, they worked together to form an artist-controlled independent company, Hieroglyphics Imperium. In lyrics, Del critiques corporate recording, stating "This is real hip hop, not your phoney phranchise" ("Phoney Phranchise," 2000), and criticizing rappers' "brown-nosing in the industry" ("Fake as Fuck," 2000). Del—who began his career writing lyrics for Ice Cube's gangsta protégés Da Lench Mob—uses his lyrics to criticize gangsta rap's aggression and pop rap's consumerism, which he argues hinder lyrical innovation. Within the rhetoric of underground hip hop, artist-owned labels achieve heightened levels of artist control. And in recording outside the influence of industry marketing strategies, artists claim to recover the individuality of their music, making it more real than the standardized corporate product. On "Jaw Gymnastics" (2000), Del rhymes, "This art form is truly in danger, so I change it, never doin' the same shit." It is through this integrity to his own aesthetic, even at times when that aesthetic wasn't selling in the mainstream, that Del maintains his personal commitment to making real hip hop music by continuing to reinvent the form.

Underground artists believe that making real hip hop music does not always make money, and that the agenda of getting rich can stand in the way of making real hip hop music. While The Notorious B.I.G. tells us that his dream of becoming a hip hop star included "lunches, brunches, interviews by the pool" ("Juicy," 1994), Del describes "sleepin' in the lobby in the Day's Inn" ("Phoney Phranchise," 2000)." Another MC, Supastition, wears his poverty as a badge of his underground status, claiming "My last show I barely made enough to pay for gas" ("The Signature," 2003). The focus on money in these lyrics represents more than the underground's reaction to MTV images of champagne parties and Cadillac Escalades. Stories of the rap career are stories about how a music culture that developed in some of the U.S.A.'s poorest neighborhoods has become one of the world's biggest-selling forms of entertainment. As artists tell stories that situate them within this journey from ghetto to industry boardroom, making money has become not only an objective for the rap artist, but a topic of lyrics. Underground artists claim that this lyrical focus on getting rich detracts from the quality of hip hop lyrics.

Criticisms of hip hop excess respond to the displays of wealth that rap artists use to prove they are living like stars. The St. Lunatics' "Real Niggas" (2001) tells a story of driving in expensive vehicles, dressing in expensive clothing, and abusing drugs and alcohol. Each verse describes specific aspects of the group's excess. The chorus of the song positions the group as real niggas, in opposition to the haters—those jealous of their display of wealth. These images of excess have drawn criticism from journalists and scholars writing about hip hop, yet these readings tend to overlook vital criticisms from within hip hop itself. Redman's "I Don't Kare" (1998) makes fun of rappers who dedicate songs to listing their possessions. Count Bass D claims, "I want an IRA, not a woman's bracelet" ("Dwight Spitz," 2002). The Lootpack assert their own realness through artistic originality and skill rather than outward displays of excess; they criticize their mainstream contemporaries for confusing "representin'" with "smoking Phillies, acting ill, getting bent." The St. Lunatics embrace the same lifestyle of excess that the Lootpack rejects, yet their performances share a basis in personal sincerity as each group presents an aesthetic of being real, and describes a lifestyle by which the group adheres to its own aesthetic. The Lootpack frames rhyme skills in opposition to mainstream sales, while the St. Lunatics emphasize the wealth they have gained selling records. This dialogue of skills and sales fits into the larger debate of what constitutes real hip hop, real niggaz, and real MCs. The next section explores the ways the potential for selling records meets with nostalgia for hip hop's origins outside the record industry. The agenda of getting paid has existed since hip hop's formative years, yet critics and MCs both tend to remember these years as an era of creative expression untainted by commercial concerns.

BACK IN THE DAY: HIP HOP'S NOSTALGIA

The concept of authenticity necessarily centers on the existence of an original. For something to be judged as authentic requires an original model with which we can make comparisons. For hip hop music, this model is the era before rap music made it big, the moment when hip hop existed in city parks and house parties instead of on MTV. This era is characterized as a pure moment of creative expression, untainted by concerns of getting rich from the music. In the beginning of this chapter, I referred to criticisms from both music journalists and scholars who understand rap artists' consumerism as a new development and a regression from the creative potential of hip hop's early years. These critics' nostalgia reflects the rejection of consumerism in lyrics from the underground artists I discussed in the previous section. Lyrics from Del and The Lootpack describe an aesthetic that they claim holds truer to hip hop's origins, and they fault "the industry" for corrupting the music. Such nostalgia forms in reaction to the threat of losing hip hop culture to the mainstream.

In telling the stories of their careers, many artists describe their interaction with hip hop culture from a young age, and narrate the changes they have watched the culture endure as it has grown into an industry. These "back in the day" narratives promote rap artists' desires to preserve real hip hop, even as they profit from its marketability in the mainstream. Several hip hop songs depict rap's formative years as less violent, more uplifting, less divisive, and most importantly, untainted by the record industry. Common Sense's "I Used to Love H.E.R" (1994) chronicles the artist's relationship with hip hop music, which he personifies as a romantic interest.[21] The song begins with a picture of Common at ten years old, first meeting a girl who was "old school" and "not about the money," but who soon shifts to a gangsta image she uses to argue her credibility through her connection to street life. Common criticizes, "Stressin' how hardcore and real she is. She was really the realest, before she got into showbiz," and blames the corporate entertainment industry for corrupting what was a pure love for him as a child. The song ends with the revelation that the woman in these lyrics is hip hop personified, and with Common's promise to "take her back" from the industry. Since the release of this song, though, Common has gone on to write hip hop songs for television commercials, most notably his collaboration with R&B singer Mya on "Real Compared To What," a commercial they recorded as part of a 2003 advertising campaign called "Coca-Cola . . . Real."[22]

My examples here illuminate two issues: First, the extent to which hip hop's discourse of realness has entered the mainstream, and second, the contradictions of this discourse's entrance by way of a TV advertisement. Common's "I Used to Love H.E.R." is one of rap music's central self-narratives, and his criticism of rap's commercialization is echoed in songs like C-Rayz Walz's "86" (2003) and Missy Elliot's "Back in the Day" (2003) that call for current artists to take their music back to the old school. The hip hop phrases "the old school" and "back in the day" can refer to a time before the music became commercial, as it does in Missy Elliot's song title. In one verse she asks "What happened to those good old days? When hip hop was so much fun?" Back in the day invariably refers to an era when hip hop was performed at house parties and block parties, such as those organized by DJ Kool Herc, the "father of hip hop." Yet

Kool Herc himself admits a commercial agenda as he charged people to attend his parties and admits his goal to make money.[23] Kool Herc was an entrepreneur, and his version of hip hop history includes profit, community, and fun as legitimate coexisting intentions, while Common and Missy Elliot point us back in the day to a time when hip hop was fun, and was for the people, but not about making money. Yet in emphasizing the fact that he was both promoter and DJ, rather than a DJ for hire by promoters, Kool Herc asserts his control over his own operation. He justifies commercial intent through his entrepreneurship, and through his working outside the system, maintaining artistic control and at the same time making more money than DJs that sold their services to other business entities. Davey D, involved in hip hop since 1977, claims a desire for profit existed from the beginning: "First, from day one people sought to get paid...if the opportunities that exist now existed then...the early 'hip hoppers' would've taken advantage...."[24]

If hip hop events began with a commercial intent, where did the culture experience the shift toward the anti-commercialism of some of today's lyrics? Missy acknowledges that rap has changed, but rap artist KRS-ONE points to one specific moment: "When 'Rapper's Delight' sold two million records in 1979, all the attention was placed on rap music as a selling tool, not on hip hop as a consciousness-raising tool, as a maturing of the community. When hip hop culture got discarded for the money to be made into rap product, we went wrong right there."[25] But for how long did rap exist as a music form unto itself before "Rapper's Delight" hit the radio in 1979? Kool Herc debuted as a DJ in 1973, which would limit "back in the day" to a six-year period during which both Missy Elliot and Common were too young to participate.

Social theorist Jean Baudrillard describes the urge to reclaim media-simulated culture through narratives of creation: "When the real is no longer what it used to be, nostalgia assumes its full meaning. There is a proliferation of myths of origin and signs of reality."[26] Auslander translates this concept to rock music as he argues that notions of rock authenticity often center on the rejection of another form perceived as inauthentic: "rock ideology is conservative: authenticity is often located in current music's relationship to an earlier, 'purer' moment in the mythic history of the music."[27] Baudrillard links such myths of origin to the escalation of the real to hyperreal, to commodified and mediatized images that have become more real than reality. Hip hop's nostalgia calls our attention to current, retrospective, constructions of the pure origins of the culture outside commercialism, and the "back in the day" narratives of top-selling artists like Missy Elliot and Common reflect Renato Rosaldo's notion of "imperialist nostalgia," by which individuals yearn for the culture they have commodified or transformed.[28] Hip hop's nostalgia yearns for a time in which the sincerity of its artistic expression could not be called into question by the marketability of the artistic product, and often emphasizes that era's focus on live performance, which has much more limited potential for circulation than a recording. In practice, nostalgic artists today turn to performance to demonstrate their connection to concepts of this earlier culture, and to assert that their vocal skills are not studio-simulated.

HIP HOP AS A PERFORMANCE CULTURE

Kool Herc and other 1970s DJs were the main attraction at early hip hop parties. They inverted the structure of musical celebrity as the audience paid not to see a performance from the group featured on the recording, but to see the neighborhood celebrities who manipulated those recordings, cutting and looping the best parts of the records into breakbeats, and eventually creating new sounds out of those recordings as DJs Grand Wizzard Theodore and Grandmaster Flash invented techniques of scratching. The DJ's presence was a central part of the performance, and initially the MC's job was to motivate the crowd, to incite them to respond to the DJ's work with the turntables. As MCs began to develop more complex rhymes, their own performance became more of a focus, and became the aspect of hip hop culture that proved most marketable. Today, more than thirty years after Kool Herc first organized his block parties, more rap listeners hear the MC's voice on recordings than in performance. Yet many MCs continue to describe the importance of performing live, and to emphasize that they began their careers performing at block parties rather than in the studio recording booth.

This emphasis on live performance connects with the nostalgia I discussed in the previous section. S.H. Fernando identifies tensions between rap performance and recording as early as Sugarhill Gang's "Rapper's Delight," the group was created by a record label, did not have a history of performing live, and did not write its own lyrics. Grandmaster Caz of the pioneering rap group Cold Crush Brothers claims that a Sugarhill MC stole the "Rapper's Delight" lyrics from him, and he argues that Sugarhill "didn't really represent what MC-ing was or what rap and hip hop was."[29] Because of this mistrust of groups created by record executives, rap vocalists must perform live to authenticate their skills as real MCs. This imperative is not unique to hip hop. In two studies of rock music, Auslander and

Theodore Gracyk agree that rock culture today centers on recording rather than performance. Although Gracyk believes today's rock artists essentially are studio musicians rather than live performers,[30] Auslander argues that live performance still plays a pivotal role in "establishing the *authenticity* of the music for the rock fan."[31] Seeing a band play live can prove that the musicians can play their instruments, and that the singer's voice can exist outside the digitized version heard on a CD. Rock differs from hip hop, though, in that hip hop performance often requires the improvisation of new rhymes, while rock groups tend to play live versions of songs that they have recorded in the studio. Although rock performance does feature improvisation in the form of live jam sessions, rap performance goes further to emphasize freestyle (improvised rhyming) and the MC battle (a competition in which two freestyle rhymers go head to head) as necessary outlets for MCs to prove their rhyme skills outside the studio.

Hip hop radio shows often call on their guests, as commercial recording artists, to freestyle live on the air. Sway and King Tech's "Wake-Up Show" on San Francisco Bay-area KMEL 106, released a CD anthology of the best freestyles from their program, from such rap luminaries as Nas, Tha Alkaholiks, and Wu-Tang Clan. A freestyle performance demonstrates the artist's roots in hip hop as a performance culture, and proves his or her skills in constructing and delivering rhymes outside the studio. While Davey D acknowledges that MCs from the 1970s, such as Melle Mel, Grand Master Caz, and Kurtis Blow, all rehearsed and prewrote much of their freestyle content, he claims what was important in performance was "to present yourself" as if the rhymes were being composed spontaneously.[32] Hip hop culture finds these early performances of spontaneous freestyle rhyme at the heart of its vocal tradition, and many MCs have built careers on their ability to improvise, to adapt the prewritten to the moment of performance, and therefore to compose, in at least some sense, spontaneously. MC Supernatural, for example, has earned a reputation for performance more than for recording, through his use of freestyle in concert. At a July 15, 2000, show in Cincinnati, Ohio, I saw Supernatural invite the crowd to hand him random items that he would incorporate into his lyrical flow without breaking rhythm or rhyme.

An extension of freestyle, the MC battle is a competition in which MCs go head to head to improvise rhymes over music that is randomly chosen and constantly changing. To win points with the audience, MCs must prove the spontaneity of their rhymes. Battle rules often specify "no written." Performers need to reference their opponent's rhymes and to react to the immediate situation in their lyrics to establish skill. The battle is a common feature of hip hop cinema, from the documentary footage of *Style Wars* (1983) to the more recent scripted battle scenes of Eminem's partially autobiographical film *8 Mile* (2002). While Eminem's scenes in *8 Mile* were scripted, they represent the documented success he saw in MC battles like Scribble Jam prior to the release of his first commercial recordings. In the film, Eminem's character B. Rabbit freezes in response to the pressure of improvising rhymes in front of a hostile crowd. In formal competition, rhymers are awarded points judged by audience reaction, and it is crucial to show that these rhymes are at least in some part spontaneous. MCs often are expected to address their opponent directly, and rhyme topics often center on jabs at the opponent's fashion style, rhyme skill, and physical appearance. To further assert the spontaneity of their rhymes, MCs can make references to their immediate situation and surroundings, often creating rhymes that incorporate the name of their opponent and the name of the venue, and referring directly to the rhymes offered by the competitor. The immediacy of detail is central to establishing a performance as freestyle.

It is important to note that many mainstream MCs do not engage in battles, but rather use their career narratives to convince the listener of the success they saw as they performed in battles on their way to the top. Eminem does not participate in battles today, but *8 Mile* works to convince the viewer that Eminem paid his dues in performance on his way to becoming a platinum-selling recording artist. While the battle traditionally is how disputes between rappers have been settled, the practice has become less common among commercial artists, perhaps because they stand to lose credibility, and therefore sales. Yet battles do still occur in the underground, and MTV has organized two separate MC battles over the past two years that invited unsigned rappers to win a recording contract by outbattling their competitors. MTV's involvement proved problematic as Roc-A-Fella Records refused to honor the contract they had promised the winner of MTV's second battle. With the MTV battles, the corporate music industry attempted to simulate a competitive process that *8 Mile* and other hip hop career narratives had presented as a forum through which MCs had paid their dues in establishing their skills in vocal performance, and fought their way up the ladder to success in the mainstream. As MTV attempted to simulate this process and offer a Roc-A-Fella Records contract as first prize, winning the competition did not establish the MC's realness in the same way.

Though many listeners may have been first introduced to the battle in its MTV form, or in the scripted battle sequence from *8 Mile*, such mainstream representations of the battle do acknowledge the importance of live vocal performance to hip hop. Because rap's vocal origins are so rooted in live performance, a real rap artist must argue his or her ability to perform not only on recordings, but in concert, freestyle, or battle. A Tribe Called Quest's "Phony Rappers" (1996) defines its subject as those "who do not write," and "who do not excite," and the song tells the story of a rap career in which Tribe has achieved some level of success as mainstream recording artists, only to find themselves challenged to perform in the streets by rap listeners who believe that "an MC that they seen on TV can't hold it down in the NYC." By Tribe's definition, the real MC pens his or her own lyrics, can excite a crowd in live performance, and can improvise lyrics to respond to an opponent. "Phony Rappers" targets those wannabe rap vocalists who approach Tribe's Q-Tip and Phife Dawg in public settings and challenge them to battle. Phife and Q-Tip claim that they must consistently prove their skills in live performance, which validates their commercial success as it proves their skills in creativity, improvisation, and crowd interaction. The question remains, though, of how these skills translate to the music industry and its emphasis on selling records more than putting on a good live show.

Lil Wayne tells a similar story from a different perspective in the skit "On the Block #1" (*Tha Carter II*, 2005), where he's approached on Miami's South Beach by a fan who wants to videotape himself battling the rapper. While Tribe's Q-Tip and Phife accept the challenge on "Phony Rappers," Lil Wayne doesn't want to waste his time. He asks "Dawg, how much we gonna make for this?" Wayne argues that, with his status in hip hop, he doesn't need to battle to prove himself anymore, and reminds his listeners that just because he's from the South and doesn't brag about his rhyme flow doesn't mean he isn't at the top of the rap game. The "On the Block #1" skit leads into and serves an introduction to the next track, "Best Rapper Alive," where Wayne illustrates his skills. When Lil Wayne brings up money in response to being asked to battle, he reflects the aesthetic of his record label, Cash Money. Cash Money artists flaunt their money and jewelry as testament to their success, and as testament to their skills. For a battle to be worth his time, Lil Wayne says he needs to get paid.

HIP HOP CAREER STORIES: THE SKILLS TO PAY THE BILLS

In the 1990s, the Beastie Boys titled a song "Skills to Pay the Bills" (1992), and Positive K titled his debut album *The Skills Dat Pay the Bills*

(1992). More recent hip hop lyrics, however, separate rhyme skills from sales. dead prez for example, claim that they're tired of "monotonous material. All ya'll records sound the same" ("Hip Hop," 2000). *Billboard*'s pop charts tend to favor less complex topics and rhyme structures, and place more emphasis on marketability for dance clubs. Crossover hits like J-Kwon's "Tipsy" (2004) or 50 Cent's "In Da Club" (2003) take on the club atmosphere as their topics. These Top 40 songs feature basic rhyme structures over sparse beats, and are lyrically very repetitive, relying heavily on the verse-chorus-verse structure of pop music. This contradiction between skills and sales recalls hip hop's narratives of an earlier, purer, hip hop culture, unadulterated by concerns of profit. These narratives tell us that back in the day MCs were not held accountable to the musical styles that sell in the mainstream. Because these back-in-the-day narratives are so pervasive, top-selling mainstream artists must prove that they maintain connections to hip hop's original culture. Artists who abandon real hip hop skills to increase sales describe getting rich in terms of getting out of, and giving back to, the ghetto.

Jay-Z justifies getting rich in terms of giving back to the ghetto communities that invented hip hop, even when getting rich means abandoning hip hop's original aesthetic. On "Moment of Clarity" (2003), Jay-Z responds to hip hop purists with a message of survivalism, invoking the question of skills versus sales, and addressing those listeners who consider the music of artists Common or Talib Kweli more real than Jay-Z's platinum-selling singles. Jay claims to "dumb down" his music in order to sell more records, and criticizes these more lyrically complex MCs for focusing on skills instead of sales. Jay claims that he chooses to produce radio-friendly music in order to get rich and give back to the community. By linking his commercial agenda to the style of hip hop he records, Jay-Z claims to put his community above his own artistry, and to simplify his rhyme style to achieve mainstream success. Yet on the same song, Jay-Z also claims "I built a dynasty by being one of the realest niggas out." This line, in context of his claims to dumb down his music, would emphasize his personal sincerity and philanthropy over his accountability to the creative expression of hip hop culture. As he responds to criticisms, Jay-Z becomes "one of the realest" rappers as he makes visible his financial agenda and the ways that agenda conflicts with his artistic production.

While I can't argue whether Jay-Z has dumbed down his music, his actions do hold true to the philanthropic agenda he proposes. He has started programs like "Team Roc" to provide scholarship opportunities and after-school programs for inner-city kids, and his annual Christmas toy drive provides $10,000 in gifts to children in the Marcy Housing Projects where Jay-Z grew up. He also hosts a Christmas dinner each year at Marcy's Recreation Center. Jay-Z's "Moment of Clarity" lyrics speak to the conflict between aesthetics and politics in black artistic production. In 1937, Richard Wright's "Blueprint for Negro Writing" argued that black writing should have a political content because of the black writer's social responsibility, and because of his or her role in creating values for the community.[33] Wright's notion of social responsibility reflects a wider tradition that goes back to Marcus Garvey, and to Booker T. Washington's idea of African-American responsibility to be "a credit to the race." William M. Banks traces the tensions between aesthetics and politics from the Harlem Renaissance through the black radicals and intellectuals of the 1960s. Banks argues that imperatives of social responsibility and a necessary political content may stand in conflict with making money in the mainstream. These historical tensions are complicated by the unprecedented commercial potential of hip hop. The global visibility of hip hop again raises questions of how African-American celebrities can, or should, speak for the African-American community.

While the black traditions Banks identifies tend to understand political content and social responsibility in their *opposition* to commercialism, and to frame political content in opposition to producing a consumer-friendly product, Jay-Z frames making commercial music as a political act in itself: Getting rich and giving back to the community does more good than producing music that holds truer to hip hop's cultural origins. Hip hop outsells every other form of popular music in the U.S., whether invented by black or white Americans. Hip hop's unprecedented sales prompt reconsideration of commercialism's influence on aesthetics and politics in black artistic production. Several black artists who make money in the mainstream emphasize the fact that they circulate that wealth within the black community. An act of philanthropy, like Jay-Z's scholarship foundation, becomes itself a form of activism, as he shows his audience he hasn't forgotten where he came from, and that he remains accountable to that community. As Jay-Z frames his sales within accountability to his community, he rejects artistry for commercialism, as does Jadakiss in his line "Screw your awardz, my son can't eat those plaques" ("Scenario 2000," 2000). Such declarations tie commercialism to politics, rather than aesthetics, as artists like Jay-Z, Jadakiss, and 50 Cent embrace their Top 40 record sales and justify getting rich as a form of survival. These and other mainstream artists frame their commercial success within a rhetoric of financial common sense. A line from Master P and Ice Cube's "You Know

I'm a Hoe" (1998), "If it don't make dollars then it don't make sense," suggests a model in which producing art that won't sell becomes a selfish and frivolous pursuit, and accountability to the community through one's aesthetics does less to support that community than do the social programs Jay-Z uses his platinum sales to fund.

SKILLS, SALES, AND CAREER LONGEVITY

Jay-Z's *Black Album* (2003) ends with the announcement of Jay's retirement from hip hop at the peak of his success. He claims the album will be his last release, and it celebrates his achievements in coming "from bricks to Billboards, grams to Grammys," and from his childhood in Marcy Projects to his sold-out concert at Madison Square Garden. In chronicling his rise to stardom, Jay-Z links his artistic achievements to a financial agenda, and as he looks back at his accomplishments, he uses the phrase "rap career." De La Soul, as well, uses "rap career" on their seventh album, *The Grind Date* (2004), which celebrates the group's longevity and perseverance even as their mainstream sales and celebrity have wavered. While written from different perspectives of success, *The Black Album* and *The Grind Date* confront the artists' interaction with the record industry, and describe a meeting of the personal and the professional in the rap career. Rap artists' experiences within the music industry become important subject matter, and an important part of hip hop's dialogue about culture and commerce.

Earlier in this chapter I mentioned De La Soul's 1988 debut video "Me, Myself, and I," in which they introduced themselves to MTV viewers by parodying the nascent culture of rap videos. Essentially, De La Soul parodied the standardization of the rap image, and the formula followed by many rap acts of that era, as standing in opposition to rap's emphasis on individuality and creativity. The "Me, Myself, and I" video features Pos, Mase, and Trugoy as high school classmates taking a class to learn to become rappers. As the group cannot fit into the formulas of rap's fashion and posturing, they are ridiculed by their classmates and instructor. The parody used in this video works to create a space for the different image De La Soul projects in their own music. De La Soul's debut album *3 Feet High and Rising* (1989) reached platinum in ten years of sales, but they have not produced another album to match that success. After sixteen years of recording, they remain on the fringe of the mainstream, but still enjoy a cult following as one of hip hop's most influential groups. While De La Soul has by no means fallen into obscurity (they performed with Gorillaz at the 2006 Grammy Awards), their sales are no match for the multiplati-num Jay-Z, and their website, Spitkicker.com, enlisted fans during 2005 to sign a petition for MTV to play their latest video, "Rock Co Kane Flow" which extends and updates their critique of mainstream rap. Along with several other tracks from *The Grind Date*, "Rock Co Kane Flow" focuses on the group's career, chronicling the reality of their current position in hip hop, the labor that went into the making of the album, and the ques-tion of their longevity in the face of those newer, less innovative acts that are selling more records through conforming to proven pop-rap formulas ("yo, let's cookie-cut the shit and get the gingerbread, man"). The album's liner notes include a month-by-month calendar that outlines the work they did to produce the album.

The Grind Date ends with De La Soul's assessment of the group's cur-rent position in the rap game: "Too old to rhyme? Too bad." ("Rock Co Kane Flow," 2004) Through this continuing critique of the rap image, De La Soul claims to have found staying power in their personal commitment to a hip hop aesthetic that lies outside commercial trends. Throughout their career they have continued to critique hip hop's commercial image, and their own image as well. Following the chart success of their debut album, the group titled their 1991 sophomore release *De La Soul is Dead*, and opened that album with a skit in which a group of kids, calling Vanilla Ice "better than any rapper I ever seen," find a De La Soul tape in the garbage. Three gangstas looking for rap with pimps, guns, and curse words, steal the tape and critique De La Soul's music in spoken interludes, until at the end of the album they return the tape to the garbage. In exten-sion of this self-effacement that stands in opposition to rap's emphasis on boasting, 1993's "Fallin" contains the line "Read the paper, the headline say 'Washed-up rapper got a song.'" In conjunction with such self-critique, De La Soul parodies the excess of popular hip hop videos in 1993's "Ego Trippin' (Part Two)," which displays the caption "It's a rental" as Trugoy cruises in an expensive car. On *The Grind Date*, De La Soul targets the much-publicized charity fundraising of Sean "P Diddy" Combs, as tele-vised on the MTV special "Diddy Runs the City." On the track "Verbal Clap," (2004), they say, "We run mics, let Sean run the marathon." As narrated in their lyrics, their career trajectory speaks for the sacrifices they have made to continue to produce real hip hop, and from this position they critique those hip hop superstars who can afford to stage charity events.

As MCs focus on where they came from, they must work to tie this history to where they've gone in their music careers. Concepts of performer realness seek consistency between an artist's origins and his or her current position in the record industry. De La Soul narrates its trajectory as a group that refuses to follow rap trends. Jay-Z tells the rags-to-riches story of a rap superstar, and ties his celebrity to stories of his younger days as a drug dealer, thereby connecting his business agenda to a streetwise mentality. As artists narrate their own careers, they revise and reclaim narratives of the self-made man (or millionaire), and frame a story of the individual's interaction with the music industry. Concepts of real hip hop center the autobiographical basis of lyrics, and on the fidelity of the performance to hip hop's original culture. These central dimensions of realness are complicated by the reality that most rap music is recorded to be sold. The conflicts between creativity and commerce lead artists to write career narratives that reconcile their backgrounds with their work as recording artists. In chapter two I will extend this discussion to show that hip hop career narratives present counterstories that challenge the accepted history of the exploitation of black music, like rock and roll, by white record companies. Hip hop counterstories complicate criticisms of materialism and excess in the music as they employ metaphors of music as a drug. Rap stars frame their rags-to-riches narratives within hip hop's criminal discourse, to present making and selling rap music as an extension of crime, and to reconcile this criminal aesthetic with their roles in the record industry. These narratives represent a social reality, one that is oversimplified by arguments that hip hop has been co-opted by the record industry, or has become too materialistic to still matter.

THE RAP LIFE

Chapter one illustrated the importance hip hop places on paying your dues along the way to success in the music industry. As rap artists use their lyrics to tell stories of how they came to be rappers, hip hop's complexities and contradictions come into focus. Rappers hold onto nostalgic concepts of "real" hip hop even as they brag about how many records they've sold. The tensions between artistry and album sales have existed since rap's first successful crossover artist, Sugarhill Gang, was assembled by a record executive and given a recording contract without an established history of performing in clubs or on street corners. Rap artists reconcile the tension between hip hop commerce and culture by taking control of their music, by starting their own record labels, becoming record executives, and taking on active roles in the promotion and distribution of their records. Lyrics from rap artists as diverse as Mike Jones, MF Grimm, and Master P describe how these rappers took charge of selling their own music.

To maintain their credibility in these new roles in production, marketing, and business, artists have to remain true to their roots in the struggle. In order to examine how wealthy, successful musicians can maintain their credibility in a form of music that started in the streets, chapter two turns its attention to hip hop as an autobiographical form, and the stories of its self-made millionaires. Stories of past struggle legitimize current success, but also hold the authors accountable to the past that shaped their identities. Hip hop artists have to stay true to themselves by using their lyrics to represent who they are and where they come from. Hip hop isn't the only music to stress the importance of the performer's identity; in country music, Hank Williams Jr.'s song "Family Tradition" (1979) poses the question, "Why must you live out the songs that you wrote?" Looking at the tragic murders of Tupac Shakur and The Notorious B.I.G., who fantasized their own murders in lyrics, this question becomes even more pertinent to hip hop.

Although the hip hop phrase "keep it real" has been co-opted by Coca-Cola, the concept of being real or staying true to one's roots still thrives in hip hop culture. Part of hip hop's appeal has always been the truths it claims to expose. Hip hop lyrics carry with them a certain quality of truth that is called into question when artists pose for the camera or adopt stage personae that do not reflect their own backgrounds. The importance of representing, staying true, and being real lends itself to a common understanding of hip hop lyrics as autobiographical in nature. Because hip hop lyrics are so often taken to be autobiographical, it is useful to draw a comparison to a recent autobiography scandal in the publishing industry. In 2006, Oprah Winfrey brought author James Frey onto her show after reports revealed that parts of Frey's memoir, *A Million Little Pieces* (Anchor, 2005), were fictionalized. Frey, whose book about overcoming addiction had been promoted as part of Oprah's Book Club, explained that in labeling his book a memoir, he did not mean to present his writing as one hundred percent factual, and that he allowed himself room to exaggerate or embellish upon his actual experiences in order to create a more compelling and sensational story. In 1991, white rapper Vanilla Ice created a similar scandal when he embellished and fabricated aspects of his biography in order to make his life story fit with those of his black peers in rap music.

The scandals of James Frey and Vanilla Ice call attention to the appeal of reality in contemporary culture, where we are inundated with claims to authenticity. In a culture that is increasingly media-driven and virtual, advertisers know we are unconsciously seeking something authentic, from the MTV series *True Life* and *The Real World*, to films based on a true story, to real hip hop. These claims to present real life have been overused to the point that they have lost their impact, and we have grown to mistrust them. Frey and Ice are well-publicized cases in which investigative journalists did research to separate fact from fiction, but every day the typical consumer judges claims to reality for herself. Chain restaurants founded in the United States advertise their food as "authentic Mexican" or "real Italian." MTV's long-running series *The Real World* opens with spoken testimonials from current cast members that "This is the *true story* of seven strangers picked to live in a house." Even with this bold statement at the start of each episode, *The Real World* devotes a retrospective episode each season to footage that was not shown, and to cast member testimonials that they were not portrayed accurately. The appeal of something real is powerful to us. We appreciate a true story, but we are also savvy about how we interpret what is real and what isn't. Viewers understand that reality television, for instance, may feature real people, but that these people were carefully chosen in casting calls that went out to thousands and that the finished shows depict constructed situations through carefully edited footage.

If fiction loses its power under a culture so obsessed with the real, then memoir, reality television, and hip hop assume new positions in the popular interest. Rap lyrics, like autobiographies and reality television, are subject to claims of what's real and what's fake. Hip hop artists assure their listeners of their realness, of the accurate correlation between their actual lived experience and the experience they present in their lyrics. I argued in chapter one that concepts of real hip hop reflect nostalgia for a culture that was created outside of the music industry, and that concepts of the real MC center on the autobiographical basis of the experiences the performer projects in lyrics. Chapter two extends that argument to study hip hop as an essentially autobiographical form in which artists write career narratives that link their lived experiences to their interaction with the music industry.

HIP HOP AUTOBIOGRAPHY

Hip hop autobiography takes shape in extension of African-American autobiographies that follow their heroes up from slavery or out of the ghetto. Yet as hip hop artists achieve commercial success, they must work to reconcile their wealth and celebrity with hip hop culture's creation outside the industry. Hip hop lyrics often trace the development of the artist through childhood poverty to wealth and celebrity in the music business. As stars such as Jay-Z or Wu-Tang Clan narrate their struggles against systemic racism in their lives and careers, they emphasize their earlier lives of crime and compare the hip hop industry to the drug trade. I argue that as rap artists juxtapose the production of hip hop music with the trafficking of illegal drugs, they challenge existing narratives of music industry appropriation of African-American music forms, and that their lyrics function as counterstories that promote rap artists as outlaw entrepreneurs, rather than as minority laborers exploited by a white-controlled record industry. MCs use autobiographical stories to frame their commercial success in terms of crime. They employ two key narratives—criminal-to-artist and music-as-drug—in order to preserve hip hop's oppositionality even as they celebrate getting rich through the corporate music industry.

Hip hop's success stories fit into a tradition of African-American autobiography. Just as autobiography centers on the development of a self, hip hop narratives focus on the development of an artist-self, whose success and celebrity are held accountable to the performer's lived experience. Hip hop lyrics are, of course, not entirely autobiographical, but they present a system of reference between self and star. *The Black Album* (2003), for example, chronicles Jay-Z's progression from selling drugs to selling more albums than almost any other hip hop star, a journey that takes him from New York's Marcy Housing Projects to Madison Square Garden, and "from bricks to Billboards, grams to Grammys" ("Dirt Off Your Shoulder" 2003). Through his journey from poverty to wealth, and from obscurity to stardom, Jay-Z narrates his hard work and personal commitment both to making hip hop music and to making money, and he connects his financial agenda to his earlier criminal involvement. In this sense, *The Black Album* becomes a *kuntslerroman*, a story about the maturation of an artist in which Jay-Z's life of crime ultimately shapes his career as a musician. Such representations of career success in hip hop have developed from African-American readings of wage labor, crime, and consumerism.[1] Crime becomes one way to make money outside the system, while the minimum wage job is devalued as wage slavery. As rap artists celebrate their wealth in lyrics, they often frame their music career as a criminal endeavor, and also confront their own hyperconsumption on songs such as "Rap Life" (1999), where Tash chronicles his lifestyle as an artist who "made a killin' and ain't got shit to show for it." Like MC Hammer, who sold multiplatinum in the early 1990s and filed for bankruptcy by the end of that decade, Tash attributes his financial losses to the friends who live off his success, and to his own desire both to support these friends financially and to impress them with his purchasing power.

Part of hip hop's goal is to use the music to bring people out of the ghetto, and as stars become rich and famous they often use their new relationship with the record industry to invite friends and family members to join their tours as members of a posse or entourage as bodyguards, hype men, and often as musicians themselves. The Notorious B.I.G., for example, promoted Lil' Kim and Junior Mafia as his protégés. Dr. Dre, long known for scouting and developing new talent such as the D.O.C., Michele, and CPO, claims on "Still D.R.E." (1999) to "still love to see young blacks get money." The rap life is one of shared extravagance. Rappers take pride in bringing their friends and families into the rap game and buying houses for their mothers. Having a large posse and the power to promote new artists stands as testament to an artist's success, but also affords him or her the opportunity to share the wealth, often to such an extreme that the wealth is spread too thin and disappears.

The rap life develops from forces of race and class, and also from a model of celebrity lifestyle for the popular musician.[2] Rock artists often emphasize the sincerity of their performance in opposition to another, more consumerist, form of the music, and this scenario has played out similarly in the punk, indie, and lo-fi movements, which have rejected the corporate rock spectacle as they present their own work as a more sincere form of expression. Hip hop, however, is unique among popular music forms in that its lyrics often work to reconcile personal sincerity with a commercial agenda. For the rap artist, internal convictions or personal sincerity can *extend* to careerism and consumerism. While hip hop rejects those artists who try to make money by diluting the original music with pop styles, artists also assert their place within hip hop culture through stories of their own poverty as part of a struggle against systemic racism. For those born into poverty, the desire for wealth becomes a more survivalist form of consumerism, and artists often connect the disadvantages of their formative years to their desire to get rich through success in the music business.

Beating the odds to achieve a career in hip hop music is the topic of several songs, from Ghostface Killah's "We Made It" (2000) to Mike Jones's "Back Then" (2005) and Biz Markie's "The Vapors" (1988). These songs tend to present a then versus now scenario in which people with low status in their neighborhoods rise to hip hop superstardom through hard work and perseverance. This trend began with Biz Markie's "The Vapors," a song that tells the story of a group of young men who rose to success in music. Playing on "catching the vapors," an old southern slang expression for feeling faint, Biz and his friends see people catch the vapors in reaction to their stardom. People who had disregarded Biz and his friends in their youth now swoon at their stardom: Biz the star is welcomed into a record store that previously refused him employment, T. J. Swan was dissed by girls until he sang on Biz's records, and Big Daddy Kane is shown a respect that he wasn't given before he left the neighborhood to become a rapper. Biz's look at how people regarded him before and after his success is echoed in Mike Jones's hit single "Back Then," which introduced this Houston underground rapper to MTV airplay. The song describes the lack of respect Jones was shown before he signed a record deal with a major label: Jones, who titled his first major-label album *Who is Mike Jones?* (2005) includes in his repertoire a call-and-response routine in which he shouts "Mike Jones" and the audience repeats "Who?" Jones presents his path to stardom as a story of hard work and perseverance. He didn't let his early audiences discourage him, and now he can flaunt his wealth and fame, and ignore the women that didn't want him before he made it as a rapper.

Again, struggle is central to a rap bio: Mike Jones and Biz Markie were told they would never make it, Jay-Z and The Notorious B.I.G. struggled to support themselves through crime, and Kanye West, 50 Cent, and The Game all overcame near-fatal accidents on their way to the top of the charts. 50 Cent survived nine bullets, the Game woke up from a coma after an attempt on his life, and Kanye had reconstructive surgery on his face after surviving a car wreck. These near-death experiences work to legitimize these artists who endured accidents and attempts on their lives as they tried to make it in hip hop. They claim to be so determined to make it that even a bullet, or a car wreck, couldn't stop them, and their appeal to listeners depends on their biographies as much as their musical talents, as they use their songs to tell the stories of how they beat the odds to become famous rappers.

As MCs use their lyrics to chronicle their paths to success, hip hop becomes more distinctly autobiographical than other popular music forms, where the performer's biography is represented primarily in press materials rather than in songs. Yet we cannot take every line from hip hop lyrics as autobiography. Rappers create complex fictions in their music through use of hyperbole, metaphor, and parody, through which rap extends black traditions of "Signifying." Yet although MCs do create fictions in their music, hip hop's Signifying also sees MCs challenge lyrics that rest too fully in fiction. MCs have called each other out for their boasting or posturing, especially as rap's performance of a physically aggressive, sexualized, and consumerist young black male has become marketable in the mainstream.[3] Boasting, however, does not grant the speaker a full reliance on fiction, and as hip hop artists become the bad men of their own legends, there arises a necessity for their stories to have a basis in autobiography, or else they'll lose credibility with their peers and listeners.

While all stories told in lyrics need not be factually accurate, they do need to be rooted in autobiography as they reflect, rather than simply chronicle, lived experience.[4] In one example, 50 Cent's "Life's on the Line" (2002) challenges a fellow artist's boasting as he issues a thinly veiled threat to Ja Rule, who 50 Cent claims lies about his life of crime on his songs. 50 Cent complains that, "These cats always escape reality when they rhyme," and he warns of the consequences of gangsta posturing for those artists who aren't really gangstas. These lyrics complicate the relationship between autobiography and fiction as they expose Ja Rule's fabulation. As 50 Cent threatens Ja Rule, he asserts that his own violent posturing is closer to autobiography, and that because of his lived experiences he can put his words into action, while Ja Rule puts on a front. The fact that 50

Cent's own life experience includes surviving a gunshot to the face becomes a selling point for him because it authenticates both his struggle in becoming a rap star, and his seeming invincibility to the forces of the street. His album title *Get Rich or Die Tryin'* (2003) references the near fatality that occurred during his rise to stardom.

While the dispute between Ja Rule and 50 Cent centers on the truthfulness of the physical aggression they each boast, songs like Kool Keith's "I Don't Believe You" (2000) and Del the Funky Homosapien's "Fake as Fuck" (2000) issue an aesthetic challenge to lyricists who hide their lack of rhyme skill behind their aggressive posturing. Del extends this theme to "Jaw Gymnastics" (2000), where his collaborator Casual rhymes "your hard boulevard façade will get you scarred … and labeled as a fable." Even as Casual attacks those rappers who play into commercial rap's image of the aggressive black male, he acknowledges his own commercial agenda. In addressing, rather than obscuring, such an agenda, Casual confronts the reality of his position as a commercial recording artist, even as he asserts the integrity of his performance in opposition to those rappers who put on a façade. In addition to asserting the MC's own integrity, such lyrics critique the way stories told in rap songs reflect on the lived experience of the performer, and his or her position in the music industry as a commodified personality. A successful performance, then, links the MC on the recording to the story of how he or she became a recording artist.

RHYMING IN FIRST PERSON

Before I move into an analysis of hip hop's criminal-to-artist narratives and the music-as-drug counterstories that stars use to frame their work in the record industry, I should further address the underlying autobiographical structures of hip hop lyrics and the power of the first-person "I." MCs bring together the performance of self and the performance of celebrity, yet the sameness of self and star comes into question as artists perform under rap names, and in some cases even obscure their legal names. I use the term "legal" here in the sense of literary critic Phillipe Lejeune's theory of the *autobiographical pact*, which argues that a contract is formed between author and reader when the name of the central character matches the name of the author on the title page. According to Lejeune, the pact works as a signature that provides textual evidence that a work is autobiographical. Although Lejeune understands autobiography as necessarily a kind of fiction, he believes readers interact differently with a fictional text than an autobiographical one, and that the name and signature are crucial to this distinction.[5]

Most hip hop lyrics are written in the first person, and this structure is not uncommon in popular music.[6] In hip hop, an artist may take on multiple nicknames, yet the sincerity of the "I" remains with each. For example, Eminem's artist name is a phonetic representation of the performer's initials: Marshall Mathers performs as Eminem. In the credits to the film *8 Mile*, "Eminem" is billed as an actor. He plays a character named B. Rabbit, and while this character shares much of Eminem's biography (including the Detroit upbringing he chronicles in his lyrics), the naming of B. Rabbit presents a clear message that the film is not fully autobiographical. On Eminem's albums, however, the play between autobiography and fantasy becomes more complicated by the first-person authenticity that Allan Moore identifies in "Authenticity as Authentication." Because Eminem uses two additional artist names along with "Eminem" and his legal name, the listener must work to distinguish what aspects of his performance are Marshall Mathers the living person, and which are "Marshall Mathers," "Eminem," or "Slim Shady." Eminem's "97 Bonnie and Clyde" (1999) presents a complex blurring of autobiography and fantasy, as Eminem first invokes his daughter, Hailey, by using her given name in lyrics, then shifts into a fantasy in which he murders Hailey's mother and kidnaps his daughter. Eminem references "97 Bonnie and Clyde" on two other songs, where he addresses the listener's potential confusion. On "I'm Shady" (1999)," he clarifies what's real and what's fiction in his lyrics, assuring the listener that he hasn't killed his ex-wife, and that "she's still alive and bitchin'." And on "Stan" (2000), Eminem interacts with a fan who wants to reenact the violent action of "97 Bonnie and Clyde." By acknowledging in his lyrics that he does write fiction, Eminem acknowledges that his stories provide a reflection of his experience, rather than a direct chronicle of his life. Though based in autobiography, "Eminem" becomes a persona, a fictional character who acts out the violent fantasies of his author. Redman takes this notion of persona further in "Redman Meets Reggie Noble" (1992), a song that takes the shape of a dialogue between Reggie Noble and his rap persona. At one point, Redman brags about bumping music in his Mercedes Benz and Reggie Noble responds, "Now you know you don't own a Benz."

The distinction between rap fiction and autobiography lies with reference. We cannot take author and persona to be one and the same, so listeners need to consider where the boundaries are between Eminem the persona and Marshall Mathers the person, or Redman the persona and Reggie Noble the person. In one theory of how autobiography operates, Paul de Man argues that the author and narrator cannot be one and the same, and that the narrator is less a representation of the author's identity than the embodiment of the author's self-reflection, like we are watching the author look at himself in a mirror. De Man describes an "illusion of reference" by which autobiography appears to depend on a simpler and more direct mode of referentiality and representation than does fiction.[7] This illusion for rap listeners complicated the 1992 *Cop Killer* scandal, which saw President George Bush and presidential candidate Bill Clinton, among other prominent politicians, criticize Ice-T for his lyrics on "Cop Killer," a song he recorded with his group Body Count. While the song itself would be classified as metal rather than hip hop, Ice-T was the frontman for the group, and his position as a prominent gangsta rapper drew criticism on the hip hop community. Barry Shank has studied the censorship of *Cop Killer* from its beginnings in a Texas police group through Ice-T's ultimate concession to allow Warner Brothers, his label, to remove the track from subsequent pressings of Body Count's album. Shank questions why such a widespread scandal was initiated by this song, and he illuminates a history of violence against police officers in folk and rock music songs like *I Shot the Sheriff* (1974) and "Pretty Boy Floyd" (1939), neither of which has sparked such controversy. While race certainly played a role in the *Cop Killer* scandal, other songs from black artists have been accepted as fiction. Bob Marley's original recording of *I Shot the Sheriff* (1973) raised no more eyebrows than Eric Clapton's version (1974). Race was central to the *Cop Killer* controversy as tensions between police departments and young black men were especially high at that time, and as the Los Angeles Police Department's beating of Rodney King had made these tensions visible to white America. Rap artists had been narrating their harassment by white officers for at least a decade, going back as far as Grandmaster Flash & the Furious Five's 1982 video for "The Message," yet Ice-T and Body Count sparked a political backlash as they inverted the violence of earlier songs to speak from the perspective of a black cop killer, rather than a black man harassed and battered by cops.

While race and the historical context of *Cop Killer* made its topic seem more real to listeners, the question of hip hop's structure of reference remains. Ice-T's defense of the song speaks to the illusion of simplistic reference in hip hop: "I'm singing in the first person as a character who is fed up with police brutality. I ain't never killed no cop. I felt like it a lot of times. But I never did it."[8] Ice-T claimed he was performing in character rather than speaking his own opinions, and argued that actors who play cop killers in films don't receive the same criticism he did. While popular music listeners can hear Johnny Cash sing "I shot a man in Reno just to watch him die" on "Folsom Prison Blues" (1956), and not take Cash at his word, listeners seemed to have a different take on Ice-T's vocals. Yet Shank identifies textual evidence from the Body Count album, where Ice-T makes clear that his is not an autobiographical performance; Ice-T, speaking in character, says "I live in South Central," while Ice-T is, in reality, a wealthy actor and rapper living in Hollywood.[9]

It is important to pay attention to rap artists' efforts to draw a line between persona and private self. Such a move from Ice-T—like the one by Eminem in *8 Mile*—is significant, because he has presented so much of his music as autobiography, chronicling his progression from a life of crime to a career in music. Hip hop's illusion of reference is formed from the music's rhetoric of lived experience. Yet to view it this way simplifies the form to direct reporting, as if it involves a simpler mode of reference than that of the country outlaw. Murder ballads from each form are reacted to very differently, as if Ice-T the artist is one and the same with the character-narrator of his song, while Johnny Cash is of course singing in persona. In fact, Johnny Cash, in performing under his legal name, establishes a more direct relationship with his narrator than does Ice-T, who is performing under an artist pseudonym (Cash's given name was J. R. Cash, but he recorded as Johnny). Yet somewhere in this play of names, hip hop alone loses the distinction between author and character.

Hip hop naming grows out of larger traditions.[10] The choosing of rap names reflects the on-air names of 1950s disc jockeys, the 1960s move for black athletes and entertainers to reject slave names, and the renaming of public figures like Muhammad Ali and Kareem Abdul Jabbar, who took Islamic names upon their conversions to Islam. Because most hip hop music is released under names invented by the performers, a particular significance is given to instances where artists invoke their given names in lyrics or album titles. Eminem protégé Obie Trice devotes a song, "Rap Name" (2003), to arguing that his performance is more authentic because he records under his legal name. Trice asserts his use of a "real name, no gimmicks" as a marker of his credibility. The use of the proper name in hip hop can attest to the sincerity of an artist, and often is invoked to emphasize an album's autobiographical structure, as with Jay-Z's *Vol. 3 The Life and Times of S. Carter* (1999). By setting aside his artist name to use his legal name, Jay-Z acknowledges that in foregrounding his given name he is becoming more personal and direct with his audience, and is stepping outside a stage name that complicates the direct relationship he wants to establish with the listener.

Yet while artists may assert a higher level of sincerity as they set aside rap names to invoke their real names, and while artists such as Obie Trice and Keith Murray record under their real names, the legal name alone does not confirm artist sincerity and verifiability. Naming is a central part of hip hop's identity play, and often names incorporate metaphor as they reference other figures, as in the Wu-Gambino names taken on by members of the Wu-Tang Clan on their second album, *Wu-Tang Forever* (1997). In addition to their original artist names, the Wu-Tang MCs assumed new names in reference to Italian mafia figures. Wu-Tang's Method Man refers to himself with so many names that it forms the basis for a Chris Rock skit on Method Man's *Tical 2000: Judgment Day* (1998). Wu-Tang's RZA is also known as Bobby Steel, in reference to Bobby Seale of the Black Panthers, to the wheels of steel, a term for turntables, and to the RZA's given name, Robert. Hip hop's focus on assumed artist names complicates its focus on lived experience, as the artist name forms a barrier of fiction between performer and listener. The idea of realness through sincerity, or of an artist's speaking directly to the listener, is complicated in the metaphors woven throughout the narratives. Yet for these metaphors to succeed, the artist first must establish a verifiable self through stories of how he or she came to *be* an artist.

In his book, *Fictions in Autobiography: Studies in the Art of Self-Invention* (1988), Paul John Eakin acknowledges the inevitable fictional content of autobiographies, yet he doesn't want to disregard truth or define autobiography as strictly a type of fiction. Instead, he argues that "autobiographical truth is not fixed but evolving" in a process of self-creation or self-discovery.[11] In hip hop, as life stories are told in lyrics, artists develop complex structures of reference between self and star, and they work to reconcile one with the other, and to assert that the self is not lost in the process of becoming a celebrity. Two central stories of the hip hop career are criminal-to-artist and music-as-drug. These stories work to reconcile careerism and consumerism with the performer's origins in poverty, and to reconcile music industry success with the oppositionality of hip hop's original culture. The criminal-to-artist story follows a rags-to-riches model of self-styled success and the rise to prominence in one's field, but with particular attention to the performer's involvement in crime. As I will show in the next section of this chapter, artists such as The Notorious B.I.G. describe how their rap careers helped them to rise from poverty and escape from the life of crime that had seemed to be their only viable means of survival. The music-as-drug narrative, on the other hand, promotes the making of rap music as a criminal act in itself. Artists like Ghostface Killah use this narrative to celebrate their roles in the *selling* of hip hop music, a legal product, yet one the government has sought to regulate through outright censorship or through programs like the Recording Industry Association of America's parental advisory labeling. In reclaiming his role in distribution, an artist such as Ghostface becomes a trafficker of the music he frames as a ghetto product distributed to the outside listener.[12] Rappers connect their performance to criminality through these stories of their rise out of crime, which demonstrate the struggle that has brought the artist to a current position of wealth and celebrity, and through metaphors that justify this wealth and celebrity in terms of crime.

CRIMINAL-TO-ARTIST

Autobiography tells the story of shaping a self. In her study of autobiography, Jill Ker Conway historicizes stories of personal development and success as they have developed from St. Augustine's *Confessions* (397), which told the story of a hero's emotional development toward a relationship with God. Jean-Jacques Rousseau then told the story of a secular hero developing a sense of personal identity, and Benjamin Franklin turned this toward the economic secular hero, "the capitalist hero" happy to achieve wealth, a tradition continued by Henry Ford and in success stories of the Horatio Alger tradition.[13] Such success stories also have been challenged and parodied within African-American literature.[14] As opposed to the Benjamin Franklin pattern, in which the statesman builds upon his success, moving steadily toward his goals, *The Autobiography of Malcolm X* (1965) follows a trajectory that seems to lead the protagonist further and further downhill before he can climb to the top. Malcolm turns to crime and spends time in prison, yet the book still presents these experiences as shaping the person he ultimately will become. In what Malcolm X called a major turning point in his youth, he rejected the white American values of diligence and delayed gratification for the excitement and immediate pay-off of crime.

In her study of black men and masculinity, bell hooks describes a similar outlaw mentality by which young black men seek purchasing power, but on their own terms and outside the wage system, which devalues them as laborers and denies them both their individuality and their control of the means of production.[15] Unlike Franklin's values of hard work and monetary prudence, which became a model for class mobility in the U.S., the values of hip hop see making music as a vehicle for the progress of the individual from poverty to wealth. To make it in hip hop requires hard work, of course, and artists acknowledge their effort and diligence, but as hip hop places itself decidedly outside the middle class, rap music is lifted above wage labor to become, like professional sports, a way to preserve individual integrity while still making money through legal means. In "Things Done Changed" (1994), The Notorious B.I.G. rejects the paths of education and hard work because he believes that crime, sports, or music are the only ways out of the ghetto: "Either you're slingin' crack rock or you got a wicked jumpshot." Biggie claims that if he weren't a rapper, he would have been a crack dealer, and his biographers confirm that before music Biggie made his living selling drugs. In fact, Diddy, who signed Biggie to Bad Boy Records, has said that Biggie doubted he could make as good a living in music.

Biggie's lyrics frame rap music as a savior from a life of crime, and downplay his material success as he breathes a sigh of relief for having escaped the life he almost led. This kind of statement is common in hip hop lyrics. Biggie's protégé Lil' Kim rhymes on "This is Who I Am" (2003) that, "without rap I probably woulda been sellin' dope in prison." Digital Underground's song, "It's a Good Thing That We're Rappin'" (1991) similarly claims that the group's members would have fallen into a criminal career (as pimps) if it had not been for their success in music. Yet even as Biggie frames hip hop as his savior from the streets, he is careful to maintain his connection to his geographical and cultural origins. On "Juicy" (1994), he claims he has "made the change from a common thief to up close and personal with Robin Leach," yet because both geographical location and artist consistency are central to hip hop credibility, other lyrics on this same song sound contradictory, as Biggie tells his listener, "Call the crib, same number, same hood." Even as a platinum-selling rapper, he claims that he hasn't changed who he was.

Biggie's narrative promotes his economic progression within geographic and cultural stability, and in this way his autobiography becomes less about the creation of a self than the maintaining of self-identity throughout his journey in becoming a recording artist. Yet a problem the rap artist may encounter with such narratives is the fact that the listener understands that the verifiable self, the living person, cannot remain wholly unchanged in the shift from poverty to wealth and stardom. Biggie's "same number, same hood" is echoed by other assertions of consistency, such as Dr. Dre's "Still D.R.E." (1999), a song that argues that even as one of rap's biggest stars, that he's "still got love for the streets." "Still D.R.E." was the lead single from Dre's comeback album, *Chronic 2001* (1999). Lyrics from the album (though many were written by stars other than Dre, such as Jay-Z) assert that while Dre may have been less visible in hip hop during the mid to late 1990s, he never left the culture and music behind. On "Guilty Conscience" (1999), Dre collaborates with his white prodigy Eminem while at the same time reaffirming his rap credentials. The song takes the frame of a dialogue between Dre and Eminem, who offer conflicting advice to three fictional characters who are considering robbing a liquor store, taking advantage of a young girl at a party, and seeking revenge on a cheating spouse. Throughout the song, the younger Eminem calls for rage and violence while an older and wiser Dre urges calm and restraint. In the final verse, Eminem calls Dre out on his contradictions, and finally rouses anger in Dre, provoking him to return momentarily to his gangsta mentality, even threatening to kill Eminem. As rap careers lengthen and artists like Dre prove their staying power across decades, this performance of the artist who's been through it all becomes common. The rise from street life to superstardom becomes a point of credibility for the artist who no longer lives that street life, and Dre exemplifies this perfectly. Eminem's verses cleverly remind listeners, some too young to have witnessed Dre's early days, of his past accomplishments, as specific as his physical attack on TV host Dee Barnes. As Eminem provokes Dre to return to his earlier hardcore identity, the artist proves that the streets are still in him.

Even as stars and millionaires, many rappers claim to still be involved in street crime. Lil Wayne, on "Carter II" (2005), claims "I'm wealthy, still fuckin' with that block shit." Lil Wayne, a top-selling artist, was recruited by Cash Money Records at age eleven, and claims that he was a millionaire by age seventeen. His involvement in crime, then, would be by choice, and would serve to keep his biography close to the drug-trade culture he depicts in his music. Wayne's extreme youth at the beginning of his career would seem to make it unlikely that he ever was involved in crime, even pre-stardom, but he tells those of us who don't believe him to "check my bio." Wayne's bio is complicated in that even after he was a wealthy and successful hip hop artist, he attended the University of Houston and talks about his higher education and his diploma in his lyrics alongside his rap career and his involvement in the drug trade. Wayne is able to justify his education in linking it to these other aspects of his personality: Rather than move up the ladder of success from street criminal to entertainer to college graduate, Wayne claims to do all three at once. The idea that wealth and fame should not change a person is prevalent in hip hop, and this mentality extends to dictate that those who were once involved in crime should not turn away from the streets. The focus on the consistency of the artist's identity pre- and post-stardom has been the basis of challenges to the truthfulness of lyrics. Pharoahe Monch, for example, on an untitled skit on De La Soul's *AOI: Mosaic Thump* (2005), questions his contemporaries' boasts about their criminal violence: "How many niggas who are actually signed still killin'?" Monch's question echoes Common's challenge to Ice Cube's truthfulness on "The Bitch in Yoo" (1996), where Common criticizes Ice Cube for his continued writing of criminal narratives after he had gotten rich in the music business: "Got the nerve to say you rob." This accusation frames a pivotal concern for hip hop counterstories. Ice Cube had not addressed his shift in perspective, and was still writing about street life from the comfort of his upscale home. To address such a concern, the selling of hip hop music can be framed as an outlaw enterprise, as an extension of, rather than an alternative to, crime.

MUSIC-AS-DRUG

Criminal-to-artist stories present music as an alternative to crime, but Jay-Z connects them as part of his same agenda, so that making and selling hip hop music becomes a crime in itself, and hip hop becomes a drug, a product circulated from the ghettoes to the masses. Jay-Z claims that his drug dealing laid a foundation for the empire building he has gone on to do with his music and his label, Roc-A-Fella Records. Jay-Z's *Black Album* (2003) links Jay-Z's drug dealing and his musical production: "I be the music biz number one supplier." Jay-Z extends a narrative of music as drug, and the MC as trafficker, that has a long history in hip hop. Beginning with Ice-T's "I'm Your Pusher" (1988), in which Ice-T intercepts a drug addict looking for a fix, then works to turn him on to hip hop records instead, the concept of music as drug has permeated hip hop lyrics. Rap lyrics' particular and unique attention to the marketing and distribution of the music see this metaphor make sense: Music as commodity and as illegal substance, making rap music out as outlaw production and distribution.

During the 1990s, rap music experienced a paradigm shift in its view of the use and sale of illegal drugs. When Dr. Dre released his debut solo album *The Chronic* (1992), named for a type of Southern California marijuana, his former N.W.A. bandmate Eazy-E was quick to sample one of Dre's decidedly anti-marijuana rhymes from N.W.A.'s "Express Yourself" (1988). Eazy-E attacks his former bandmate's inconsistency by sampling Dre's lyrics on "Down 2 Tha Last Roach" (1993), a song celebrating marijuana, which was almost requisite for a rap record released during that time. Dre's *The Chronic* was followed by Cypress Hill's "I Wanna Get High" (1993) and "Hits from the Bong" (1993), and Redman's "How to

Roll a Blunt" (1992), as well as marijuana-themed rap groups like Funk-doobiest. Artists like Dre's protégé Snoop Dogg made smoking marijuana a key part of their personae.

Yet even with the 1990s popularity of marijuana in hip hop, Dre's earlier statement against drug abuse was not at all uncommon for rap music during the 1980s, the time of the crack epidemic. Songs about drugs, like Ice-T's, tended to speak against using and dealing. N.W.A.'s song "Dopeman" (1988) chronicles the group's take on various neighborhood figures who have had their lives negatively affected by crack. The Beastie Boys removed the line "I smoke my crack" from their song "Rhyming and Stealing" (1986) before their debut album *Licensed to Ill* (1986) was released. Although there were exceptions, most notably the Geto Boys, who wrote about selling cocaine, the majority of rap artists in the 1980s spoke against drug abuse. As crack faded in popularity during the mid-90s, though, MCs began to write stories of themselves as traffickers. The Lost Boyz titled their 1994 debut *Legal Drug Money*, in reference to the selling of their music. Tracks like "Music Makes Me High" extend this metaphor, and on an interlude titled "Legal Drug Money", Mr. Cheeks describes his group as "legal drug thugs selling the most addictive drug in the world, music." This metaphor is also used by artists such as MF Grimm—who compares his independent record label, Day by Day Entertainment, to a drug cartel—and by two Wu-Tang members: Inspectah Deck, who titled his solo album *Uncontrolled Substance* (1999), and Ghostface Killah, who in a verse from Raekwon's "Guillotinz (Swordz)" (1995) reminds the listener that if rap were crack, he'd be "the kingpin of the rap drug traffickin'." This metaphor of rappers as traffickers is particularly significant in that the "substance," "product," or "goods" that hip hop circulates include lyrics presented as autobiography. MCs sell stories of ghetto life in America.

Kanye West's "Crack Music" (2005) takes on this metaphor of trafficking as its subject. Kanye suggests that hip hop music has hooked American listeners to such a degree that white listeners have adopted black styles and slang. This same song claims that white American Presidents Ronald Reagan and George Bush designed the crack epidemic to "stop the Black Panthers" and further plague black ghettoes, while "crack music" (i.e. hip hop) is created by African-Americans and circulated to white listeners. West's song becomes a revenge fantasy in which he reverses the racialized structures of power in America through the impact of his music. West's political statement fits into a tradition of dissent in songs like Public Enemy's "By the Time I Get to Arizona" (1991), in which Chuck D takes action to force the state to observe the Martin Luther King, Jr. holiday. Yet in his lyrics, West presents his music *itself* as his activism, rather than a vehicle for voicing his dissent. For West, the very act of producing hip hop music is revolutionary. Other such music-as-drug narratives that position the MC as trafficker claim selling music as a legitimate extension of street life. These songs frame the production and distribution of records as an outlaw enterprise. This framework is complicated, however, in a song such as dead prez's *Hip Hop* (2000), where the group claims, "These record labels slang our tapes like dope," giving agency to the corporation as trafficker of the MC's product. While dead prez criticizes a history of exploitation of black artists by a white record industry, lyrics from other artists invert this dominant notion as they claim an active role in the distribution of their own product. As traffickers, MCs take on entrepreneurial, criminal identities, even as they work within a music industry that historically has exploited black forms. In these songs, the racialized power dynamic of the record industry is presented as a smaller version of the world at large. West and Wu-Tang present a model in which they take over the record industry and then take over the world. On the radio interview included as an interlude on their debut album *Enter the Wu-Tang* (1993), Raekwon states that the group's goal is "domination, baby."

These drug trafficking metaphors are fueled by attempts on the part of the U.S. government to censor hip hop music and regulate its production and circulation. From sampling lawsuits, to the reaction of police groups and the FBI to Body Count's *Cop Killer* and N.W.A's "Fuck tha Police" (1988), to Vice President Dan Quayle's claim that Tupac's music has "no place in our society," to the censoring of 2 Live Crew's *As Nasty As They Wanna Be* (1989) as the first album officially declared legally obscene—which led to Supreme Court hearings and 2 Live Crew's subsequent single, "Banned in the U.S.A." (1990)—the U.S. government consistently has branded hip hop music as an outlaw form.

In January 2007, however, the focus shifted from the content of the music and lyrics to the production and distribution of the recordings. Mixtapes, which from hip hop's birth in the seventies have been a central part of marketing the music, were targeted by the government, and DJ Drama, a Southern mixtape hero, was arrested for racketeering. Mixtapes are unofficial releases, produced and distributed outside the support of a record label. Although they are generally branded "for promotional use only," mixtapes are sold to listeners online, at shows, and in local record stores. Although mixtapes generally contain a wealth of unpublished vocals and music from underground and mainstream artists, they frequently remix pieces of music and vocals that were released by major labels, often without securing the label's permission.

Mixtapes began in the seventies as cassette tape recordings of live DJ routines from hip hop club shows and block parties. Today, they retain the name mixtape even though they are now created and distributed digitally on CDs instead of cassettes. Because mixtapes allow up-and-coming artists the freedom to record and distribute their music independently of a label, and permit established artists to break out of the album and single format and maintain their connection to hip hop's roots, they have played a key role in building the names and careers of rap artists from Kool Herc and The Cold Crush Brothers to 50 Cent and Lil Wayne. DJ Drama, who had produced several popular mixtapes for Lil Wayne, Young Jeezy, and T.I., among others, was charged with racketeering: In January 2007, the government seized thousands of mixtape CDs from Drama's house, along with vehicles and other possessions they claimed he had bought from the sale of illegal goods. The story of this mixtape raid, the biggest yet, sounds very much like a drug raid. It confirms that the stories rap artists write about themselves as outlaws goes beyond fantasy to reflect the outlaw position that rap music continues to hold more than thirty years into its history.

SELLING VS. SELLING OUT

By telling these types of stories about their involvement with hip hop music, successful commercial artists claim agency in the selling of hip hop. By framing their business within criminal metaphors, the artists I've studied claim their selling of hip hop to be an oppositional act. Their act of selling is made distinct from selling *out*, which met with backlash in the early 1990s, when artists like MC Hammer and Vanilla Ice were accused of diluting hip hop with pop or dance music to give it crossover appeal. The 1990s phrase "keep it real," though now archaic within hip hop, does demonstrate that realness is an ongoing project. Once artists establish realness through the performance of self in their first releases, they must work to remain true to an artist identity that they have successfully negotiated with the audience. To change their image is to sell out, and artists whose careers span multiple years often face such accusations.[16] Writing autobiography is a process of self-creation, but in hip hop, self-development is held accountable to an original performance of self that becomes the authentic model by which future performance is judged.

As selling out means giving up some part of self-identity in order to increase profit, even those artists who celebrate their ability to sell records make specific distinctions between selling and selling out, which in hip hop means sacrificing artistic control, and therefore individual and artistic integrity, to the record label. During the 1990s, the Geto Boys, De La Soul, and 3rd Bass, among others, were assertive in their criticism of the sell-out. In "Do it Like a G.O." (1989), the Geto Boys parody a phone call from a corporate record executive, "the president of White-Owned Records," who attempts to buy out their independent Rap-A-Lot Records, suggesting that the white-owned label can make the group famous: "It would take you a lifetime by yourself because you know your people don't stick together." The Geto Boys claim that they are black-owned and will never sell out. Today the group's Mr. Scarface is himself CEO of Def Jam South. He has joined corporate ranks while maintaining black ownership and artist control, and achieved success without sacrificing his integrity.

Autobiography's success stories often follow the author-character's journey toward an eventual position of wealth, celebrity, emancipation, or some other self-actualization through exterior forces. In addition to this model, Stone suggests a second pattern for black autobiography that focuses not on journeying, but on "standing fast" (Stone, 177). As a classic example, Stone cites Booker T. Washington's *Up From Slavery* (1901), where the author confronts American racism by staying in Alabama and Mississippi, rather than journeying to a more egalitarian promised land. Earlier, I discussed the importance of the stability of individual identity for the hip hop artist, and a similar "standing fast" narrative has been employed by artists who narrate their work in the music industry. Most notably, this structure is used to challenge rap's success stories in one of hip hop's most vibrant and overlooked albums, Masta Ace's *Disposable Arts* (2001). Ace uses the album to reflect on his thirteen years in the music industry without a gold album, and his lyrics reveal an anxiety about sales and career longevity that challenges rap's emphasis on boasting.

In structure, *Disposable Arts* is both autobiography and fiction, and narrates Masta Ace's career both through lyrical retrospection from Masta Ace, and through skits that follow a younger "Ace" as he matriculates at the Institute of Disposable Arts, where he will learn to become a successful hip hop artist. His class roster includes "Street Promo," "Bronx History," and "MPC 101," where his final grade will depend on his using the MPC-3000 machine to produce a beat. Through songs and skits, *Disposable Arts* juxtaposes the stories of the two Aces, one several years into a music career and the other beginning his education in the trade. The younger, fictionalized Ace reflects the lived experiences of Masta Ace himself both at the University of Rhode Island, where the New York City native found his classmates out of touch with hip hop culture, and in the music business, which Ace has navigated with no formal training. On "Dear Diary" (2001), Ace voices his anxiety about his future in the music business. Upon hearing of Ace's plan to return to hip hop in his late thirties, Ace's personal journal voices his anxieties back to him: "When will you old cats ever learn?" Ace's diary reminds him he has been dropped by his record label, who tells him he can't sell albums, and the diary accuses Ace of being washed up, of being too old to rely on his rhyme skills, and tells him he's going to make his few remaining fans waste their money on *Disposable Arts.*

Throughout *Disposable Arts,* Masta Ace debates leaving the rap business, having seen his greatest successes early in his career. In the album's last three songs, however, Ace makes clear that his involvement in hip hop has not been about commercial success. The album ends with the younger Ace earning his degree, then moving back to Brooklyn to start his own label and artist management company. On the final track, "No Regrets," Masta Ace tells us he wouldn't have done things differently, and that he is fully satisfied with his career, even "If the luxuries in life I can't of course afford," and even if he never receives major awards for his music. Ace shows that commercial success and industry dominance are not the only progressive outcomes of hip hop's autobiographical journey, and he speaks for the continuing dialogue between underground hip hop and Top 40 artists. In "Something's Wrong," Ace comments on the drug narratives of his contemporaries: "I'm an incredible rhymer, why I wanna sell crack for? I'm real, you an ac-tor."

Such assertions of realness from hip hop artists make autobiographical veracity a central dimension of credibility in performing the music, yet the play between Masta Ace and his character Ace illustrate that hip hop lyrics create complex structures of reference that go beyond a simple chronicle of the lives of its artists. As hip hop's emphasis on realness through lived experience leads listeners and critics to understand the music as autobiography, lyrics can create an illusion of reference that has led certain listeners (like the politicians who criticized *Cop Killer*) to forget or ignore the fact that hip hop artists also perform first-person vocals as characters, often switching between these narrative modes as they construct narratives that preserve self-identity throughout their interaction with commercial forces. The play of autobiography and fiction in the music shows a complexity of story structure and narrative perspectives that warrants more attention to hip hop as an autobiographical, narrative form, as well as one that challenges the roles of culture and industry in the production of popular music.

LIFE, DEATH, AND LIFE AFTER DEATH

In writing their lives into their lyrics, MCs also often recall their own births and fantasize about their own deaths, encapsulating their lives in the same way autobiography does. Tupac Shakur and The Notorious B.I.G., two of rap's biggest stars, both wrote songs about dying, and both were murdered before age twenty-five. This focus on one's own mortality finds precedent in Dr. Martin Luther King, Jr.'s speech in which he seemed to predict his own death one day before his assassination in Memphis, Tennessee, on April 4, 1968, and in the end of *The Autobiography of Malcolm X* (1965). Both Malcolm X and Dr. King sensed and predicted that they were not long for this world. This sense of impending death gave their messages a power of urgency during their lives, and a power of supernatural wisdom after their murders, recalling Jesus's speech in the Garden of Gethsemane, in which he informed his disciples that his enemies would kill him the next morning. The documentary, *Tupac: Resurrection* (2003), and the The Notorious B.I.G.'s album, *Life After Death* (1997), employ similar biblical allusions.

The murders of Tupac and Biggie mark the pinnacle, and some say the end, of the age of gangsta rap. Their deaths were the music's violence and fatalism taken to their fullest—taken out of lyrics and into the lives and deaths of the performers. Yet these incidents were not the first time hip hop life had seemed eerily to imitate hip hop art. Slick Rick was released from prison in 1998 after serving five years for attempted murder (he had participated in a shooting and then evaded police). Slick Rick's crime seemed to follow the script from his hit song, "Children's Story" (1988). Released in 1988 and structured as a bedtime story that Uncle Ricky is telling his young nephew and niece, "Children's Story" is a cautionary tale about a young man who shoots someone and attempts to evade police before he is killed in a shootout. As the song ends, Slick Rick reminds his listeners to stick to the straight and narrow, which becomes a haunting message in context of Rick's prison term. In another case of life imitating art, in 1994, Snoop Dogg faced charges for his role in the shooting death of Phillip Woldermarian, an event that occurred after his song "Murder Was the Case" was recorded for his 1993 album *DoggyStyle*. In Snoop's case, the song's lyrics actually fantasized Snoop Dogg's own death at the hands of murderers; Snoop is mortally wounded in a drive-by shooting, but makes a pact with the devil for eternal life. The appeal of a rap star facing murder charges while rhyming about his own murder set the stage for Snoop's performance at the 1994 MTV Video Music Awards, where he began the song rapping from a wheelchair in front of an open coffin and ended it chanting "I'm innocent, I'm innocent."

Snoop's fantasy of his own death set the stage for the extended death narratives of Tupac and The Notorious B.I.G., both of whom imagined their murders in songs.

In one sense, Tupac and Biggie's focus on death in their lyrics reflects the high mortality rates of young black males living in urban settings in the U.S. Yet their lyrical depictions of their murders were so detailed that they have spawned conspiracy theories and a culture of tribute for each artist. When Tupac and Biggie were murdered, hip hop became a culture of death, with several artists paying tribute to these stars on their albums. Puff Daddy's "I'll Be Missin' You" (1997) eulogizes Biggie, and Lil' Kim proclaims herself "the legacy of B.I.G." Though Tupac was murdered in 1996, and B.I.G. in 1997, previously unheard vocals from each artist have been released as late as 2003, when Eminem produced the track "Runnin," which spliced together unreleased studio recordings to simulate a collaboration between Biggie and Tupac. Such recordings attest to the artistic productivity of these two performers during their lives. And through the release of new records, often in which their vocals appear with stars who have emerged since their deaths, these performers maintain their star status. The cult of tribute that surrounds these two artists becomes more powerful in the fact that neither murder has been solved, and in the focus on mortality in their lyrics, as each of them narrated their own deaths on multiple songs. They have become larger than life.

This preoccupation with death speaks to a history of African-American autobiographies, which often convey a particular fatalism. Roger Rosenblatt reads black autobiography as a genre in which "blackness becomes a variation of fate."[17] The black autobiographers of Rosenblatt's study narrate a sense of the inevitability of oppression, poverty, violence, and death. This sense of inevitability influences the endings of many African-American autobiographies and novels, where the narrators obscure or eliminate the self-identity they have constructed throughout the story. As examples of this phenomenon, Rosenblatt points to the ending of Ralph Ellison's *Invisible Man* (1953), where the narrator goes underground; James Weldon Johnson's ultimate choice to pass for white; and the endings of the autobiographies of Richard Wright, Eldridge Cleaver, and Malcolm X, all of whom acknowledge a disappearance of self. Most directly, Malcolm X, in the end of his autobiography, addresses the end of his life:

> Anyway, now, each day I live as if I am already dead, and I tell you what I would like for you to do. When I *am* dead—I say it that way because from the things I *know,* I do not expect to live long enough to read this book in

its finished form—I want you to just watch and see if I'm right in what I say: that the white man, in his press, is going to identify me with "hate."[18]

As most autobiography centers on the creation of a self, the conventional narrative tends to stop when the author feels he or she has accomplished a goal, when she has grown into an acceptable selfhood, and at a point where the author-character is not expected to undergo significant development or change. The self dies in that its narrative development is complete, and as such, endings indicate that the self will remain stable and unchanging. In black autobiography, though, characters often progress not only into selfhood, but also from their lived experience toward disappearance, death, or ascendance to a new life. Rosenblatt argues that the killing of the black self anticipates a state of grace in an afterlife: "Unlike his white counterpart, he dies but has a future."[19]

Death creates a future for Tupac and Biggie in that their legends are preserved in their posthumous releases, starting with Tupac's *Makaveli* (1996) and Biggie's *Life After Death* (1997), both of which were released shortly after their respective murders. Each album carries a feeling of foreboding: Biggie's title is a follow-up to his debut album, *Ready to Die* (1994), and Tupac's album cover features a painting of himself being crucified. De Man believes the quality of autobiography lies in its power to shake up how we view plot and endings, because any ending is simply a choice, and the life is still in motion. Tupac and The Notorious B.I.G. each narrate a life cycle and an anxiety about death that makes them seem vulnerable to their listener, yet death does not end their stories. Tupac's songs "I Wonder if Heaven Got a Ghetto" (1997) and "Thug 2 Mansion" (2002) speculate the carrying-over of his lived experience to the afterlife. Most haunting is Tupac's video for "I Ain't Mad at Cha" (1996), in which he seems to forgive his killer. Recorded only weeks before his murder, and released posthumously, the video depicts the artist's being shot and fatally wounded after leaving a movie theater with a friend. Tupac performs in heaven, dressed in all white. The image of Tupac's speaking from the afterlife was a common structure for his music, and it carries over to the 2003 MTV Films release *Tupac: Resurrection,* which is narrated by Tupac Shakur himself. While Tupac was murdered seven years earlier, he had talked extensively in interviews about his birth, life, and death, and from these interviews the film's directors created voice-overs that frame the film as an autobiography in which Tupac narrates the story of his life, from his in utero stage to his murder at age twenty-five.

The lyrics of Tupac and The Notorious B.I.G. balanced death imagery with stories of their childhoods. When looked at as a whole, Biggie's music

presents a narrative arc that takes him from impoverished child to street corner drug dealer to rap superstar to murdered icon. Tupac's music presents a
similar trajectory, but with more focus on himself as a martyr, or a symbol
for the plight of young black men everywhere in America faced with absent
fathers, the allure of making money through street crime, and police brutality. Tupac's "Dear Mama" (1995) video makes clear that Tupac was born out
of struggle as it tells the story of his mother's incarceration while pregnant
with him. Afeni Shakur was incarcerated because of her involvement with
the black militant group the Black Panthers, and the fact that the unborn
Tupac spent time in jail with her sets the stage for his militant stance in his
lyrics and his future prison terms. Like Malcolm X and Dr. Martin Luther
King, Jr., Tupac believed that his message made him a target, and he attributed his legal trouble to "crooked cops" (on "Point tha Finga" 1993). Images
of Tupac's origins contrast with the death imagery that became a central focus
in his music after a first, unsuccessful attempt on his life. In his music, his
birth and death form a continuum, and as his career progressed, his lyrics
became increasingly concerned with his own mortality, with the afterlife, and
with resurrection. Tupac's artistic attention to his origins and to his mortality
creates a life story that makes him vitally real to his audience.

Both Tupac's mother, Afeni Shakur, and Biggie's mother, Voletta Wal-
lace, have taken active roles in preserving their son's legacies, which is interesting because each woman featured prominently in her son's lyrics. Biggie
bragged about the mink coats, houses, and cars he was able to buy for his
mother, and about her pride in seeing her son become a superstar. Tupac's
music contextualized his own message and actions as a legacy of his mother's involvement with the Black Panthers. Tupac most directly explored his
connection with his mother in "Dear Mama" (1995), which chronicles his
troubled youth with a mother who was often absent in his early childhood
because of her activist involvement, and during his teenage years because of
her addiction to crack cocaine. Afeni Shakur appeared in the video for
"Dear Mama," which reenacts her reconciliation with Tupac. Afeni's place
in her son's music works to establish two key facets of his credibility with
listeners. First, Tupac connects himself to black radical history through his
mother's affiliation with the Black Panthers. Second, her appearance in his
music and videos confirms Tupac's music as autobiography, and confirms
that his life and performance form an organic whole, as she proves to the
audience that 2Pac the artist is one and the same with Tupac the performer,
and that the two share a common history and identity.

The role of the mother is important to hip hop autobiography, as invoking your mother proves that you're telling the truth. "I swear on my mama"

is a common phrase used to convince someone that you aren't lying, and rappers feature their mothers and grandmothers in songs and videos. LL Cool J wrote "Mama Said Knock You Out" (1991) in response to his grandmother's advice for him to take out other, inferior rappers. Through the figure of the mother, performers appear to take themselves offstage and trace their origins. Eminem's negative portrayal of his mother has drawn a lawsuit from her. Ghostface Killah's "All That I Got is You" (1996) is a tribute to his mother. Nas's *God's Son* (2002) album chronicles his mother's death from cancer. In bringing their mothers into their music, hip hop artists show themselves as real and vulnerable, and in this way begin to go beyond speaking from lived experience to construct the story of a life.

Jay-Z's *Black Album* (2003) follows a structure that draws from the birth-death continuum written into the lyrics of Tupac and B.I.G. Jay's mother introduces *The Black Album* with a spoken piece that tells the story of her son's birth, troubled childhood, and his musical virtuosity at a young age. The songs on the album chronicle Jay's childhood in a single-parent home, his early forays into crime and music, and finally, his rap stardom. Throughout the album, Jay-Z says this record is his farewell to hip hop; the album ends on a high note, with Jay listing his plans for retirement. This progressive ending, in which things turn out well for Jay-Z, would appear to stand in contrast to the sense of inevitable doom built into the lyrics of Tupac and Biggie. Ultimately, though, Jay-Z's video for "99 Problems," the last single released from *The Black Album*, depicts him being shot to death in front of the Marcy Housing Projects in which he grew up, linking his death to his place of origin. Jay-Z claims that the video depicts the symbolic death of the artist Jay-Z, who has released his final album, and his rebirth into Shawn Carter, which is the performer's given name, which would indicate that to become himself again, Shawn Carter has to kill off his Jay-Z persona. In an MTV interview, Jay-Z said "the whole [being] shot thing is just really symbolic to the whole retirement thing and putting the whole Jay-Z thing to rest."[20] All life ends in death, and in writing the end to an autobiography, the writer makes a choice in how to present the person he or she has become, and to indicate what the future might hold for that person. When hip hop stars use their music to tell the stories of their lives, deaths, and murders, they imbue their life stories with a sense of urgency, as if they are striving to get out their message before the inevitable happens. At the same time, however, there is the sense that being murdered can make that message larger than life, and can help ensure the legacy of the artist.

THE RAP PERSONA

In depicting his murder in front of the Marcy Projects at the end of his "99 Problems" video (2004), Jay-Z intended to kill off the Jay-Z phenomenon, in effect killing off his persona so that he could retire from being a hip hop superstar and return to being Shawn Carter. The split between performer and persona is complicated in hip hop, where artists claim to present their lives in their lyrics. Jay-Z makes claims to be the realest throughout his music, and he uses his lyrics to tell the story of his life, yet his intent to separate his personal life from the iconic figure of Jay-Z reveals that Shawn Carter and Jay-Z are not one and the same. Jay-Z's retirement was short-lived, and with the 2006 release of a new Jay-Z album, *Kingdom Come*, Shawn Carter proves that his character lives on. To think about rap artists as fictional characters or dramatic personae would seem to contradict the autobiographical nature of the music. However, many stars use personae as a mirror image to reflect on the performer, so that Jay-Z *reflects*, rather than depicts, the life of Shawn Carter, and 2Pac reflects, rather than depicts, the life of Tupac Shakur.

All hip hop is not autobiographical, but the majority of its lyrics are linked to the performer's life story. Tupac Shakur and Shawn Carter created personae that are deeply rooted in their own biographies, and this strong basis in reality afforded them the credibility to write fantasies based on their own experiences. Jay-Z's lyrics tell stories that Shawn Carter did not live out, and 2Pac's lyrics tell stories that Tupac Shakur did not live out. Yet these stories are built from the personal experiences of the performers; 2Pac's fictional stories were so tied to Tupac Shakur's life that the lyrics often seemed to precede, or even predict, events in his life, including his own murder. Typically, the stories told in hip hop lyrics are tied to everyday life in the city, and to a form of literary realism that leads many listeners to understand hip hop as street reporting. However, hip hop identity is created through more than lyrics that are rooted in reality. Certain rap artists create fictional characters and perform as comic-book supervillains, space aliens, or mechanized rappers from the future. Rappers often distinguish between themselves and their new personae by wearing costumes and masks.

In literature, the concept of the mask is tied to discussions of sincerity, truth, and authenticity. In his Harvard University Charles Elliot Norton Lecture, *Sincerity and Authenticity*, Lionel Trilling traced the history of "the doctrine of impersonality of the artist," which led readers and critics to view the poet's voice not as the voice of a person, but as the voice of a *persona* constructed on the page.[1] This view of literature was challenged in modernist literature by critics like Richard Ellman, whose biography of James Joyce examined the roots of Joyce's fiction in his lived experiences. In the 1950s and 1960s, poets such as Allen Ginsberg abandoned persona altogether to speak to the reader as themselves. This privileging of the author's stripping away artifice to speak as himself is a recent literary development; Trilling showed that earlier authors and thinkers such as Ralph Waldo Emerson, Oscar Wilde, and Frederick Nietzsche believed that adopting a mask could help writers more directly express the truth. Wilde and Nietzsche held that wearing a mask allows a speaker to adopt an ironic stance, and to develop a psychic distance between the author and narrator "in order to establish a disconnect between the speaker and his interlocutor, or between the speaker and that which is being spoken about, or even between the speaker and himself."[2] In hip hop, where lyrics typically take on the artist's life and the culture of hip hop music as part of their topic, using a mask or persona to adopt an ironic stance allows rappers to become more critical toward the culture while they still remain rooted in it.

To continue my literary comparisons, hip hop's techniques of constructing personae lie closest to the metafiction employed by the postmodern author Kurt Vonnegut, Jr., who in *Breakfast of Champions* (1973) presents the reader with two versions of himself: Kurt Vonnegut the author, and his fictional alter ego Kilgore Trout, who is an underappreciated science fiction writer. In this novel, Vonnegut tells the reader that he is tired of pretending and putting on puppet shows as a fiction writer. Breaking the fourth wall, he addresses his reader directly to reveal the process by which he has created his fiction. Vonnegut acknowledges that he has created a fictional character, Trout, who reflects several aspects of his own personality, but is also a distinct entity from Vonnegut the author. As I showed in chapter two, Redman makes a similar move in "Redman Meets Reggie Noble" (1992), and Eminem acknowledges his personae as imagined versions of himself who can live out his violent fantasies. While all hip hop persona artists may not follow Vonnegut's pattern in revealing how they created their persona, many of them follow his pattern in existing alongside their persona, and even interacting with it. Because of hip hop's focus on authenticity and autobiography that I have discussed in my previous chapters, it is unusual for a hip hop artist to rhyme strictly in persona. I demonstrated in chapter two that hip hop autobiography can depend on fictions of selfhood, and on complex structures of reference between author and character, and because of this already complex negotiation of self and star, the rappers who do develop personae tend to create them as a fictional counterpart to their established career. These rappers split their identities to perform as two or more different characters, complicating hip hop's basis in autobiography. Artists like Kool Keith, Digital Underground, Bobby Digital, and MF DOOM use personae and costume to critique the hip hop career and its focus on marketing the image of the self. Rapping in persona, these artists confront and redefine hip hop's standards of authenticity, which require performers to represent their actual backgrounds while at the same time engaging with industry standardization of the hip hop image: their biographies have to fit within hip hop culture, but they also have to prove that they are unique. As I discussed in the preceding chapters, rap artists value consistency between the identities of the living person and the artist on stage.[3]

Hip hop identity is built not only from the biographies of the performers, but from other cultural sites. MCs borrow characters from sites as varied as comic books, martial arts, mobster films, and outlaw histories of the Italian mafia, European monarchy, and the Old West. Artists layer their performances with personalities that reflect the identities they want to project to the audience. These personalities coexist with the performer's autobiography through naming (like Scarface, Capone-N-Noreaga, Young Gunz, Tupac's Makaveli), through sampling (Ill Bill begins and ends his 2003 album *Ill Bill is the Future* with samples from the film *Seven*), and through simile (LL Cool J claims he's "just like Muhammad Ali" on "Mama Said Knock You Out"). Digital Underground and MF DOOM extend this identity play to perform in personae, a tradition which has its roots in funk and rock music. Phillip Auslander identifies a form of theatricality in rock performance, and argues that during the 1970s artists like Alice Cooper and David Bowie worked to develop stage personae rather than to construct in themselves an image of the authentic rocker.[4] These personae developed during the era of the rock concept album, which is an album of songs structured around a common theme, and often, as in the cases of The Who's *Tommy* (1969) or Pink Floyd's *The Wall* (1979), take on a narrative structure as they develop characters and follow a linear storyline (these albums were labeled "rock operas" because of their narrative structures).

As rock concept albums began to present fictional characters, develop consistent themes, and follow a plotline, rock musicians began to create personae. In the 1960s, Vincent Damon Furnier created the persona of Alice Cooper, whose horror-themed albums and stage shows saw his music labeled "shock rock" because the character Alice Cooper was a horror-obsessed psychopath. In 1974, Furnier legally changed his name to Alice Cooper (which had originally been the name of his band), and in 1975 he released the concept album *Welcome to My Nightmare*, which brought the storylines and narrative threads of his stage show to record. Cooper's contemporary, David Bowie, created his own persona, Ziggy Stardust. Bowie's 1972 concept album, *The Rise and Fall of Ziggy Stardust and the Spiders From Mars,* tells the story of a spaceman sent to save Earth, but who succumbs to the excesses of being a rock star. Also during the 1970s, concept albums began to appear in country music and funk: Willie Nelson's *The Redheaded Stranger* (1975) told the story of a wife-killing country preacher on the run from the law; the funk group Parliament Funkadelic created a P-Funk mythology that involved a cast of fictional characters played by the group. George Clinton became Dr. Funkenstein, a funk doctor from outer space. As part of their concerts, Parliament included a giant "mothership" from which the group emerged to perform, as if they had been transported from outer space direct to the stage. Parliament's 1976 album *Mothership Connection* tells the story of Dr. Funkenstein, whose ancestors had hidden the secrets of funk in the Egyptian pyramids, to be released when humans were ready for funk. P-Funk also created the characters of Starchild, a spaceman sent to bring funk to the Earth, and his nemesis Sir Nose D'Voidoffunk, who wants to deprive the Earth of funk music.

The influences of 1970s funk and rock concept albums are evident in hip hop music. Alice Cooper's horror-movie imagery may have inspired the hip hop genre known as horrorcore, in which artists like Ganxsta N.I.P., Gravediggaz, and The Flatlinerz imbue their lyrics with stories of horrific torture and murder. The Geto Boys pioneered this subgenre in 1991 with their album, *We Can't Be Stopped*. The album's cover featured two of the Geto Boys, Scarface and Willie D, flanking a third member, Bushwick Bill, who sits on a hospital gurney, having taken a gunshot to the eye in a suicide attempt. The Geto Boys matched the social realities of Houston's 5th Ward with horror-movie images on songs like "Chuckie," in which Bushwick Bill takes on the persona of the talking, killing doll from the *Child's Play* movies. Horrorcore tends to blend fiction with reality, exaggerating violence and gore but keeping one foot, unlike Cooper, in the realities of life in the ghetto. This blend of horrific fantasy and reality was reinforced for listeners when Ganxsta N.I.P.'s album, *South Park Psycho* (1992), was found in the tape deck of a teenager who killed a police officer. In hip hop, the artist's identity is conveyed in autobiographical lyrics, as I have shown, but these lyrics combine with skits, samples, costumes, and album liner notes to create a backstory for the artist. Typically, the setting for this backstory is an impoverished urban neighborhood, but like the rock, funk, and country music stars listed above, MCs who perform in persona often create a different setting for the story of their origins.

While hip hop's horror themes may have been inspired by Alice Cooper, the science fiction themes of 1970s funk and rock concept albums have even stronger connections in hip hop music. Since the early days of rap music in the 1970s, hip hop has been obsessed with outer space. One of hip hop's three founding fathers, Afrika Bambaataa, released Afrika Bambaataa and the Soul Sonic Force's *Planet Rock* in 1982. Borrowing from P-Funk's outer space themes and outlandish costumes, Bambaataa's performance fused electronic beats and keyboards with African Zulu warrior outfits. Bambaataa formed the Zulu Nation, a collective of rap artists devoted to promoting social and political awareness in their listeners. The Zulu Nation led to the formation of the Native Tongues collective, which consisted originally of De La Soul, A Tribe Called Quest, Queen Latifah, and the Jungle Brothers. Each group drew its philosophy from Bambaataa's Zulu Nation, but De La Soul borrowed Bambaataa's outer space imagery as well. The liner notes of De La Soul's debut album, *3 Feet High and Rising* (1989), present in a comic strip the story of the group's origins: Producer Prince Paul teleports De La Soul from Mars to record an album for Tommy Boy records. De La Soul extended this outer space theme on "Transmitting Live From Mars," a song that overlays vocals from a French language tutorial onto a sample of "You Showed Me," a 1968 single from the rock group The Turtles, and a song that ties together De La Soul's Afrocentric fashion, outer space themes, and 1960s hippie imagery to complete the package of *3 Feet High and Rising*, an album loosely structured around a fictional game show.

De La Soul shows their thematic indebtedness to their hip hop predecessor Afrika Bambaataa, but Digital Underground took their tribute to P-Funk even further in titling their 1991 sophomore album *Sons of the P.* The album's hit single, "Kiss You Back" was co-written by P-Funk's George Clinton, and the *Sons of the P* liner notes depict, in comic strip form, the origins of Digital Underground, linking this hip hop group to the P-Funk mythology created by Parliament in the 1970s. Adapting such themes from their musical predecessors, hip hop artists develop personae that allow them to step outside the normal boundaries of hip hop identity and posturing to critique the culture as an outsider—in fact, most hip hop personae are outcasts, space aliens, and comic book super villains sent to rescue hip hop from itself. However, because hip hop is so concerned with autobiography and authentic identity, these personae tend to exist alongside other, more autobiographical versions of the same rapper.

THE HIP HOP PERSONA

Like George Clinton performing as Dr. Funkenstein or David Bowie performing as Ziggy Stardust in the 1970s, or Garth Brooks performing as Chris Gaines in the 1990s, certain hip hop acts perform as a second artist persona. This performance, through costumes, lyrics, and samples, can critique the material conditions of the musician. Rose and Potter explore the often subversive politics of hip hop as it grew from an oppressed culture.[5] Rap artists use costumes to obscure or split their identities and challenge the often conflicting imperatives of authenticity and marketability. A hip hop persona may be composed in response to the conflict inherent in selling one's identity while maintaining in lyrics that this artist's identity matches the performer's. In the example of Digital Underground, a persona may allow the artist behind the mask to perform as a more marketable alter ego while at the same time performing as a traditional artist. Such identity play has a complex history within African-American culture.[6] Digital Underground extends this phenomenon to attack the music industry's focus on the marketable rap image, even as they construct one of rap's most memorable, and marketable, characters. The persona artist constructs a second, distinct identity that goes beyond a change in name. Although a mainstream artist like Eminem may alternate names to form his trinity of Eminem, Slim Shady, and Marshall Mathers, these characters do not constitute separate personae, but rather different aspects of the same artist. In one example of such identity play, Gregory E. Jacobs performs in the group Digital Underground both as Shock-G and MC Humpty Hump, two distinct artists with individual personalities, vocal styles, and physical images, their identities distinguished visually through Humpty's trademark mask. Jacobs preserves in Shock-G a traditional, consistent identity that is presented as authentic both to the performer's experience and to hip hop culture, while at the same time he performs through Humpty Hump a comic-sexual persona that has proven appeal for the mainstream listener.[7] Digital Underground uses the Humpty Hump persona to increase the group's commercial appeal, and at the same time to criticize the mainstream's emphasis on image rather than rhyme skill, thereby aligning themselves with a real hip hop aesthetic even as they enjoy widespread commercial success.

The question of hip hop's participation in its own selling often is at the heart of debates about its resistance. When a song like Body Count's "Cop Killer," N.W.A.'s "Fuck tha Police" or Public Enemy's "Fight the Power" (1989) sells albums for corporations, how does this selling change the nature of the resistance, and to what extent do artists construct a marketable image through their very resistance? Even the artists can sound contradictory. In 1988, N.W.A. warned of artists who "forget about the ghetto and rap for the pop charts," and expressed their own pride in being banned from several radio stations ("Express Yourself" 1988) even as their own album *Straight Outta Compton* (1988) sold over one million copies, and the "Express Yourself" video was played on MTV. The audience dichotomy emphasized in such lyrics maintains that an authentic rap artist must direct his or her performance to the ghetto listener rather than to the mainstream, yet N.W.A.'s performance was directed at the mainstream. As they called out the police force and the FBI on their songs, they drew national attention. While several artists (like N.W.A., Paris, and The Coup) have engaged in a more overt form of resistance to commercial radio through their musical style, subject matter, and lyrical content, another hidden transcript of resistance through the identity play of personae may also allow rap performers to challenge the dichotomy of authentic versus marketable music. MC Humpty Hump and MF DOOM create personae that explicitly critique the imperatives of authenticity and marketability within hip hop music.

Kool Keith Thornton, after the break-up of his group Ultramagnetic MCs, resurfaced to release his 1996 solo album *Dr. Octagonecologyst* under the persona of Dr. Octagon. Kool Keith was already known for his non sequiturs and surrealist imagery in his work with Ultramagnetic MCs, but his transition to Dr. Octagon constitutes more than a change in name; Keith constructs a persona and maintains it across the album, rhyming not as himself, an established old school MC, but as Dr. Octagon, a gynecologist from outer space. Songs, skits, and samples on *Dr. Octagonecologyst* work together to construct a narrative history for the character. "Real Raw" describes Dr. Octagon's "yellow eyes, green skin, and pink and white Afro." "Earth People" is a message from Dr. Octagon to the citizens of

Earth, whom he tells "I was born on Jupiter." "General Hospital," "A Visit to the Gynecologist," and "Elective Surgery" offer Dr. Octagon's services in treating such ailments as chimpanzee acne and moose bumps, or "relocating saliva glands." *Dr. Octagonecologyst* combines surreal images such as "it's raining green" and "oh shit, there's a horse in the hospital!" with scatological humor, samples from pornographic films, and a story about a futuristic outer space doctor who also raps. The album's beginning and ending tie together the stories of the fictional character Dr. Octagon and the rap career of Kool Keith Thornton himself: We begin with "3000" and end with "1977," which purports to be an audio recording from an early rap performance by Kool Keith. "1977" is the final track on *Dr. Octagonecologyst*, and the first to mention the name Kool Keith. The track serves to reveal to the uninitiated the man behind the mask, and to link the surreal, futuristic Dr. Octagon to Keith's roots in old school hip hop. Thus, the album that opened by telling us "rap moves on to the year 3000" closes with Kool Keith announcing a 1977 rap show featuring hip hop pioneers Grandmaster Flash, Kool Herc, The L Brothers, and the original scratch creator Grand Wizzard Theodore. The message is clear: Kool Keith is part of hip hop history, and even as rap moves on to the future, Dr. Octagon does not replace Kool Keith.

In fact, since *Dr. Octagonecologyst,* Keith has since gone on to record as the new characters Mr. Gerbik (who appears on the Dr. Octagon album), and Robbie Analog, as well as Dr. Dooom, who kills Dr. Octagon in the opening track of his album *First Come, First Served* (1999). Dr. Octagon came back to life, however, in 2006's *The Return of Dr. Octagon.* Outside these different personae, Keith Thornton has also recorded new albums, and an adult video, as Kool Keith, including 2000's *Matthew,* which takes its title from Keith's middle name, suggesting that the Keith on the album is closer to Keith's offstage identity. Keith's Robbie Analog persona was a directed response to the Wu-Tang's RZA, who borrowed Keith's idea in titling his 1998 solo album *RZA as Bobby Digital.* Bobby Digital is a rap hero from the future, but his identity lies close to RZA's. In fact, Bobby Digital has become less a persona than a nickname, as RZA has gone on to use the personae almost interchangeably on his 2003 release, *Birth of a Prince.* In the 2004 Jim Jarmusch film *Coffee and Cigarettes,* RZA refers to himself as "aka Bobby Digital."

Kool Keith was only one half of the Dr. Octagon project; he collaborated with Dan the Automator, who produced the album and created the music over which Keith rhymed. After Dan and Keith parted ways over creative differences, Keith went on to create new personae and Dan went on to produce a second space-themed hip hop album, *Delton 3030*. The album is a futuristic dystopian opera with production from Dan the Automator, turntable scratching from DJ Kid Koala, and rhymes from the Bay Area rapper Del the Funky Homosapien. *Deltron 3030* contains twenty-one tracks, nine of which are narrative interludes that help advance the storyline between songs. In keeping with the album's narrative format, the liner notes present a cast of characters: Dan the Automator as The Cantankerous Captain Aptos, Kid Koala as Skizoid the Boy Wonder, and Del the Funky Homosapien as Deltron Zero (Del also plays Quzar and Battle Song Receptionist). Deltron Zero, the album's protagonist, enters an intergalactic rap battle in an attempt to take hip hop back from the corporations who even control time in 3030: The album opens with a statement from The Corporate Institutional Bank of Time, and the track "Time Keeps on Slipping" furthers this concept of a future where time has literally become money. In its focus on a futuristic, space alien savior of hip hop, *Deltron 3030* recalls both P-Funk and Ziggy Stardust. Deltron wants to save hip hop, but MF DOOM says he came to destroy it. The rest of this chapter turns its attention to DOOM, the rap super villain whose costume and identity are modeled after the Marvel Comics villain Dr. Doom, and to MC Humpty Hump, a hip hop clown who undermines hip hop's emphasis on the performer's image and fashion. In undermining a standardized rap image and seeking to destroy rap, respectively, these two artists take hip hop personae in a new direction from the rock and roll savior Ziggy Stardust or the funk liberators of Parliament. DOOM and Humpty Hump also complicate the way personae relate to the person behind the mask. Dr. Octagon and Deltron 3030 are fictional characters played by Kool Keith and Del the Funky Homosapien, who continue to release non-persona albums under their own names. Digital Underground and MF DOOM, on the other hand, use identity play to obscure performer identity, and to form multiple personae that they, at least initially, do not connect.

SHOCK G AND MC HUMPTY HUMP

Gregory E. Jacobs, founder of Digital Underground, maintains two distinct personae. Digital Underground liner notes list both Shock-G and MC Humpty Hump as group members. Jacobs also makes guest appearance on albums, like Murs's *End of the Beginning* (2003), billed both as Shock-G and MC Humpty Hump, and he created a fake biography for Eddie "Humpty Hump" Humphrey, a fry cook who burned and disfigured his face in a kitchen fire. This story explains the fake nose Humpty wears, which is the most identifiable part of his costume. Humphrey wears the mask to hide his surgical scars from skin grafts. The intent of such a bio, and of other tactics like hiring a body double to wear Humpty's costume and pose next to Shock-G (see Ernie Paniccioli's *Who Shot Ya? Three Decades of Hip Hop Photography* for one example of such a photograph), is to fool the audience into believing that Shock-G and Humpty Hump are two different people. By intentionally splitting his performer identities and making up a fake history for his persona, Jacobs avoids the necessary sameness between the artist and the performer that is dictated by rap's emphasis on autobiography. He challenges commercial representations of hip hop artists and the standards by which their marketability and authenticity are judged.

As I described in chapter one, hip hop's imperatives of authenticity require that the MC appears to be the same person offstage as he or she is onstage or on record. As hip hop entered the mainstream, this emphasis on parity between performer and artist met with standardization of the rap image, and with the question of marketing this image to the mainstream listener. As rapper's personalities were marketed, they maintained that their identities were authentic. McLeod's interviews of MCs found that many of them asserted their realness through a connection between their onstage and offstage identities. Method Man, for example, told McLeod "I make music that represents me. Who I am."[8] Peterson has described a similar "lack of affectation" for country artists, and he claims that this lack of affectation can be so pronounced that it becomes itself an affectation.[9] Within popular music, stars often become recognized and appreciated more for the personalities they exude than for traditional musical skills or talents. Hip hop culture, however, values lyrical creativity and originality as well as showmanship. Yet concern with the performer's image has overshadowed lyrical and musical skill as hip hop has shifted from its earlier basis in live performance to the sales of recordings. Before rap singles proved to be more than a novelty on commercial radio, as both their frequency of presence and their chart positions increased in 1990–91, vocalists were judged more by their rhyme skill than by a sense of performed authenticity. With the development of shows like *Yo! MTV Raps*, and the increasing chart presence of rap music, the 1990s promoted an image of the rap artist disconnected from the culture many artists claimed to represent. A key dimension of that culture, as I discussed in chapter one, is the MC battle, which was won based on crowd reaction, and where lyrics generally centered on the rhyme style and skill of the performers involved. In one famous example from 1981, Kool Moe Dee defeated Busy Bee with a direct reference to his overuse of his signature Diggy-Dang routine. Similarly focusing on rhyme skill, pioneering Top 40 rap act Run DMC's 1983 song "Sucker MCs" issued a challenge to the unskilled rap vocalist who didn't know how to put together lyrics or rhyme to the beat. In the early 1990s, however, after both MC Hammer and Vanilla Ice spent several weeks at the number one position on the 1990 Billboard pop album charts, rap lyrics began to shift to a focus on a performed authenticity and the *image* of the individual as equally if not more important than skill. Not only did Eazy-E attack Dr. Dre's shifting position on the use of marijuana, but he also included in his liner notes for *187 Um (Killa)* (1993) a captioned photo of Dre in very non-gangsta attire from his 1980s performance with the dance group World Class Wreckin Cru, and he captioned the photo with attacks on Dre's masculinity, his sexual orientation, and his personal integrity, but none on his musical skill. Eazy then completed his challenge to Dre's authenticity by calling Dre's new partner Snoop Dogg a "studio gangsta," borrowing a tactic from old country-western stars who often discredited each other as studio cowboys. None of Eazy's attacks address Dre's musical skill, but only his credibility as hip hop performer. Eazy's implication that Dre follows trends is a serious charge as hip hop culture struggles to maintain its identity in the face of commercialization.

Rap's unprecedented sales during 1990–92 prompted a widespread lyrical shift from claims of performer skill to concerns of crossing over, selling out, and keeping hip hop pure. A Tribe Called Quest called out MC Hammer on their song "Jazz" (1991), reminding him "rap is not pop, if you call it that, then stop." White hip hop artists 3rd Bass yelled for Hammer to "shut the fuck up," and directly challenged Vanilla Ice's contribution to rap music in their single "Pop Goes the Weasel" (1989), taking the insult further by claiming to have followed Vanilla's "formula" to ensure their response song would be a hit even as it criticized his success.[10] In their lyrics to "Pop Goes the Weasel," MC Serch says that with Vanilla Ice's success, "Hip hop got turned into hit pop." Several songs of that same era also relate a mistrust of the record industry through stories of shady dealings with record executives, A&R staff, and concert promoters. This historical and ongoing tension creates an anxiety for the rap performer, who must at the same time market himself and maintain ownership and control of his identity. Hip hop rejected crossover artists in the 1990s, but by the end of that same decade, artists like Jay-Z, Wu-Tang Clan, and Master P devoted lyrical attention to their business roles and asserted their control over their own careers through entrepreneurialism in self-marketing, industry dealings, or operating an artist-owned record label.

In an extension of this lyrical critique of the image standardization that came with rap's entrance into the mainstream, Digital Underground constructed a persona as a visual statement about identity. Digital Underground's Humpty Hump is identified by his trademark Groucho Marx-style novelty glasses with an oversized brown nose. Digital Underground reached number eleven on the Billboard pop charts with their 1990 single, "The Humpty Dance," a song that showcased Humpty as the sole MC. The track was the second single from *Sex Packets*, one of the three out of a total of fourteen tracks to feature Humpty, and the only song to showcase his vocals exclusively. The song's video depicts a live Digital Underground performance in which Humpty takes center stage, in full costume, while Shock-G and the several other members of the group take the position of backup singers. Subsequent Digital Underground singles have been very Humpty-centered as well ("No Nose Job" 1991, "The Return of the Crazy One" 1993). "The Humpty Dance" pushed *Sex Packets* to sell platinum, but the group's use of persona goes beyond sales gimmick. Dressed in costume, Jacobs used his Humpty persona to speak against the importance of physical image for the popular hip hop artist. "The Humpty Dance" begins with a rhyme that opposes a uniform, stylized appearance for Top 40 rappers: "I'm about to ruin the image and the style that you're used to." Jacobs balances Humpty's playful appearance and vocal style with his performance as the smoothed-out and soulful Shock-G. Although Jacobs performs both characters, his identity as performer is collapsed only onto Shock-G, and is distanced from the Humpty Hump persona. He can preserve a level of authenticity in Shock-G while selling records to the mainstream listener through Humpty's humor.

Rap artists cannot step out of character without risking a central element of their credibility.[11] But as MCs split their identities to perform in persona, Potter's idea of staged blackness becomes more relevant. The costume then goes beyond identification of character to take on an additional role as disguise. Digital Underground videos often show Humpty and Shock-G performing side by side, which further confounds the identity of the two MCs. Humpty Hump's nose and glasses also play a crucial role in Digital Underground's live show, as Shock-G sneaks offstage to change into his Humpty costume, which can also include a feathered headdress and leopard-print miniskirt. As Humpty stages his difference, his oversized nose does "look funny," but at the same time it is a tactic of resistance to the commodification of black bodies in music videos.[12]

In "No Nose Job," Humpty argues against plastic surgery at both a literal and figurative level, as he struggles to maintain the black features of his identity in the face of mainstream success. The 1991 single, from Digital Underground's second album, *Sons of the P,* opens with a verse from Money-B, who recalls Humpty's success with "The Humpty Dance," urging Humpty to get plastic surgery to whiten his features now that he's making money: "Yo, your face has gotta change, Hump!" The dilemma presented in this verse speaks to a wider crisis for the hip hop artist: Does acceptance by mainstream culture mean the hip hop artist should embrace the dominant culture entirely, or change his identity by stepping across the boundary of blackness? To do so would be to ensure commercial success at the cost of losing credibility in his culture of origin, but through the Humpty Hump persona, Digital Underground is able to straddle this boundary, to participate in and profit from mass commercialization of hip hop even as they make their listener more critically aware of its dangers.

"I ONLY PLAY THE GAMES THAT I WIN AT": MF DOOM

Digital Underground generally is not regarded as a resistant or political hip hop group, and certainly is not placed in the same political category as Public Enemy or N.W.A. Yet the Humpty Hump persona was an early strategy of resistance in its critique of hip hop's emerging struggle with market forces. Jacobs has said that he intended to create a group based more in Black Panther imagery than P-Funk hijinks, but when Public Enemy beat him to the punch, he decided to go a different route with Digital Underground. Hip hop's struggle with the pop charts would intensify as gangsta rap became both villain and selling point for rap music in the mainstream. Amy Binder examines contradictory reactions to explicit content in the music of black rap groups versus white heavy metal groups on the part of moral watchdog organizations like the PMRC in the 1990s, yet Potter cites cases in which "negative publicity added measurable market value."[13] The 1992 controversy that arose in response to the violent, anti-establishment lyrics of Body Count's "Cop Killer" and Paris's "Bush Killa" (1992) and "Coffee, Donuts, and Death" (1992) increased sales for certain hip hop artists, while posing to others what Potter acknowledges as a "material threat."[14] In one important case, the group KMD lost their recording contract because of political messages in cover art for their second album, *Black Bastards* (originally scheduled for release in 1994, but actually released in 2001). Backing away from potential controversy, the Elektra label pulled KMD's single "What a Niggy Know," and refused to release *Black Bastards* because of cover art, drawn by Dumile, which depicted a cartoon blackface performer in a hangman's noose. According to Dante Ross, Artist & Repertoire Vice President at Elektra, the artwork "represented the hanging of stereotypes. It was a parody of the game hangman—you get it wrong enough times and you die."[15]

Through the very outright resistance of their album cover, KMD urged listeners to kill the stereotype, to do away with this white representation of the black man, a message that became even more powerful in a moment in which hip hop was experiencing an unprecedented level of commercialization as it embraced, through gangsta, the very stereotype of black male violence and misogyny. Elektra's refusal to release the album remains one of the more telling examples of major label treatment of rap artists. Though not one copy was officially sold (until 2001, when MF DOOM's own Metal Face Records released *Black Bastards*), *Black Bastards* became an underground classic via bootlegs of early promotional copies. After the loss of his record contract and the death of his bandmate and brother DJ Subroc, KMD vocalist Zev Love X dropped out of sight. Seven years later, as a musician whose once-mainstream career had moved not only underground, but away from the music industry altogether, Zev Love X had a unique opportunity to reinvent himself and reemerge as a new persona, MF DOOM.

MF DOOM has enacted an identity shift from Zev Love X of the group KMD to his current incarnation, DOOM. As MF DOOM, Daniel Dumile performs in a mask and refuses to be photographed out of his costume, thereby avoiding a physical connection to his earlier persona. MF DOOM recorded his return to hip hop on the tiny and now-defunct Fondle 'Em label, in association with his own Metal Face Records. DOOM produced his album single-handedly, creating the beats in his home studio and writing lyrics that interact with samples to tell the story of an artist injured by commercial forces, now back in mask to seek revenge on the record industry. Brian Goedde reads *Operation DOOMsday* (1999) as an "album of continuous meaning," which is to say it plays like a concept album: It follows a character through a storyline and/or it develops a theme. DOOM's lyrics are interwoven with samples from two sources: *Fantastic Four* cartoons featuring Dr. Victor Von Doom as sympathetic villain, and the hip hop film *Wild Style* (1982), in which graffiti artist Lee Quinones struggles to keep his art pure in the face of commercial forces. So hero and antihero are juxtaposed with Dumile's own history as a musician to situate MF DOOM as both rap's savior and destroyer.

Unlike Humpy Hump, MF DOOM is in some sense a borrowed persona. Greg Dimitriadus has studied performance in hip hop culture through its connection to popular texts such as mobster movies, comic books, and martial arts films. Christopher Holmes Smith says narratives of the Italian mafia promote the gangster as a figure of American consumerism who built his wealth outside the lines of society. For hip hop artists who trace their rise from poverty, this figure of the outsider who still benefits from consumer culture can hold a position of particular importance. Similarly, the figure of the comic book superhero or super villain, also often outsiders, is drawn into lyrics.[16] MF DOOM's persona links his own artistic trajectory to figures from popular culture. He borrows both a revenge narrative and disguise from Marvel Comics' Dr. Doom. Marvel's Dr. Doom puts on a metal mask after his face is injured in a scientific experiment. MF DOOM samples Dr. Doom's dialogue from an episode of *Fantastic Four* in which his experiment goes wrong: "Now I must hide my face from all mankind." Dr. Doom's experiment blew up in his face, and MF DOOM draws a parallel to Elektra's reaction to KMD's pushing industry boundaries with *Black Bastards*. Dumile's visage as the artist Zev Love X is irreversibly connected to this experiment, and to his status as industry outcast. His metal mask hides a figurative injury and allows him to anonymously stage his comeback as a new artist. "Hey (1999)," DOOM's first single, was released to New York hip hop stations as a debut single from a new artist, and was promoted with no connection to KMD. Further obscuring the link between his past and present artist identities, MF DOOM never performs live or appears in photographs or videos without wearing his mask. Although DOOM's vocal style and production sound nothing like his earlier incarnation, without the mask he could not have avoided critical comparison, and could not have as successfully negotiated his return to the world of hip hop.

MF DOOM's first album, *Operation DOOMsday*, is a multitiered autobiography composed through persona, samples, and lyrics. At the level of samples, the performer's own musical career, aesthetic, and agenda are chronicled in Dr. Von Doom's dialogue from *Fantastic Four* and Quinones's narration from *Wild Style*. The two alternate throughout the five skits (three from Dr. Von Doom and two from Quinones) and build up to the track "Hero vs. Villain," labeled in the track listing as an epilogue, adding narrative terminology to the album's continuous narrative structure. "Hero vs. Villain" connects two narrative strands by interspersing dialogue from a seemingly victorious Fantastic Four, who have stopped Dr. Doom's attempt at world domination, with *Wild Style* dialogue in which Quinones argues against media exposure for his graffiti. "I don't want no fucking picture taken of my shit." Spoken narration from E. Mason reinforces this connection with a challenge to cultural definitions of hero and villain. Mason's spoken verse adds a third narrative voice to the album's already complex lyrical storytelling. At the lyrical level, MF DOOM plays with narrative perspective. Hip hop's standard self-referential lyrics here are delivered in both first- and third-person ("He cleans his metal mask with gasoline"). DOOM's lyrics are playfully evasive, and he challenges the listener to follow the narrative strand. In another third-person sequence, DOOM says of himself, "He's like a ventriloquist with his fist in the speaker's back," and track ten is especially revealing in its chorus of "Who you think I am? Who you want me to be?"

On "DOOMsday," DOOM rhymes that he "came to destroy rap," and in the following verse identifies the contradictions of his character as a "killer who loves children." DOOM has resurfaced to take revenge on the industry that injured him, that forced him to wear his mask. His grudge is with not only the record industry, but with artists and producers he feels are controlled by this industry, who are doing exactly what record companies want. KMD lost their contract for pushing the political envelope in their music. Now in this verse from "Hey!," MF DOOM calls out more complacent and derivative artists as trained monkeys to the record executive's ferret, specifically attacking pop rap's watered-down lyrics and use of existing hit music intact, rather than the cut-and-paste mixes so important to hip hop: "I heard beats that sound like karaoke." Like the Dadaists of the early 20th century, who sought to create anti-art or to fight art with art, claiming "Dada destroys everything," DOOM fights rap with rap. He fights commercial rap's formula for producing crossover pop hits—instead of hiring well-known R&B singers to do his choruses, DOOM sings them himself, deliberately off-key on tracks like "I Hear Voices" and "Dead Bent." Dada was in part a reaction against World War I, and its proponents believed that a culture that could create such carnage did not deserve beauty; Dada artists attacked the aesthetic principles of art in such works as Marcel Duchamp's "Fountain" (1917), which was a urinal unadorned and unmodified by the artist. In hanging this piece of what he called "readymade" or "found art" on a museum wall, Duchamp challenged the intent of art itself. DOOM, with his off-key singing and wavering voice on his song's choruses, challenges the blending of hip hop and R&B on the pop charts, a combination that also was attacked by Native Tongues artists De La Soul and A Tribe Called Quest in the early 1990s, before each of these groups adopted the same pop formula for hits in the late 1990s.

DOOM's disgust with commercial rappers is further evident in other tracks, such as "Rhymes Like Dimes" ("A lot of em sound like they're in a talent show"), and is representative of contemporary underground hip hop's mistrust of the record industry. Underground MCs often lyrically dissociate themselves from mainstream rap music, and claim to be not only more authentic, but more lyrically skilled than the mainstream artists they often attack for rhyming about expensive cars and clothes (listen to Sage Francis's "Narscissist" (2002) for an example of an underground hip hop song that criticizes the fashion industry). MF DOOM's perspective as a corporate label's outcast fosters a level of authenticity to less commercial-minded hip hop culture, and his identity play proves an effective strategy of resistance to corporate music in this new stage of his career.

Since *Operation: DOOMsday*, DOOM has gone on to record a second album as MF DOOM, 2004's *MM ... FOOD*, as well as one album under another persona, King Geedorah, three collaborations (2000's *MF DOOM & MF Grimm*, 2004's *Madvillainy* with Stones Throw's Madlib, and 2005's *DangerDOOM* with Danger Mouse), and two albums from a third persona, Viktor Vaughn. In keeping with his grudge against major labels, DOOM has released his albums on several different indie labels: *Operation: DOOMsday* on Fondle 'Em, King Geedorah's *Take Me to Your Leader* and MF DOOM's *Live From Planet X* on Nature Sounds, *Madvillainy* on Stones Throw, *MM ... FOOD* on Rhymesayers, Viktor Vaughn's *Venomous Villain* on Insomniac Music, Viktor Vaughn's *Vaudeville Villain* on Traffic, and the EP *MF DOOM & MF Grimm* on Brick, and *DangerDoom* on the punk rock label Epitaph. Along with these releases, DOOM has released ten volumes of beats (instrumentals), from the labels High Times, Nature Sounds, and Shaman Works. DOOM's excessive level of production over seven years, and his spreading releases across nine different labels, reflects his desire to take over the industry. He borrows from Wu-Tang's divide-and-conquer tactic to allow their nine members to sign freely with several different labels, making the brand Wu-Tang Clan larger than any one label.

DOOM continues to build his mystique through interactions among his personae. Many of his albums connect one persona to his other incarnations: The cover of Viktor Vaughn's *V2: Venomous Villain* (2004) features a marquee that reads "Tonight: MF DOOM," and the back cover of MF DOOM's *Operation: DOOMsday* features a picture of KMD's Zev Love X and D.J. Subroc, but with a black bar over Zev's eyes, obscuring DOOM's earlier identity. In even more direct interaction, MF DOOM is credited as a guest star on King Geedorah's album, Viktor Vaughn is credited as a guest star on *Madvillainy*, and Viktor Vaughn's *Venomous Villain* album features the track "DOOM on Vik," where DOOM speaks on Viktor Vaughn and complains that people compare the vocal styles of the two personae without realizing the subtle distinctions between the two figures.

THE BACK END SUCKS: PERSONA MEETS RECORD DEALS

On the opening verse of his album *Venomous Villain*, Viktor Vaughn urges his listeners to burn a copy of their friend's CD, rather than spend ten dollars to buy *Venomous Villain* themselves. In encouraging fans to bootleg copies of his CD, he assures them that they'll be taking money from the label instead of from DOOM himself: "I did it for the advance, the back end sucks." This is a different tactic from the outright resistance of Public Enemy's "Burn Hollywood Burn," (1989) for example, but it is a resistant act. DOOM's disregard for record labels proves effective because he maintains multiple artist identities and releases his music through several different independent labels. If one label drops him, another will pick him up. Taking a page from Wu-Tang Clan's playbook, DOOM diversifies his bonds, spreading his music across as many labels as possible, just like Wu-Tang's nine members have done since 1993 as part of their agenda to take over the record industry. Like Wu-Tang, DOOM refuses to sign an exclusive contract with any one company.

This tactic used by DOOM and Wu-Tang preserves a level of control over one's music that typical recording contracts seek to prevent. In fact, there are stories of artists who have worked to emancipate themselves from record companies, whose contracts typically state that the record label owns full rights to any music recorded by that artist, including guest vocals on releases from other artists—this is why in CD liner notes, you see disclaimers like, "Q-Tip appears courtesy of Jive Records." In the liner notes to the Beastie Boys' *Ill Communication* (1994), Q-Tip's disclaimer appears directly above the statement "Biz Markie appears courtesy of his own damn self." Biz Markie, who was dropped from Cold Chillin' Records after he lost a 1991 lawsuit over his unauthorized sampling of Gilbert O'Sullivan's "Alone Again (Naturally)" (more on this case in chapter four), flaunts his liberation from label control: Even as this obviously makes it more difficult for him to release his own records, it allows him more freedom of creativity, and allows him to guest star on any album he wants.

In 1999, rap group The Lox launched an emancipation campaign to urge Bad Boy Records to release them from their contract. The Lox were unhappy with the pop rap image that Bad Boy had crafted for them, and printed t-shirts, made picket signs, and protested outside Bad Boy's headquarters until the label agreed to release them. This protest has precedent in the case of the pop artist Prince, who throughout the mid to late 1990s made a statement about the unfair practices of his record label, Warner Brothers Records. After disputes over the recording and release of his 1994 album *The Gold Experience*, Prince wanted to emancipate himself from his record company. What is most troubling about Prince's situation is that his given name, Prince Rogers Nelson, had been contracted to his record label, so that in effect, they owned his name. Prince could not release music under his own name outside his label. In further protest, Prince wrote the word "Slave" on his face for public appearances. Prince reclaimed his identity by legally changing his name to an unpronounceable symbol, leading fans and critics to start calling him "The Artist Formerly Known as Prince," and later simply, "The Artist." Prince had begun his identity play in the liner notes for several musical projects; he billed himself as Alexander Nevermind as the writer of Sheena Easton's "Sugar Walls" (1984), Joey Coco as the writer or producer of other Easton songs, Christopher as the writer of The Bangles' "Manic Monday" (1986), and Gemini on the *Batman* soundtrack (1989). Yet his greatest statement was dropping his given name, Prince, and adopting a symbol for his name to comment on the level of control record labels can exert over artists.

Hip hop's resistance to record label control responds to those same conditions that Prince brought to the public's attention, but they level this critique in the music itself, devoting lyrics to criticisms of record contracts, and even to their business dealings meant to achieve more artist control. Theorists have disagreed about the effectiveness of such critiques, and whether in fact they even can be labeled as "resistance."[17] In the public transcript, the political performance of rap music often is seen as a strategy of marketing and promotion, rather than as one of resistance. Several scholars have examined rap's selling in the corporate marketplace as a central dilemma of the discourse between hip hop and capitalist society at large.[18] In rap performance, the artist himself often takes on the role of entrepreneur. Rap music indeed is sold, and the process of selling records is acknowledged more directly within rap performance than in perhaps any other form of music. Through lyrical references to recording contracts, album advances, and royalties, rap artists foreground their material conditions, often as a form of resistance. A Tribe Called Quest's "Show Business" (1991) takes the form of a warning to aspiring MCs not to be exploited by industry practices. 3rd Bass's "The Gas Face" (1989) follows a rap group into the industry as a record executive tells them, "Sign your life on the X. Trust me," and the Beastie Boys assure the listener "If you don't buy my album I got my advance" ("Brass Monkey" 1986). Through a similar approach, MF DOOM's "Rhymes Like Dimes" fits into a larger history of rap songs that share a metaphor of rap music as drug. In likening the selling of his art to the selling of dime bags of marijuana, MF

DOOM turns a critical eye toward the act of marketing his music, which hip hop historically has positioned as a positive, life-affirming alternative to the drug trade. Rap artists, however, traffic in the ghetto itself, as they must sell as part of their images the same material conditions that have placed them outside the mainstream. DOOM claims that he's following the American path to success by coming up with the means to "earn a healthy buck" from a self-destructive attitude.

While still rooted in this entrepreneurial artistic tradition, through personae, rap performers can step outside the marketing of a performed authentic self to traffic not in the reality of the ghetto, but in fantasy via MF DOOM's artist–as-comic-book-villain, or the various sci-fi identities assumed by persona artists like Dr. Octagon, Bobby Digital, or Deltron 3030. As hidden transcript, the fantasy of persona constructs a valuable commentary on hip hop reality. The persona artist is uniquely positioned to critique the cultural and commercial image by which the rap performer is judged. Jacobs constructs a Humpty Hump persona through which he can at the same time increase Digital Underground's commercial appeal and critique hip hop's concern with image. Dumile uses his MF DOOM persona to critique the industry that wronged him in an earlier stage of his career when he performed as a different artist. These personae, as they split the performer's identity, can at the same time work to strengthen and preserve the rap self that is strained by the differing criteria of the music business and a culture that grew out of the streets. Hip hop has increased artist control within the corporate industry.[19] Persona artists strategize their positions in relation to this industry, and their lyrics and identity play simultaneously reflects a sense of cultural ownership and an understanding of their music as commodity. Through their construction of multiple artist identities, they position themselves to critique such contradictions, and the playful nature of their critique allows them also to benefit as artists and entrepreneurs from the contradictory economics of hip hop music.

4

SAMPLING AND STEALING

Along with the stories told in lyrics, skits, and interludes, a central part of hip hop's contradictory economics is digital sampling, which complicates hip hop's notions of music as crime, as well as concepts of intellectual property and the creative nature of making rap music. Hip hop DJs and producers have long been criticized for stealing the work of other musicians, and some hip hop producers have embraced the concept of sampling as theft. Like Jay-Z's plan to get rich and give back to his community, hip hop sampling can become a Robin Hood narrative in which hip hop producers place sounds recorded by black studio musicians back into the hands of rap artists. Robin Hood versions of success stories are characterized by the means through which the protagonists achieve their goals. In English folklore legends dating back to the 1450s, Robin Hood is a heroic criminal who stole from the rich and gave to the poor, thereby making the man who is a villain in the eyes of the powerful a hero in the eyes of the powerless. In chapter two, I discussed Malcolm X's winding path to success that led him through a life of crime, and framed this stage of his life as a necessary step in developing the outlook that led to his success. But while Malcolm learned lessons as a criminal and then moved onto loftier pursuits, Jay-Z and many other hip hop artists create metaphors of making music as a criminal act in itself. Digital sampling becomes a way to rip off a music industry with a history of ripping off black artists.

At the same time that DJs and producers describe sampling as crime, however, they also maintain that it is a creative act. Like graffiti artists overlaying a railroad car or bridge with their murals, hip hop producers overlay sounds as they cut, loop, and recombine existing records. When hip hop producers sample, they insert segments of recorded music into their own songs, often truncating the sample to extract its most useful section, syncopating the sample to fit a new rhythm, and looping the sample so that the segment, which may have appeared once in the original recording, repeats throughout the entirety of the new song. This process differs from interpolation, in which a hip hop artist acquires the rights to a musical composition, or sheet music, but plays the music himself or hires studio musicians to play it. Afrika Bambaataa and the Soul Sonic Force were pioneers of interpolation in their 1982 single "Planet Rock," in which Bambaataa replayed a keyboard sequence from Kraftwerk's "Trans Europe Express" (1977), speeding up the tempo and changing the pitch of the original. Interpolation is limited to musical instruments, but samples may be music or vocals from other songs, or may be borrowed from non-musical sources such as films, political speeches, or television commercials. Hip hop values creativity in finding unique sources, recombining unlikely sources, and putting recognizable material into new context.

By recombining and recontextualizing sources, hip hop producers create powerful juxtapositions. GM Grimm, for example, samples the line "those were the days" from the Lee Adams and Charles Strouse theme song to the sitcom *All in the Family* (1970), and makes it the refrain for "Digital Tears" (2004), a song about his experiences as a black man who sold drugs, was paralyzed in a shootout, and spent years in prison. The line "those were the days" feeds into Grimm's own lyrics, which juxtapose his social struggle with a theme song from a show about a white American bigot. The fact that the theme song's original lyrics contained racially motivated lines such as "didn't need no welfare states" only adds to the impact of Grimm's recontextualization of its refrain into a story about poverty, crime, drugs, prison, and desperation. Grimm also juxtaposes sampling and citing as he samples the *All in the Family* theme song without crediting it to its authors, but attributes a reference to Niccolo Machiavelli in the song's opening line: "Machiavelli said you better treat fortune like it's a woman." In Grimm's song, "those were the days" takes on a different meaning that it had in the Adams and Strouse original. Grimm uses the line to refer to the ways he tempted fate in his youth, but in the context of how his reckless youth led to his incarceration and paralyzation, the line creates irony.

Sampling, at its best, uses sources to create new meaning. Sampling, as in the example of MF Grimm's song, often comments on and critiques sources through juxtaposition. I believe that to equate sampling with plagiarism ignores the ways that sampling transforms and responds to the sources it uses. Because sound and print are often compared to each other in cases of plagiarism or copyright violation, it is important to understand where sampling and writing may differ in goals and aesthetics. The most important distinction lies in the attribution of source material. In scholarly writing, listing sources builds one's credibility as an author who reads widely and understands the current conversation surrounding her topic, but hip hop producers often guard or disguise their sources to avoid copyright litigation or so that their style can't be imitated by other artists. In sampling, a DJ's credibility is built from discovering unused material, and to reveal sources is to give away the secrets of the trade.

This idea of guarding one's sources goes back to the three founding fathers of hip hop: Kool Herc, Afrika Bambaataa, and Grandmaster Flash, all of whom at some point removed the labels from their records so that competitors couldn't copy their catalog. The process of not attributing sources may sound unethical, or at least foreign, to those of us who have taken a course in freshman college composition in the United States. The concept, though, is not entirely foreign to Western scholars. In a 1980 interview, Michel Foucault described his citation practices in regard to Marx and Marxism:

> I often quote concepts, texts, and phrases from Marx, but without feeling obliged to add the authenticating label of a footnote with a laudatory phrase to accompany the quotation. As long as one does that, one is regarded as someone who knows and reveres Marx, and will be suitably honoured in the so-called Marxist journals. But I quote Marx without saying so, without quotation marks, and because people are incapable of recognising Marx's texts I am thought to be someone who doesn't quote Marx.[1]

Foucault indicates distinctions between citation and use—and between quoting and attribution—which highlight the reverence that often accompanies source use in academic citation systems. Foucault avoided attributing ideas to Marx, yet he built his own work from these ideas. Foucault's citation process fits with his notion that the author is a product of capitalism. In his influential essay "What is an Author?," Foucault argued that the author-figure is tied to an individualization of ideas and to the concept of private property because authorship functions to brand works with the name of their author. Foucault did not apologize for using Marx's work separate from his name, but instead faults his reader for not being able to recognize the text separate from the label or brand of Marx.

In the precapitalist societies Foucault described in "What is an Author?," discourse was not a product but an act. With capitalism came intellectual property guidelines that necessitated an author's proving ownership of his or her work. Foucault's understanding of the author as a function of ownership, and his connecting of authorship to copyright laws, are important in order to understand hip hop sampling, which over the past twenty-five years has complicated copyright laws designed for the printed word.[2] To write off sampling as stealing is to ignore the complex legal system in place for clearing samples, which generally requires the backing of a corporate record label to purchase rights from another corporate record label. Clearing samples is big business. Aside from legal concerns, to call sampling stealing also ignores the aesthetic quality of sampling: The way it makes something new out of existing materials.

SAMPLING OR STEALING?

The stigma of sampling as theft overshadows the role of sampling as a citation system where sources are transformed for new use. This negative view of sampling finds it roots in the court cases that applied to hip hop music a copyright system designed for print. In 1991, Judge Kevin Thomas Duffy—in granting a preliminary injunction against rap artist Biz Markie, who sampled Gilbert O'Sullivan's "Alone Again (Naturally)" (1972)—invoked the biblical commandment "thou shalt not steal." Yet Biz's own lyrics, when juxtaposed with the music and chorus of O'Sullivan's original song, created irony. Under Section 107 of the U.S. Copyright Law, Biz's song should have been protected as a parodic commentary on O'Sullivan's song. Such court cases highlight the limits that copyright litigation can place on new sound compositions. In 1994, the U.S. Supreme Court held that 2 Live Crew's "Pretty Woman" (1989) was protected as a parody of Roy Orbison's "Oh, Pretty Woman" (1964), and that even though 2 Live Crew's song was a commercial release, Orbison was not entitled to royalties. The Supreme Court held that:

> The more transformative the new work, the less will be the significance of other factors, like commercialism, that may weigh against a finding of fair use. The heart of any parodist's claim to quote from existing material is the use of some elements of a prior author's composition to create a new one that, at least in part, comments on that author's work.

Sampling transforms sources by placing them in the new context of hip hop lyrics and other samples. Rather than copying the original source, hip hop producers critique and respond to the original through juxtaposition, parody, and direct commentary.

Sampling builds upon existing texts by making new connections and responding to them with new ideas. Sampling differs, though, from citation systems for the printed word that require attribution via footnotes or a list of references. Joseph G. Schloss, in his book *Making Beats: The Art of Sample-Based Hip-Hop* (2004), outlined an ethics and aesthetic that many hip hop producers share. Schloss interviewed several hip hop artists about their approaches to making music. His interviews revealed that the musicians were concerned both with discovering unique material and with using it in unique ways. Hip hop producers sample small segments of records, then often change the pitch, slow them down, speed them up, and combine them with other pieces of other recordings. Just as Foucault felt he could build from Marx's ideas without providing an in-text citation to attribute those ideas to Marx, hip hop producers build from the work of musicians such as Prince, James Brown, or Parliament Funkadelic without necessarily listing those musicians' names in their lyrics or liner notes. Hip hop producers value the discovery of unique source material, which can make producers reluctant to share their sources. Schloss outlined a professional ethics of digital sampling by which producers avoid copyright litigation from record companies by not attributing samples or disguising them by altering their original sound. Likewise, producers guard their source material from "biters," who Schloss defined as those producers who "sample material that has recently been used by someone else."[3] Producer Jake One complained that biting devalues the time hip hop producers spend searching for unique source material.[4] This notion of guarding one's source seems foreign to academic writing, where we rely on an open network of information and even gain credibility by connecting our ideas to a tradition of thought. Yet Foucault, like the hip hop producers in Schloss's study, was concerned less with preserving the name of the source's author than with building a new composition in response to the source.

The problem with Foucault's approach to citation, of course, is that without his attributing the source material, even expert readers may find it difficult to separate Foucault's own ideas from Marx's, or to determine where the two diverge. Reverence to Marx aside, the issue is whether readers can distinguish Foucault's new ideas from his reference to another source, or distinguish Marx's voice from Foucault's. Without seeing a citation for a source, how do readers know which part is Foucault and which is the source? Sampling, on the other hand, allows listeners to *hear* source material in a way that is unavailable to writing. When I listen to "Digital Tears," I can hear that GM Grimm's voice sounds different from *All in the Family*'s Edith Bunker. Because I know that hip hop is sample-based music, when I hear a Jay-Z song on the radio, I don't marvel at Jay-Z's skills as a drummer and bassist. I know I am listening to his voice over sampled music. In fact, sampled music is so standard for hip hop that

RZA from Wu-Tang Clan reports that listeners often mistake for samples the organ and piano that he played himself on Wu-Tang's first album.[5] When I listen to hip hop, I expect to hear songs built from multiple sources. Hip hop producers don't try to pretend that they wrote or performed all the sounds on their records, but instead pride themselves on their unique recombination of sources within a new composition.

The obscurity of much of the material hip hop samples fosters a new aesthetics of citation, one based on discovery of unique sources and putting recognizable sources to new use. Of course, not all hip hop producers embrace this aesthetic, and in fact, many of hip hop's crossover hits heard on mainstream radio deviate from this modernist, make-it-new aesthetic to produce songs that are much more derivative of past radio hits—this is a proven pop rap formula. Sampling hit songs is a marketable, yet contentious, practice. Pop rap producer Puff Daddy has sampled recognizable and sizeable pieces of rock and pop hits such as The Police's "Every Breath You Take" (1983), for "I'll Be Missin You" (1997), and Led Zeppelin's "Kashmir" (1975), for "Come with Me" (1998). Even with these songs, however, sampling is not stealing. Puff Daddy's record label paid for the use of these recordings, and members of The Police and Led Zeppelin have shown their approval by performing these songs with Puff Daddy in concert.

Puff Daddy isn't stealing, but other hip hop producers might argue that he isn't sampling either. Underground hip hop producer MF DOOM, for example, criticizes such sampling practices on "Hey" (1999), where he says, "I heard beats that sound like karaoke," meaning that a beat, or the music to a hip hop track, should be an original composition that doesn't copy another song's structure. Producers like DOOM value the discovery and digital manipulation of multiple sounds from multiple sources, rather than the use of pop hits intact. Several producers boast in lyrics about the time they spend digging in the crates in record stores for obscure material, and resent artists like Puff Daddy for giving sampling a bad name. One group calls itself D.I.T.C., the Diggin' in the Crates Crew, and the Lootpack released the song "Crate Diggin," (1999), in which they claim that hip hop producers are "searching for the unordinary sounding loop" which they can put to use in a hip hop track. In short, the responsible hip hop producer must create original new compositions, even if these are built from pieces of several different existing recordings. If responsible sampling hinges on doing something new with the source material, it comes to look less like plagiarism than citation.

In his history of citation systems designed for the printed word, Robert Connors describes the restrictive nature of systematic citation formats such as MLA and APA, which he says are adopted at the cost of "readability and prose style."[6] Connors argued that these systems were developed to showcase the author's knowledge of related texts, and to allow the author to speak to those texts he or she "embraces or rejects"; footnotes function to "show off the author's wide reading or membership in a discourse community,"[7] and to build upon the work of other scholars.[8] Connors notes that citations can attest to the expertise of an author by connecting the author to a tradition of thought or a body of thinkers. Foucault said he never felt obligated, when citing Marx, to add the "authenticating label of a footnote."[9] Foucault's use of "authenticating" takes on two meanings: Attribution can authenticate the quote as Marx, and authenticate the writer as a Marxist scholar. In the first sense, attribution of a quote provides readers with a link to the original source by naming its author and showcasing that author as an expert. In certain hip hop songs, MCs use their lyrics to attribute a sample. For instance, Defari's "Keep it on the Rise" (1999) samples B Real's vocals from Cypress Hill's "Hole in Your Head" (1992), and Defari's lyrics attribute the quote to B Real:

> Defari vocals: "I got the phuncky feel like B Real. I'll put a"
> B Real sample: "hole in your head"

It is rare for a hip hop artist to so directly attribute a sample to its author. In Defari's song, sampling works very much like quoting would in a book: He uses his own language to introduce and attribute the quote, and then pares it down to the most essential words. Defari's new composition enters into dialogue with the source, and it is important to preserve or capture the source's voice through a quote, or in this case, a sample. Importantly, Defari credits B Real, another hip hop star, in his lyrics, yet he never mentions the musicians who composed and performed the instrumental sounds from which his song is built. In quoting B Real, Defari shows himself to be part of hip hop's discourse community, just as LL Cool J does in "The Boomin' System" (1990), where he cites old school rappers like Big Daddy Kane, Eric B. & Rakim, and EPMD, in lines such as "Like Rakim said, I wanna move the crowd." In short, because LL and Defari are making hip hop music, it is important for them to show their awareness of hip hop's lyrical history. Defari and LL are showing off their knowledge of hip hop history, or their wide reading (or listening), and using samples to speak to texts that they embrace.

In keeping with this notion of citation as tribute, there is a long tradition in literature of authors borrowing and adapting phrases from the work of writers they admire: For example, Lawrence Ferlinghetti's seminal poetry collection *A Coney Island of the Mind* (1958) takes its title from a line written by Henry Miller, and Ernest Hemingway's *For Whom the Bell Tolls* (1940) borrows its title from "Meditation XVII," a poem by John Donne. In his song "Sanctuary" (2002), Count Bass D samples Jim Morrison's vocals from the Doors song, "The Soft Parade" (1969). Count Bass D extracts one line, "can you give me sanctuary," which lasts six seconds and occurs only once in the Doors's original. He combines his own keyboard and drums with a loop of Morrison's singing to create a musical track that runs behind his own vocals. In this way, Morrison's voice functions as an instrument in the song, yet his phrase is preserved in the chorus and title of "Sanctuary."

Returning to Foucault's second sense of authentication—that of supplying credibility to an author within a particular field of study—popular music, and hip hop in particular, has a long history related to authentication as proving credibility.[10] Like the way Eminem achieves credibility by working with gangsta rap veteran Dr. Dre, sampling can take on an authenticating function as rap artists use samples to establish their connections to an original source of hip hop. By sampling an MC's voice, they can link themselves to a tradition much in the way scholars link themselves to Marx's thought. For instance, musicians might add the authenticating label of a vocal sample from Rakim (often named top MC in history) without stating Rakim's name in their lyrics; an ideal listener should be able to recognize Rakim's voice, just as Foucault's ideal reader should be able to recognize Marx's words.

SAMPLING AND PLAGIARISM

Analogies drawn between sampling and print writing in recent sampling lawsuits and plagiarism scandals make these events a strong starting point for complicating our views of sourcework in print and sound. To conclude, I'll turn my attention to a recent case where sound was invoked in defense of print, when an author's plagiarism was defended as sampling. In 2005, The University of Georgia Press stripped Brad Vice of his Flannery O'Connor Award and pulped his short story collection *The Bear Bryant Funeral Train* (2005) after a librarian discovered several phrases were borrowed from Carl Carmer's book *Stars Fell on Alabama* (1934). Jason Sanford, writing in defense of Vice, compared Vice's use of Carmer to sampling:

> All I know is that throughout history all types of artists, including writers, have used variations of sampling. Shakespeare was famous for this. (In fact, Shakespeare may have done much more than sample. Hamlet,

for example, was supposedly based on a so-called Ur-Hamlet play written a few years earlier by another playwright, possibly Thomas Kyd.)

Vice's case illuminates how many people misunderstand sampling as plagiarism. While Sanford is right that all types of artists have used sampling (for example, Salvador Dali, Andy Warhol, Donald Barthelme, William S. Burroughs), what Sanford is describing is not sampling. The works to which he refers are not transformative. They do not engage in textual revision. Shakespeare wrote in an age before the concept of intellectual property that Foucault shows coincided with the concept of authorship. Sanford's analogy is flawed in that Vice employed none of the recombination or recontextualization demonstrated in my earlier examples of hip hop sampling. Vice's story does not revise or parody Carmer, or transform his work in any substantial way. Vice adapted several phrases, including his story's title, from Carmer's original story, and changed some of them very slightly (see Young, 2005, for side-by-side examples of text from Carmer and Vice). In this sense, Vice comes much closer to writing a cover version of Carmer's story. Cover songs maintain the original song's essential structures, both musical and lyrical, but may adapt the song for new audiences, changing the style of the performance while keeping these essential structures intact. When the Ataris released a pop-punk cover of Don Henley's "Boys of Summer" (1984), they sped up the song and shifted their intended audience by changing one line (from "I saw a Deadhead sticker on a Cadillac" to "I saw a Black Flag sticker on a Cadillac") to distinguish Henley's 1960s rock nostalgia from their own 1980s punk nostalgia. The cover song is in many ways a tribute to the power of the original; although the modes of performance and audience may change, the original composition is preserved to an extent that does not fit with hip hop producers' descriptions of sampling.

Vice's writing is not sampling because it is not transformative. He does not engage in juxtaposition, parody, or textual revision. Sampling is an odd choice to use in defending Vice's work; sampling remains a maligned practice, one often equated with theft rather than creativity. Vice's case is more about the stigma of plagiarism. In keeping with my reading of his story as more like a cover song than a sample-based composition, Vice has explained that he intended the story to be a tribute to Carmer. The problem is, his book never mentions that author's name. Although Vice titled his story "Tuscaloosa Knights" in reference to Carmer's chapter "Tuscaloosa Nights," the reference to the title was not sufficient attribution for readers not intimately familiar with Carmer's work. Here we return to the audience question posed in Foucault's statement about using Marx. If Carmer were well-known enough, or if I were well-read enough, I would not need to see attribution to know that the words were his. Unlike listening to a sample, I can't hear the difference between Vice's voice and Carmer's. There is nothing to indicate what comes from the source and what comes from Vice. As I argued earlier, while sampling does not attribute the source by providing an author's name, as a listener I can distinguish between what is original composition and what is source. Knowing the author's name is secondary. What is most important is that the reader can distinguish source from new composition.

Yet the most interesting aspect of this case is that Vice's University of Cincinnati doctoral dissertation included an epigraph from Carmer at the beginning of "Tuscaloosa Knights." This epigraph did not appear with the story in his book. Both sides of the debate have used this epigraph as evidence. Either Vice intended to credit Carmer, and the epigraph was somehow cut before publication, or Vice intentionally removed the epigraph to hide his reliance on Carmer. The consensus seems to be that a plagiarism case would be more difficult to build if Vice had included *any* mention of Carmer's name, anywhere in the book. Plagiarism, then, hinges on Vice's intent. Did Vice intend to present Carmer's work as his own, or was it a poorly-attributed tribute? Obviously, short stories do not traditionally follow a citation system such as MLA or APA. How, then, should such sourcework be attributed? Does a general acknowledgement of another author indicate that certain phrases throughout will be quoted or borrowed without citation? Print authors and some hip hop artists have relied on copyright pages and liner notes to cite their sources without interrupting the aesthetics of their piece with in-text citations or footnotes.

SAMPLING AS REVISION

I am describing sampling in terms of writing, but this phenomenon of texts speaking to texts has a deeper history within the African-American oral traditions of Signifying. Henry Louis Gates, in *The Signifyin(g) Monkey*, defined Signifying as "a metaphor for textual revision" through repetition and recontextualization.[11] Gates interrogated a history of African-American literature in which authors such as Ishmael Reed Signify upon the work of other authors. Reed himself said that his "gumbo style" or his "mixing and sampling" technique "might be the constant in African American culture, that of making something whole from scraps."[12] Extending this tradition to the hip hop producers who use digital sampling to reassemble pieces of existing recordings, Paul Gilroy explained that "the aesthetic rules which govern [sampling] are premised on a dialectic of rescuing appropriation and recombination."[13] Thomas Porcello defined sampling's key capabilities as "the mimetic/reproductive, the manipulative, and the extractive."[14] Each of these capabilities relies on context. A mimetic/reproductive parody, like 2 Live Crew's "Pretty Woman," can rely on the repetition, in new context, of key elements of the original song. The manipulative capability is illustrated in Kanye West's sampling of Chaka Khan's line "through the fire," which he sped up and manipulated to say "through the wire" for his hit single "Through the Wire" (2003). The extractive power of sampling is revealed in the Beastie Boys' "Hello Brooklyn" (1989), where the line "I shot a man in Brooklyn" is followed by the Johnny Cash sample "just to watch him die." In extracting just these five words from Cash's "Folsom Prison Blues" (1956), the Beastie Boys changed the setting from Reno to Brooklyn and removed the context of consequences and regret from Cash's original murder ballad. In each of these examples, sampling transforms the original by placing it into new context.

Sampling's textual revision extends the tradition of Signifying in that hip hop as an aural form allows the listener to hear the original in new context, often digitally manipulated to fit a new rhythm, or even given a new tone to match its desired usage. While the history of Signifying provides important context for the advent of sampling, I wanted to better understand sampling's unique aesthetics of textual revision, specifically what it can do via sound that cannot be done in print or oral storytelling. I interviewed Count Bass D, a Nashville-based hip hop artist. Count Bass D is uniquely positioned to discuss sampling. His debut album, *Pre-Life Crisis* (1995) was celebrated by critics in *Rolling Stone* and *The Source* for his use of traditional instrumentation rather than samples. A self-trained musician, Count played every instrument on his debut album, yet after earning warm critical reception for his instrumentation, Count felt he had to learn sampling in order to prove himself to other hip hop artists: "Everybody was kind of looking at me like, well that's great that you can play an instrument or whatnot, but it means nothing unless you can actually make a beat too." Making beats via samplers and drum machines is so central to the production of hip hop music that making a live instrument album can call into question an artist's authenticity and raise questions of audience and reception. Count said, in my interview with him:

The purists want to keep hip-hop for themselves. They're afraid the machine is gonna get it. And the machine, by praising me they were tearing down all the other artists and saying what they did was nonsense, when nothing could be further from the truth.

In response to this pressure to prove himself as a hip hop artist, Count taught himself to use a sampler for his 2002 album *Dwight Spitz*, where his textual revision is most evident in two songs: "Truth to Light" and "Just Say No."

"Truth to Light" begins with the correction of another artist, Greg Nice of the group Nice & Smooth. Nice's opening verse from "Funky for You" (1990) contains the misinformation "Dizzy Gillespie plays the sax," and Count revises this statement through use of Nice's vocals. Like Defari in my earlier example, Count attributes his sample. "Truth to Light" opens with a sample of Greg Nice saying his own name, "Nice." Then, Count sets up the vocal sample with his own lyrics:

> Greg Nice sample: "Nice"
> Count Bass D vocals: "Lester Young was on the tip of his tongue when he said"
> Greg Nice sample: "Hey yo Dizzy Gillespie"
> Count Bass D vocals: "played the trumpet."

In tying these lyrics to trumpeter Lester Young, Count uses his jazz expertise to revise Greg Nice's vocals. Count described his composition process in terms of sampling:

> Songs that really I like a whole lot, that I've liked over the years, kind of run through my head all the time and so they kind of creep into songs. They get used that way, like in lyrics or something like that. And oftentimes I'll try to accent it by using the original. Unless you know [Nice & Smooth's "Funky for You"], you don't know who I'm talking about or what I'm talking about, but I think to the people who are in the know, I think it strengthens their faith that the things I'm talking about that they don't understand may have some relevance to them in time."

Count believes his ideal listener should be able to recognize his source. This concept of audience is important to understanding sampling's revision function. If listeners cannot recognize the *All in the Family* theme song, or the Nice & Smooth lyrics, or Johnny Cash's "Folsom Prison Blues," is the impact of the revision lost? Foucault faulted his reader for not catching his allusions to Marx, and because sampling deals more in popular culture than philosophy, the responsibility rests with the listener. As I discussed in a previous section, hip hop producers enjoy discovering and reclaiming obscure material. With "Truth to Light," Count seems more interested in strengthening his bond with those listeners who are "in the know" than with explaining his sample and revision to the less savvy listener. As Foucault argued, physicists use the ideas of Newton and Einstein in their work without providing footnotes to guide the reader through physics' founding principles. Count directs "Truth to Light" toward those listeners familiar with old school hip hop lyrics, but on "Just Say No," he borrows from more familiar territory in juxtaposing a 1980s antidrug slogan with a thirty-second voiceover from a 1980s sugar commercial: "Do you think things that taste good are fattening?," the commercial begins, enticing the listener to give in to the pleasures of sugar. "Come on, you're not using one of those substitutes, are you?" With my listening guided by the title, "Just Say No," I can't help hearing the sugar spokesman as a pusher.

SAMPLING AS CRIME

Court decisions that reduce sampling to theft recall Foucault's idea that the concept of authorship had less to do with writing than with private property. I have illustrated sampling's transformative power and the new meanings it can create through recombination, parodic repetition, and juxtaposition. Because copyright laws were designed for print, the act of sampling often is articulated through print metaphors to show that sampling can function as quoting or citation. Yet several lawsuits over sampling have seen musicians and record companies seek damages for the use of their sounds in hip hop songs. As copyright laws criminalize sampling, hip hop artists have embraced sampling-as-crime to write a Robin Hood narrative of musicians freeing sounds from the bonds of record company litigation. Foucault's concept of authorship as ownership comes into play as the name on the recording contract often doesn't match the name of the musician who recorded the actual sound. As I illuminate these issues through my interview with Count Bass D and a study of a sampling lawsuit against the Beastie Boys, this section will examine the contradictions between sampling's alternative roles as a creative and a transgressive act.

Count Bass D identified a bias against sampling. As an artist who felt he had to learn sampling in order to prove himself to his peers, and found it more difficult than any of the traditional instruments (like bass, drums, and keyboards) that he'd learned to play, Count recognizes that sampling is widely criticized as a creative shortcut, even as audiences appreciate similar digital recombination in the visual arts:

> Sampling is like photography, and drum machines are like Photoshop, or Quark, or Illustrator. But because the things we use are so obscure,

they don't even understand that this is coming from this place, and this is coming from that place, because it all comes together and makes musical sense. So people think you just get one record and you get some drums and voilà.

Count described the technical and cultural knowledge that sampling requires, from understanding musical composition, to learning sampling technologies (like truncating and looping samples, converting digital sound to analog, and manipulating samples to fit the rhythm of the new song), to understanding the types of records and drum patterns from which hip hop music is built.

Yet even as Count Bass D defends sampling's creativity, he also promotes making rap music as a criminal act: "We're renegades, man. What we're doing is illegal. That's one of the main reasons why I like it too. It *is* hip hop when you're doing it my way. You know? It's got to be renegade. Hip hop started as a writing culture, as a graffiti culture, which is not legal." Just as graffiti artists overlay existing structures (railroad cars, billboards, buildings) with their own art, so that the structure becomes part of the artwork, rap producers without the financial and legal backing of a major record label have to find ways around the intricate process of sample clearance. As an artist who currently records independently, Count feels a distinct tension between his ideology of sampling from musicians he admires, and the profit agenda of the corporate recording industry. Count makes a clear distinction between ethics and legalities as he makes the point that rap producers often steal from the record companies that gave studio musicians unfair contracts, rather than the musicians themselves. He feels that industry regulations on sampling can hinder creativity as they require musicians to go through the proper legal channels to make sure those entities who own publishing rights are properly compensated:

> We duck around trying to find a manufacturer that'll press up this record or press up that record, because we don't have time to wait on the RIAA and record companies to decide how much more they want to fuck people in the ass. I'm sampling this man's drums and the drummer's not even getting fuckin' paid. How am I supposed to feel guilty when James Brown is getting the money and not [Brown's "Funky Drummers"] Clyde Stubblefield and Jabo Starks? When I've *talked* to Jabo Starks. I've *talked* to Clyde Stubblefield. I've talked personally to them and discussed it, and I know that they're not seeing a dime off that. How am I supposed to I feel guilty if I use their drums? It's their work. Nobody told them to play that pattern. Nobody gave them

writer's credit and they didn't get any publishing [rights], so they don't get any money.

As a commercial product, popular music is granted an author function, but the name on the record and the name on the publishing contract often don't match. Studio musicians cede their publishing rights to the artist on the album cover, and artists cede licensing rights to record labels. Clearing samples is a complicated business, because rights to the composition (the sheet music) and the performance (the sound recording) often are held by different entities, even when the composer and performer are the same person. In the late 1980s and early 1990s, before there was a defined legal system of clearing samples, artists such as De La Soul, Biz Markie, and the Beastie Boys were sued by the musicians they sampled. Media attention to hip hop sampling tended to label it a transgressive act by which rappers, who didn't play instruments, infringed on the copyrights of more legitimate musicians. In conjunction with the early backlash against sampling, hip hop artists often frame sampling as a transgressive act. As sampling was outlawed, many rap artists embraced this outlaw identity.

Sampling as theft fits with Tricia Rose's description of hip hop's "sociology-based crime discourse."[15] In the legal realm, however, sampling is a white-collar crime, contained to lawsuits over intellectual property. As stated earlier, legal issues regarding sampling often get articulated through comparisons to written text. In 2002, for example, the Beastie Boys issued a statement after being sued unsuccessfully by composer James Newton for not having cleared the rights to a sequence of three notes (C/D-flat/C) Newton composed for his song "Chorus." The group had cleared all rights to the recorded music with Newton's record label, ECM, but had not cleared their use of the musical composition, for which Newton still owned the rights. This distinction between recorded performance and written composition proved pivotal to the judge's decision in favor of the Beastie Boys. In their own statement, issued online at www.beastieboys.com, the group defined a crucial distinction between the written and the performed:

> A composition is a combination of words and musical notes, generally presented as sheet music. The copyright of the recording on the other hand, has to do with the uniqueness of the performance on that particular recording. The system exists because often songwriting and performing are two different lines of work.

The Beastie Boys offered an analogy to literature, where the sound recording of a book on tape constitutes a very different copyright than the words printed on the page. The Beastie Boys argued that their sampling of only three successive notes, originally composed by Newton, on their song "Pass the Mic," did not breach copyright because a sequence so brief (six seconds) does not constitute a musical composition. The group argued, "If one could copyright the basic building blocks of music or grammar then there would be no room for making new compositions or books." The Beastie Boys extended their print analogy to argue that in digitally manipulating Newton's recorded flute performance to change its tone and duration, they effectively changed the notes Newton composed. They compare this kind of digital manipulation to paraphrasing.

As the Beastie Boys defended their digital sampling on "Pass the Mic," they called into question distinctions between print, recording, and performance. These distinctions are complicated by hip hop's existence as a commercial music form, and also by the crime-based discourse that still pervades the musicians' concepts of identity performance. The Beastie Boys argue that copyright regulations exist to protect musicians, rather than limit them, and that when Newton sought what they considered an unfair payment of more than $100,000 (and as he refused an out-of-court settlement), he attempted to manipulate the intent of copyright laws that protect transformative works. As I discussed in my introduction, sampling is subjected to the fair use regulations of U.S. copyright law, section 107, which outlines four factors to consider in determining if an infringement occurred: "the purpose and character of the use" (i.e., commercial or nonprofit), "the nature of the copyrighted work," "the amount and substantiality of the portion used," and "the effect of the use upon the potential market for or value of the copyrighted work." Earlier I mentioned the U.S. Supreme Court's decision that upheld 2 Live Crew's right to parody Roy Orbison's "Oh, Pretty Woman." This decision stated that "The more transformative the new work, the less will be the significance of other factors." The Beastie Boys' "Pass the Mic" bore very little resemblance to Newton's "Chorus." The Beastie Boys transformed the original by manipulating its sound and combining it into a new composition.

The Beastie Boys's case is important for students to examine to understand how copyright laws are applied. The C/D-Flat/C heard on "Pass the Mic" is so transformed from Newton's sheet music that it is impossible to prove that they stole his composition. But the case played out in court for nearly three years, and the Beastie Boys report that their legal costs were more than $100,000. In the statement on their website, they urge musicians to avoid such frivolous lawsuits, and remind their readers that copyright laws exist to protect artists, not to hinder their creativity. Musicians and record companies have been very litigious over sampling, which reminds me of Foucault's claim that authorship has less to do with writing than the law, and who has the right to claim ownership of words, ideas, and sounds. Count Bass D's concept of sampling-as-crime works to put these words and sounds back into the hands of musicians.

THE TAKEOVER

Since the 1980s, hip hop's digital sampling has raised new issues regarding intellectual property and brought to light the contractual dealings of the music industry, which often divvies up rights among different entities, and which rarely grants artists full rights to their own work. Rather than continue to fall victim to lawsuits like those levied against Biz Markie, De La Soul, and the Beastie Boys, or continue to sign away their rights to their music, as so many rap artists did in the 1980s, several of today's rap artists instead study the ins and outs of the music business, and eventually move into roles as record label CEOs or owners of their own production companies. These new roles necessitate manipulating the rules of the industry to the artist's advantage, and rappers even brag about knowing the music business better than their contemporaries. The rivalry between Jay-Z and Nas, for instance, featured a lot of lyrical attention on which one of them best knew the music business. On "The Stillmatic Freestyle" (an unofficial release in 2001), Nas claims that he makes money from Jay-Z's music when Jay-Z samples his voice. But on "The Takeover" (2001), Jay-Z brags about making out the royalty check to Serchlite Publishing rather than Nasir Jones, making clear that Nas doesn't own the rights to his vocals. Jay-Z tells Nas that he's been in the music business for ten years and needs to "smarten up."

Jay-Z also claims that he used Nas's voice to better effect than Nas did: "You made it a hot line, I made it a hot song." Jay-Z sampled the line in question—from Q-Tip's remix of Nas's "The World is Yours" (1994) in his 1996 song "Dead Presidents,"—five years before he and Nas began to wage a war of words with several diss songs beginning in 2001. Jay-Z's "Super Ugly" (2002), and Nas's "Ether" (2001) took rap beef to a new level, as both artists included their business savvy as one of their strengths over their opponent. In Jay-Z's verse about sampling Nas's vocals, his expertise in copyright law and contract negotiation becomes a dimension of credibility; Jay brags about business smarts just as other rappers brag about their aggressiveness, murderous natures, physical prowess, or rhyme skills.

Manipulation of the rules of the music business to one's personal gain is evident in the way rap artists use sampling and interpolation. As I described in the beginning of this chapter, digital sampling differs from interpolation in that sampling clips and inserts a piece of an original recording into a new record, even if it manipulates the tone, pitch, or rhythm of that original. Interpolation, on the other hand, involves working from original sheet music but playing the sound in a new performance. Before digital sampling became the standard for hip hop production, pioneering acts of the late 1970s and early 1980s, like Sugarhill Gang and Afrika Bambaataa, relied on interpolation, hiring live musicians to play basslines, drum breaks, and keyboard segments from sheet music originally composed and performed by other bands. Because copyrights to sheet music often are held by different entities from the owners of the sound recordings, interpolation offers hip hop producers a method for working from existing songs without paying record companies royalties for the sound recording, and instead paying the musician who composed the work. In this way, rap producers circulate money to musicians instead of corporations, and typically pay a much smaller fee.

In my previous section, I discussed the case of James Newton versus The Beastie Boys. When the Beastie Boys sampled James Newton's "Chorus" on their song "Pass the Mic," they had secured the rights to the sound recording with Newton's record label, ECM, but had not secured the rights to the sheet music from Newton as the composer. Newton, as the musician who played and recorded the notes, was entitled to a royalty check from ECM, but he said he never received it. Because the Beastie Boys were sampling, the sound was what was a stake rather than the composition of three notes. However, in some cases producers can avoid paying record labels higher fees by securing the rights to sheet music from composers, and then either playing the music themselves or hiring studio musicians to play it. Dr. Dre, one of hip hop's biggest producers, says that he prefers this type of interpolation to sampling because working from sheet music allows him more control of the sound: he can ask studio musicians to play it the way he wants it.[16]

Interpolation isn't the only way Dre has been involved in issues of intellectual property. By manipulating the copyright system to their advantage, hip hop producers, managers, and label owners have become savvy about publishing rights and the U.S. copyright system. A prime example of this is Dre's former partner Suge Knight, who used business savvy, threats, and force to get Dre released from his contract with Ruthless Records and to secure the rights to the master recording of Vanilla Ice's *To the Extreme*, a platinum-selling album that Knight had nothing to do with. Suge Knight's history in hip hop is tied to the breakup of N.W.A. When

Dr. Dre split from the group, he was still under contract as an artist for
Ruthless Records, a company co-owned by his N.W.A. bandmate Eazy E
and N.W.A.'s former manager Jerry Heller. On *It's On: 187 Um (Killa)*
(1993), Eazy calls Dre his bitch and samples his N.W.A. vocals (to which
Eazy owned the rights) in order to mock him. At the same time, on "Dre
Day," Dre claimed Eazy E was a yes man for N.W.A.'s white manager Jerry
Heller. According to Heller, Knight secured Dre's release from Ruthless
Records by threatening him and Eazy with pipes and baseball bats. After
Eazy and Heller released Dre, he and Knight formed Death Row Records
together. Eazy-E wasn't the only rap artist Suge is said to have threatened.
Vanilla Ice says that Knight hung him by his ankles from a balcony to
scare him into signing over the rights to *To the Extreme*, which contained
his hit song "Ice Ice Baby."

   The racial implications of Knight laying claim to Vanilla Ice's music are
vast, and are tied to concepts of making rap music as a Robin Hood
endeavor. If sampling takes sounds out of the hands of the record companies
and puts them back into the hands of the musicians, the process of sampling
fits with hip hop's Robin Hood stories of stealing from the rich and giving
to the poor. Jay-Z talks about getting rich and giving back, Chuck D talks
about the responsibility to keep rap money in the community, and Count
Bass D talks about freeing the sounds that black musicians signed away to
their bandleaders or record labels for an unfair price. In effect, Knight scared
Vanilla Ice into paying a black man some of the money he made from rap
music. Though the Suge Knight/Vanilla Ice conflict is an extreme example,
a friendlier version of this racialized Robin Hood story is found in Dr. Dre's
role in building the career of Eminem. Dre, a black rapper and producer,
claims that he had been seeking a white rap star to sign to his label, and
with Eminem he found someone who could market as so authentic to the
rap model that he could make people forget Vanilla Ice. As I will show in
my next chapter, Eazy-E, Queen Latifah, and Ice-T have echoed Dre's sentiment about the marketability of a white rapper. This recalls the 1950s trend
for white label owners to pay white musicians to rerecord songs from black
groups to reach a wider audience. But in hip hop, the black stars maintain
control as the producers, label owners, and sponsors that lend the white
artists credibility. Upon its release in 1991, Vanilla Ice's "Ice Ice Baby" outsold any black rap song before it by co-opting the stories of crime, gangs,
and social struggle told in the lyrics of black artists. Vanilla Ice borrowed
African-American struggle and style in order to sell rap music to white
America, and Suge Knight, a true-life member of the street gang M.O.B.
Piru Bloods, took back what he felt was his.

Although Knight and Dre have parted ways, Dre's work with Eminem on his own label Aftermath Records is in some ways an extension of this same approach to shifting the racial power structures of the music industry. In attaching his name to Eminem, Dre helped the young white rapper move past the Vanilla Ice stereotype and achieve the credibility necessary to succeed in hip hop. Dre worked to help Eminem forge a unique brand of white credibility that is more careful not to poach on black territory. In this way, Dre ensured that even as Eminem became an international star, his music made clear that hip hop remains black-owned. In keeping with this theme, my next chapter examines the ways white rappers from the Beastie Boys to Vanilla Ice to Eminem to Paul Wall, have worked to establish their credibility in a black-created form, and the ways in which their interaction with black stars have shaped their careers in a music form that seeks to right some of the racial wrongs of the music industry. The business savvy that began in hip hop as a survival tactic for stars and as a necessary component of digital sampling has transcended that form to bring street smarts not only to sampling and interpolation, but to contract negotiation, founding and running record labels, and the A&R duties of recruiting and developing new talent.

WHITE RAPPERS

Hip hop music has become a global force, yet fans, critics, and artists continue to frame hip hop as part of African-American culture.[1] It makes sense to consider hip hop music an African-American form, given the roles of African-Americans in the creation of the music. More than thirty years into its history, the majority of hip hop recording artists remain African-American, and when white artists are accepted by listeners, they tend to gain this acceptance through their association with an established black artist—in two important examples, Run DMC and Russell Simmons sponsored the success of the Beastie Boys, and Dr. Dre sponsored Eminem. Along with African-American dominance on the performance side of hip hop culture, African-American entrepreneurs have founded record labels, recording studios, concert promotion firms, clothing companies, bodyguard services, and other businesses that support hip hop music and culture. In their lyrics, hip hop artists emphasize their goal to maintain control of their music and reverse the white-black power structures that so affected rock and roll, blues, and jazz as these forms went mainstream, and many African-American musicians signed away their rights to music they wrote or performed.

Because hip hop music tells the story of black artists learning from this history and taking control of the business side of their music, white people involved in hip hop today feel a need to acknowledge their place as outsiders, as if to anticipate criticisms that they are treading on black turf: Vanilla Ice made whiteness a part of his artist name, Eminem used his lyrics and the film *8 Mile* (2002) to show us that his white skin didn't guarantee social or economic advantage, and made him have to work twice as hard to gain acceptance as a rapper. Even white critics and scholars writing about hip hop are careful to be up front about their racial position. To make sure it doesn't look like they're poaching on African-American territory, white hip hop critics often make excuses for their white skin and their interest in hip hop in the introductions to their books. Rather than standing behind his author bio, which states his credentials as a musicologist and professor, Adam Krims introduces his book *Rap Music and the Poetics of Identity* (2000) with an attempt to establish his personal relationship to hip hop culture. He makes clear to the reader that he understands his position as a cultural outsider:

> Any claim I could make to hip hop authenticity would be preposterous. So I do not make it. My connection to rap music and hip hop culture is that of an ardent fan, someone whose musical life has been saturated by rap music since (roughly) 1990, who is at times a rap performer (as instrumentalist and producer), who is both a producer and a consumer, but who is by no means close either to hip hop's original cultural existence or to rap's current source of authenticity.[2]

Because the notion of authenticity is so important to hip hop, Krims feels an anxiety about his position as researcher. Crispin Sartwell is even more forthright with his apology for whiteness in *Act Like You Know: African-American Autobiography and White Identity* (1998), which includes a chapter on hip hop. He states in his introduction: "I cannot hope to escape the possibility that some of what follows—or even all of it—is racist."[3] Sartwell argues that it is impossible for a white American man not to be racist, and tells his reader "what follows is written in the *anxiety* that it could be interpreted to express racist attitudes."[4] In putting their anxieties into their introductions, these white scholars let themselves off the hook, as though acknowledging the racial tensions that exist in hip hop somehow lessens these tensions.[5] Revealing their anxiety is crucial to the authenticating strategies of these white critics. This image of white speakers tiptoeing around black issues is rooted in the political correctness of the 1990s, which is to say it is rooted in fear of a political backlash. These critics foreground their political anxiety and at the same time assert their immersion in African-American culture. Sartwell's long introduction about his own racial position also tells the reader about Sartwell's leftist parents who took him to race rallies and to a Martin Luther King, Jr. vigil in Washington, D.C. He relates stories of his childhood, when he went to school with black kids and "was intensely attracted to some of the black girls."[6] Even as he emphasizes his anxiety, Sartwell authenticates himself through stories of his immersion with black culture, just as Vanilla Ice and Eminem did. As musicians and critics address their white skin, the message is clear: Hip hop culture is African-American culture.

Of course this is dangerous ground to tread. On one hand, to defend hip hop culture as black-owned is a sort of cultural preservation, but on the other it essentializes aspects of African-American identity: If rap equals black, does black also equal rap? This problem came out in Tempe, Arizona, on November 30, 2006, when Mayor Hugh Hallman and Police Chief Tom Ryff apologized for a segment of *Tempe Street Beat*, a cable access reality show that follows Tempe police officers on duty. In the segment, Sergeant Chuck Schoville pulls over two young black men in a shopping mall parking lot, then offers to let them go if they perform a rap about littering. The two men agree to rap for Schoville, who claims that off-camera they had told him they were aspiring hip hop artists. Reverend Jarrett Maupin of the National Action Network said of the incident, "It's important for police officers to realize that black people do not speak hip hop. We're not all rappers and thugs and gangbangers. We speak the English language and we're entitled to the same amount of respect."[7]

A similar sort of essentializing of African-American identity caused controversy in 1988, when the CBS network fired sports commentator Jimmy "the Greek" Snyder for saying on the air that African-American men were naturally better athletes because white slave-masters had bred their ancestors to be bigger and stronger workers. CBS executives and viewers called for Jimmy the Greek's dismissal, but on a Boston radio talk show, a black man calling himself Ali phoned in to speak to the sports commentator's defense, claiming that "Jimmy the Greek said nothing but what was true," and that his critics "do not want to hear the truth."[8] Greek's statements on slave-era breeding may well be historically accurate. But his sentiment seemed to characterize African-Americans as naturally physically powerful, as if to say that black athletes don't have to work as hard as white athletes (even though Greek stated explicitly that black athletes tend to work harder than whites). Greek's description of how race influences athletic skill caused an uproar and led to his firing, but his sentiment was mirrored in the 1992 film *White Men Can't Jump*, in which a character played by Wesley Snipes explains to a character played by Woody Harrelson why black men are endowed with certain athletic skills that white men are not.

Hip hop exploits similar preconceptions about African-American identity: That black men are by nature aggressive and criminal. Hip hop created a paradigm of African-American experience that is drawn from the impoverished, urban communities where rap music was invented. Rappers from inner-city New York housing projects expose truths about life in these projects. Rappers who sold drugs on street corners tell vivid stories about selling drugs on street corners, and how that experience shaped the outlook that led them to their careers in rap. But hip hop music also is a form of

entertainment, and as my previous chapters have shown, listeners should
not accept lyrics as factual reporting or as straight autobiography. Rappers
use hyperbole, fictionalize their experiences, and write stories about fictional characters. Rappers invent personae like MF DOOM and MC
Humpty Hump to comment on the racial stereotypes that hip hop can
reinforce. Hip hop is entertainment, and such artistic license is present in
any form of entertainment. Yet no matter the degree to which their lyrics
are fictional, each hip hop artist must show that his or her outlook was
shaped by his or her experiences in life. All rappers must achieve credibility
with their listeners and peers, and this credibility is drawn from struggle
tied most directly to the experiences of African-Americans in urban settings
facing poverty, crime, violence, and lack of opportunities for employment
and education.

Hip hop is defended as an African-American form. African-American
artists often extend this image of the authentic to present hip hop as a
black expressive culture faced with appropriation by a white-controlled
record industry. This concept of white-black interaction has led white
artists either to imitate the rags-to-riches narratives of black artists, as
Vanilla Ice did in the fabricated biography he released to the press in
1990, or to invert these narratives, as Eminem does to frame his whiteness
as part of his struggle to succeed as a hip hop artist. Because hip hop's representations of racial identity are so tied to class, each of these white artists
tells stories of his class struggle to counter hip hop's representations of
white privilege. Eminem, however, also succeeds in attending to the privilege his whiteness affords him with listeners. I argue that the reaction
against Vanilla Ice changed the way white rap artists confront their whiteness, and that newer artists have developed a more critical awareness of the
problem of constructing white hip hop as "real," even as the success of
white artists would indicate hip hop's assimilation. Specifically, Eminem
frames his performance in response to Ice's discrediting. Rather than imitate a model of hip hop blackness, Eminem emphasizes the autobiographical basis of his lyrics and his struggle to succeed as a rap artist, to present a
new model of white hip hop authenticity where being true to yourself and
to your lived experiences can eclipse notions of hip hop as explicitly black-
owned.

This chapter studies hip hop as black American music, and looks at
the ways white artists have addressed their minority status in rap. A look at
rap's three decades of history reveals that white rappers have moved from
the cultural immersion enjoyed by the Beastie Boys as the first white act
among Def Jam's roster of established black rappers, to Vanilla Ice's failed

imitation of black rappers' life stories, to Eminem's lyrical focus on his own whiteness, and finally to Paul Wall, whose success indicates that a white rapper can once again make it without rhyming about being white. The problem with gaining credibility as a white rapper traces back to the 1990–92 scandal that reduced Vanilla Ice from rap's top-selling artist to rap's most discredited. An examination of journalists' treatment of Vanilla Ice illustrates that Ice became a scapegoat for a history of white appropriation of black music forms; his discrediting changed the ways that white rap artists address their whiteness in lyrics. Earlier white artists such as the Beastie Boys relied on narratives of cultural immersion, yet white artists after Vanilla Ice have shown a more critical awareness of their whiteness as minority position within the music. The chapter also examines rap's representations of white listeners, and the ways black artists and executives sponsor white artists and market their music to a white audience even as hip hop remains African-American music.

The relationship of white identity to hip hop became complicated when SBK Records marketed Vanilla Ice as a white artist who maintained credibility in the black community. Ice was not the first white artist to achieve crossover success with hip hop, yet his performance marked the first time a rap artist had so deliberately articulated his own whiteness in marketing, beginning with his name and the title of his first single, "Play That Funky Music (White Boy)" (1990). Vanilla Ice turned his minority position as a white rapper into a point of pop marketability. Yet, at the same time, his lyrics and the official SBK artist biography appealed to a "real" hip hop image through his claims to an urban upbringing, criminal involvement, and gang affiliation; the bio even claimed he had been stabbed in a gang fight. Ice's biography seemed to fit with the stories of many black rap artists who were his contemporaries, but his background became a point of investigation for Ken Parish Perkins of *The Dallas Morning News*, who on November 18, 1990, published a story that disproved much of what SBK had claimed about Ice. According to Perkins, SBK press materials "portray a colorful teen-age background full of gangs, motorcycles, and rough-and-tumble street life in lower-class Miami neighborhoods, culminating with his success in a genre dominated by young black males."[9] In reality, Rob Van Winkle, who performed as Vanilla Ice, spent his teen years primarily in the Dallas suburbs, and was both wealthier and less involved with crime than his bio had claimed. For example, Perkins revealed that Van Winkle attended R.L. Turner High School in Carrollton, Texas, rather than Miami's Palmetto High. When Perkins contacted Vanilla Ice's manager, Tommy Quon, to question this contradiction,

Quon acknowledged that Ice's upbringing "could have been well-off.... it may not be true that he grew up in the ghetto—but maybe he spent a lot of time there."[10]

Because hip hop lyrics are rooted in autobiography and often narrate black artists' struggles against systemic racism, Vanilla Ice's false claims to a background of ghetto poverty and crime breached the norms of rap rhetoric. Vanilla Ice asked the listener to look past his whiteness to see a kind of social blackness that would authenticate him because his rise to stardom fit with black rappers' success stories. He failed, however, because his lying and his selling of hip hop to the pop charts made his performance look like an imitation of black artists to make a white artist rich. Although Vanilla Ice broke hip hop sales records with his 1990 hit single "Ice Ice Baby" and his album *To the Extreme*, Perkins initiated a backlash. By 1992, newspapers referred to Vanilla Ice's career as "a travesty" and to Ice himself as "questionable" and "a bad memory, a one-man joke."[11] Over the course of two years, such responses to Vanilla Ice signaled a shift in the public perception of Ice himself, and heightened attention to the importance of racial identity to constructing hip hop authenticity.

As I discussed in chapter one, within popular music studies, the concept of authenticity often centers on the performance's proximity to notions of an original culture that at one time existed outside the record industry. Concepts of "real" hip hop, as this term is used in lyrics, frame hip hop as a black-created culture threatened with assimilation into a white mainstream. McLeod identifies the semantic dimensions of hip hop realness as it is constructed to resist assimilation. He presents a model of urban black masculinity, which emphasizes, in part, "staying true to yourself vs. following trends."[12] Armstrong, who theorizes the authenticating strategies of Eminem, updated McLeod's model as he identified three "initially evident" forms of hip hop authenticity: Being true to oneself, claiming "local allegiances and territorial identities," and establishing a connection to "an original source of rap" through locale, style, or links to an established artist.[13] Hip hop realness, then, is conveyed when an artist performs as a unique individual while maintaining a connection with the original culture of hip hop.[14] For white artists, authenticity is constructed in response to the performances of black artists. Yet constructions of white authenticity have changed most distinctly with the success of key white artists, first with Vanilla Ice, and then with Eminem, and now extending to white Southern rappers like Paul Wall, Haystak, and Bubba Sparxxx.

White authenticity became more difficult to negotiate in the nine years between Vanilla Ice's discrediting and Eminem's debut. The scandal over

Ice's bio effectively separated white artists from mainstream rap until 1999, when Eminem released *The Slim Shady LP.* In fact, white artist involvement in hip hop can be divided into three distinct eras, each with its own authenticating strategies; pre-Vanilla Ice (1973–1990), Vanilla Ice (1990–1999), and Eminem (1999-present). I will use the terms immersion, imitation, and inversion to describe the ways white artists in each era have worked to frame their whiteness as part of real hip hop. As notions of hip hop authenticity have changed, white artists have moved from immersing themselves in a nascent music culture, to imitating an explicit model of the black authentic, to inverting the narratives of black artists to frame their whiteness as a career disadvantage in a form that remains dominated by black artists.

HIP HOP AS BLACK AMERICAN MUSIC

Hip hop music is a black form, given the involvement of African-Americans in its creation, and because its concepts of authenticity are so tied to the roots of its culture. As I discussed in chapter one, hip hop authenticity is rooted in African-American rhetoric; its emphasis on the performer's staying true to himself grows out of black rhetorical traditions such as testifying and bearing witness, in which authority to speak is negotiated through claims to knowledge gained through lived experience. White artists are regaining a foothold lost by Vanilla Ice, who breached this tradition of truth, as their performances remain accountable to the music's black traditions.[15] As I present a counterhistory of the white artist, though, I want to be clear that central characteristics of hip hop's language, musical traditions, oral culture, and political location make it a black American form. In fact, the history of white artists is a history of their speaking to the black Americans who continue to dominate the music.

Of course, issues of race and ethnicity are oversimplified in a discussion of black-white interaction that does not account for the multiple racial positions reflected in hip hop. For instance, Puerto Rican involvement in the creation and development of hip hop has been well-documented. However, Puerto Rican and female pioneers are primarily graffiti artists and breakdancers, rather than the MCs or rappers who are the focal element of commercial hip hop, and who are the figures I study here. Also, Latino MCs like Kid Frost, Big Pun, and Fat Joe have had less trouble than white artists in establishing their legitimacy. Because hip hop remains a resistant culture, and because the dominant culture is white, whiteness stands outside hip hop as a force that threatens to appropriate its culture.

Hip hop has been, and remains, very conscious of the long-standing threat of appropriation, and of the loss of black control of the music and culture to a white record industry. This tension between African-American artists and white record executives fosters representations of whites as appropriative toward black music.[16] Inevitably, record labels co-opt new forms invented in black communities, and there is a history of white artists topping the charts with black music they have adapted for a white mainstream, and making more money than the African-Americans who invented the form. This tension grew within hip hop culture with the success of Vanilla Ice, who made his whiteness a selling point even as he obscured his upbringing in white suburbs.

While other, earlier, white rap artists had met with general acceptance, Vanilla Ice made whiteness, as difference, fully visible within hip hop.[17] During the 1980s, white artists asserted their immersion in hip hop culture without imitating a model of black authenticity. Although most commercial rap was recorded by black artists, white artists such as the Beastie Boys met with acceptance from their peers. Nelson George credits the Beastie Boys's 1986 debut *Licensed to Ill* with creating a "racial chauvinism...making the Beasties the first whites (but hardly the last) to be accused of treading on 100 percent black turf."[18] At the same time, George contends that rap culture never was exclusively black culture, that it was never "solely African-American created, owned, controlled, and consumed."[19] Mike Rubin describes rap's reception of the Beastie Boys: "Back in the early '80s the Beasties were just New York City kids taking advantage of the nascent hip hop scene's any-and-all-welcome attitude to enroll as the first minority students in the old school."[20] The group's acceptance among black artists would seem to support this claim. Black rap artists like Run DMC and Public Enemy shared the stage with the Beastie Boys, and LL Cool J credits them for discovering him. The group was black-managed, by Russell Simmons, and in a reversal of a typical story of white-black interaction in the record industry, the Beastie Boys claim Simmons signed them to an unfair contract.

Black MC Q-Tip, who recorded and toured with the Beastie Boys, says: "You know why I could fuck with [the Beastie Boys]? They don't try to be black. They're just themselves."[21] While newer white rap groups like Lordz of Brooklyn and Insane Clown Posse have adopted Beastie Boys vocal styles, in particular Adrock's nasal delivery, the Beasties didn't so much attempt to sound white as they established a performative frame of reference for white acts to come. In fact, Q-Tip and the Latino rapper B Real planned to record with Adrock in a group called The Nasal Poets[22]; and on MC Milk's "Spam" (1994), Adrock refers to himself and Milk as "the high-pitched brothers from the East Coast." These collaborations with black artists complicate readings of the Beastie Boys's "white" vocal styles as a way to foreground their racial identity. "Spam" is notable also because it contains more explicit references to race than Beastie Boys lyrics; Milk refers to Adrock as "white boy," and Adrock refers to Milk as "black guy." The Beastie Boys never directly confronted their whiteness in lyrics, although they did speak against racism on *Paul's Boutique* on the songs "B-Boy Bouillabaisse" and "Lookin' Down the Barrel of a Gun" (1989). By not calling attention to their whiteness, the Beasties did not make their minority status a gimmick. But they did encounter resistance when they treated their whiteness as invisible to a black audience. In one incident in the 1980s, the Boys themselves seemed almost ignorant of their minority status. Former Beastie DJ Dr. Dre (from *Yo! MTV Raps*, rather than Dr. Dre from N.W.A.) told *Spin* magazine about a Beastie Boys performance at New York's Apollo Theater, during which Adrock yelled to the crowd, "All you niggers wave your hands in the air!"[23] Although this type of crowd incitement is common for hip hop artists, Dr. Dre claims he could feel an immediate shift away from the audience's warm reception of the Beasties, who were so much a part of hip hop culture that in the excitement of performing they forgot they were still outsiders. Dre says that the Beasties used the term "not maliciously, but out of warmth for their audience."[24] Yet while he claims the incident is recorded on videotape, the Beasties wrote to *Spin* alleging that Dre made up the story.[25] Whether true or not, the incident became a footnote to the Beastie Boys's long history of acceptance in hip hop.

The Beastie Boys's interaction with black artists has been key to their career. The white MCs of 3rd Bass also promoted their acceptance by black rappers in their debut single, "The Gas Face" (1989). The song was produced by black producer Prince Paul. Zev Love X, the black MC who would later perform as MF DOOM, appears on the song, and the video features prominent black artists like Erick Sermon of EPMD. Like the Beastie Boys, 3rd Bass included a black DJ, but Vanilla Ice did as well, so a group's integration cannot alone establish its authenticity. Aligning themselves with established hip hop artists, 3rd Bass used the song to criticize MC Hammer for selling out the form as a pop crossover. In 1992, in joining the criticism of Vanilla Ice, 3rd Bass saw its biggest chart success with "Pop Goes the Weasel," a single dedicated to lampooning Vanilla Ice's performance of hip hop realness. The song compares Ice to Elvis and accuses him of stealing his hit song's chorus from a black fraternity. The video depicts 3rd Bass beating Vanilla Ice (as played by punk rock icon

Henry Rollins) with baseball bats. Through their connections to black artists and black topics, 3rd Bass asserted that they belonged to hip hop culture. They confronted issues of racial identity in "The Gas Face," when MC Serch rhymes, "Black cat is bad luck, bad guys wear black, Must have been a white guy who thought of all that." He then urges black listeners to embrace their racial identity and avoid hair-straightening products and blue-colored contact lenses. In 1990, *The Village Voice* ran Playthell Benjamin's story "Two Funky White Boys." As the title indicates, the story's tone was positive, and it established 3rd Bass's hip hop legitimacy. One year later, an article celebrating hip hop whiteness would be difficult to find.

VANILLA ICE: THE ELVIS OF RAP

Two months after Perkins exposed lies in the Vanilla Ice bio, *Washington Post* writer Joe Brown assessed the change in Ice's reception in the press: "Now, making the Ice slip on his own stories is getting to be a favorite pastime of pop journalists."[26] Following Perkins's lead, journalists questioned Vanilla Ice about several aspects of his biography such as the schools he attended, the neighborhoods he grew up in, and how he was occupied before he made it big as a rapper. The investigation extended to Ice's use of a sample from the Queen and David Bowie song "Under Pressure" (1981) for the hook of "Ice Ice Baby." Sampling disputes, as I discussed in chapter four, were not uncommon for hip hop artists in the early 1990s, but the lies in Ice's biography made him an easy scapegoat for critics who believed sampling was less than artistry. Brown identified a trend among journalists to react not only against Ice's ethnic border crossing, but also against simulated performance in popular music. Vanilla Ice debuted in 1990, when rap singles had begun to regularly cross over to the pop charts. The year was rife with debates over authenticity in popular music. Rap's mainstream market was increasing, which raised fears of losing its original culture; the pop group Milli Vanilli was stripped of its 1989 Grammy award for Best New Artist after the group's manager made public that Fab and Rob, who performed as Milli Vanilli, did not sing a single note on their recorded album, and lip-synched in their concerts.[27] The context of Milli Vanilli is important to understanding the Vanilla Ice scandal. Ice himself told the *San Francisco Chronicle* "I ain't no Milli Vanilli."[28] The crucial distinction between the two scandals is that Vanilla Ice *did* record his own vocals, yet his critics were concerned with a different kind of musical authenticity, one that focused on how the performer's biography was reflected in his music.[29]

Vanilla Ice's false claims to ghetto credibility made him more of a scapegoat than Hammer. While Hammer marketed a culture from which he came, Ice was selling a culture in which his own experience was not rooted. Print journalists linked Vanilla Ice to a history of white appropriation of black music, comparing him to Elvis Presley (Mills, "White Thing"; Coady) and calling him "the Elvis of rap" (Brown). As journalists connected Ice to Elvis, they linked him to rock and roll's history of white performers who achieved success by adopting black sounds. Print journalists or the scholars they interviewed referred to the way Ice "gets criticized for imitating blacks."[30] They raised issues of white mimicry and appropriation of black culture, and assessed the Vanilla Ice phenomenon as history repeating itself: "Vanilla Ice is merely the latest chapter in a recurring American dream, in which a good-looking white kid borrows a black sound and style...and walks off with the prize."[31] These journalists criticized whites' poaching on black culture, and as they reacted against Ice's circulation of a fake biography, their inquiry extended to Ice's credibility in several aspects of his performance, from his name to his fashion style. In this way, Vanilla Ice became a scapegoat for the history of white exploitation of black sounds in American music.

Several newspaper stories published 1991–92 covered the difficulties of emerging white rappers trying to establish their credibility in the Vanilla Ice era. I studied thirteen newspaper articles published between November 19, 1990 (the day after Perkins's article ran) and August 30, 1992. Six make direct, negative assessments of Vanilla Ice. Six raise questions of Ice's authenticity but remain neutral in their assessment, and only one, from *The London Times*, offers a defense of his performance. Of six newspaper articles to cover new white rap artists in 1991–92, all mention Vanilla Ice. Four articles make negative comments about Ice, and two are neutral.[32] Two articles present a positive view of 3rd Bass and the Beastie Boys. Journalists framed new acts in negative comparison with Vanilla Ice: "Unlike Vanilla Ice (aka Robert Van Winkle), Marky Mark doesn't feel the need to pad his biography with street-wise fibs to prove to the world he's got the right to rap."[33] New white artists themselves expressed uncertainty about their prospects for success. Icy Blu, a rare example of a white woman rapper, told the *Miami Herald Sun*, "Sometimes I get nervous when I'm playing at a club and the crowd is all black people. I get the feeling they are not going to like me because I'm white. It's like I'm going to get this horrid backlash. I get scared."[34] J.T. similarly reported feeling "a strong need to be accepted by the black audience, because it is a black industry."[35] The schism created by Vanilla Ice is most obvious in examining the careers of white artists who debuted between Vanilla Ice's 1990 debut and the release of Eminem's *Slim Shady LP* in 1999. Ice's discrediting affected the sales of subsequent white artists, as well as the ways they dealt with their white skin as something inauthentic to hip hop.

In the nine years between the debuts of Vanilla Ice and Eminem, one-hundred-nineteen singles from sixty-four black hip hop artists made the *Billboard* Hot 100 Chart. For white artists, six singles charted, from Vanilla Ice (1990, 1991), Marky Mark and the Funky Bunch (two singles in 1991), House of Pain (1992), and the Beastie Boys (1998) (Bronson, 2003). (I exclude Snow, a white pop-reggae artist who I do not categorize as hip hop because of the style of his music [he sings rather than raps]; I also exclude Shaggy, a black pop-reggae artist, for this same reason.) Most revealing are the authenticating strategies of Marky Mark and House of Pain, the two white artists who made their chart debut after Vanilla Ice, and a fourth white group, Young Black Teenagers, who saw MTV airplay with "Nobody Knows (Kelli)" in 1991. Marky Mark and the Funky Bunch's pop rap debut, *Music for the People* (1991), sold more units than any other white rap album between Vanilla Ice's *To the Extreme* and Eminem's *The Slim Shady LP.* Marky Mark's album cover features Mark Wahlberg surrounded by his posse of black and white friends. The album's title even has a note of harmony to it. Designed for pop crossover success, and marketed in connection to Mark's brother, Donnie Wahlberg, from New Kids on the Block, *Music for the People* sold over one million copies. Although his group toured with New Kids, a bubblegum pop group and one of the world's biggest-selling artists, Marky Mark framed his hip hop authenticity within his history of criminal involvement as a youth in Boston. This move turned against him when it was revealed that his background included two racial incidents. In 1993, Marky Mark issued this statement to the press:

> In 1986, I harassed a group of school kids on a field trip, many of them were African American. In 1988, I assaulted two Vietnamese men over a case of beer. I used racist language during these encounters and people were seriously hurt by what I did. I am truly sorry. I was a teen-ager and intoxicated when I did these things. But that's no excuse.... (Kelly, 2D)

While he went on to enjoy success as an actor in films such as *Fear* (1996), *Boogie Nights* (1997), and *Invincible* (2006), and as the producer of the HBO series *Entourage*, Mark Wahlberg's rap career was short-lived. Sales for his second album, *You Gotta Believe* (1992), were low enough to make it his final album release.

Young Black Teenagers, a group of five white kids, released their first album only six months after Vanilla Ice's *To the Extreme*, and asserted their cultural immersion more directly than any white artist before them. YBT's track listing included "Proud to Be Black" and "Daddy Kalled Me Niga Cause I Likeded to Rhyme." Their album was recorded, although not released, before Vanilla Ice's stardom, and the two artists employ a similar strategy to claim realness despite their whiteness—through immersion in black culture. YBT argued that their love for hip hop culture was so strong that they could consider themselves black. Like 3rd Bass two years earlier, YBT claimed to be white performers who were *down* with black listeners, so much that whites criticized them for their interest in black culture ("Daddy Called Me Niga"). Claiming authenticity through immersion became more difficult after the reaction against Vanilla Ice, when white artists began to employ authenticating strategies which redefined their whiteness outside privilege. This discursive shift is best evidenced by House of Pain, whose self-titled debut album emphasized the ethnic character of their whiteness as they promoted their Irish heritage as distinct from a generic "white" identity. The album's cover featured a picture of the three white group members along with a shamrock, the group's logo. They had shamrock tattoos and wore green Celtics jerseys. The album included tracks like "Shamrocks and Shenanigans," "Top O' the Mornin' to Ya," and "Danny Boy, Danny Boy." The video for their first single, "Jump Around," was set at the Boston St. Patrick's Day Parade, although no member of the group was from Boston. To avoid all accusations of attempting a performance of blackness, House of Pain focused on another racial position: not white, but Irish. This performance recalls Noel Ignatiev's *How the Irish Became White*, which traces the history of Irish heritage as a racial identity in the U.S. Like the Beastie Boys and the Latino group Cypress Hill during this same era, House of Pain marketed themselves to alternative rock listeners via their fashion (nose rings, tattoos, and green flannel) and their music, most notably in the guitar-heavy version of "Shamrocks and Shenanigans," remixed by Nirvana producer Butch Vig. House of Pain released Vig's remix as a single rather than the original album's more distinctly hip hop version.

With the 1992 release of *Check Your Head*, the Beasties made live rock instrumentation a key component of their performances as they moved away from the strictly hip hop styles of their first two albums. The Beasties didn't release another complete album of hip hop tracks until 2004's *To the 5 Boroughs*. By aligning themselves with new trends in white rock music, these groups did not so much distance themselves from hip hop as they did play it safe with their audience. This created a further split between "hip hop" and "rap," and ultimately fueled the rap-rock movement that would see white bands like Korn, Limp Bizkit, and Linkin Park borrow hip hop's fashion, vocal styles, and turntable scratching to incorporate hip hop styles into rock music.

Rap-rock is a form of rock music, and therefore lies outside my focus on hip hop music here. However, the most pertinent connection to hip hop music, and the most intriguing figure of rap-rock music undoubtedly is Kid Rock, a Detroit-area native who languished in obscurity as a hip hop artist before he turned to rock. Kid Rock learned rhyming and turntable scratching at house parties in the Detroit suburbs, and in 1990, at nineteen years old, Kid Rock released his debut album, *Grits Sandwiches for Breakfast*, on Jive Records, the hip hop label that housed rap heavyweights like Kool Moe Dee and groundbreaking artists like A Tribe Called Quest. Hip hop legend Too $hort produced the album. That same year, Kid Rock toured with Too $hort, D-Nice, Ice Cube, and Yo-Yo. Faced with the public scrutiny of Vanilla Ice, however, Jive did not sign Kid Rock to record a second album. Kid Rock continued to make rap records in the underground, and in 1993, he released his sophomore effort, *The Polyfuze Method*, on Continuum Records, an indie label. *Polyfuze* anticipated Kid Rock's later success in rap-rock as it combined heavy metal styles with rap. In 1994, Kid Rock started his own record label to release *Early Mornin' Stoned Pimp*, an album that solidified the unique rap-rock style that would lead him to a new major-label deal. The album continued the rap-metal style of *The Polyfuze Method*, but also included classic rock, even featuring one track titled "Classic Rock." Emphasizing his focus on rock, the album's cover featured a long-haired Kid Rock lying in bed playing a guitar. This cover stands in stark contrast to the cover of his first album, which featured a cartoon drawing of Kid Rock with a high-top fade haircut and gold rope chain, standing with a black friend in front of a soul food restaurant.

Kid Rock sold several copies of *Early Mornin' Stoned Pimp* out of his basement, and the success of his self-published album gained the attention of Atlantic Records, who signed him to record 1998's *Devil Without a Cause*. From his first two albums to *Devil*, Kid Rock's style had moved from straight, sample-based rap music to more guitar-driven alternative rock. More importantly, he had discovered his hook: fusing hip hop beats, hip hop boasting, and hip hop fashion with hard rock guitar and Southern rock attitude. Although Kid Rock himself is from Romeo, Michigan, a suburb of Detroit, the Southern rock connection is important to his appeal as an artist. In lyrics and interviews, he reminds listeners of his love for country stars like Johnny Cash and Hank Williams, even claiming that "the only book I've ever read is the autobiography of Hank Williams."[36] The country-themed song "Cowboy," and "Picture," a collaboration with country artist Sheryl Crow, emphasized Kid Rock's love of and links to country music, although he grew up in a less-than-country locale. While his Detroit-area contemporary, Eminem, was rebuilding the urban credibility that Vanilla Ice had lost for white rappers, Kid Rock built a new type of credibility from the image of the white, Southern, good ol' boy.

While Kid Rock's commercial success was founded on the hybrid persona of a white kid from suburban Detroit who loves country music and plays hip hop, a study of Kid Rock's album covers reveals that he settled on this hybrid after making several changes to his persona throughout his early career, up until the point he hit MTV with his single, "I am the Bullgod" in 1997. Since this mainstream success, Kid Rock's fashion style has remained consistent, but the Beastie Boys's *Grand Royal Magazine* (1995) featured a profile of Kid Rock that traced his changes across different trends in music in the early to mid 1990s. The cover art of Kid Rock's 1990 debut album *Grits Sandwiches for Breakfast* obviously employs signifiers of black culture, and suggests that Kid Rock is a welcomed participant in black hip hop culture, even welcomed into soul food restaurants by black men. It is important to keep in mind that this album was released *before* the Vanilla Ice scandal, when Kid Rock was well aware of how he could use being white as a gimmick. He told *Grand Royal*: "I remember seeing the fuckin' Beasties at Cobo (Arena, Detroit) and being the only white kid there...and going 'Oh fuck man, there's some white kids on stage, someone beat me to it.'" Kid Rock told *Grand Royal* he got "lots of shit" for being a white rapper in the wake of Vanilla Ice.[37]

After Vanilla Ice, white artists turned to different constructions of white identity. The Young Black Teenagers rejected their whiteness in their name, and claimed that their love for hip hop culture made them black, while House of Pain emphasized their Irish heritage. The problem with studying the character of whiteness is defining what it means to be a "white" person in the first place. Duster historicizes the debate between scholars who argue that racial classification is biologically arbitrary versus those who argue that, even if race is a biological fiction, racial identity remains a deep structure that guides our social experiences.[38] In the face of shifting definitions of what makes a person "white," there still exist social constructs of whiteness, as with all racial classifications, that individuals carry with them. Hip hop's representations of whites' privilege leads to mistrust of the white artist who performs within a music culture created in underprivileged minority communities, and one where authenticity remains tied to the performer's biography of social disadvantage. In the overarching social structure of the United States, white people are born with a social advantage. The question, then, becomes one of how white Americans treat this advantage when they record hip hop music, where artists draw credibility from social disadvantage.[39] In early 1990s hip hop, Vanilla Ice lied to conceal his white privilege and Young Black Teenagers claimed a cultural blackness that set them at a disadvantage among whites. Since the late 1990s, subsequent white artists have confronted and redefined their whiteness in different ways.

EMINEM'S MOVE TOWARD REINTEGRATION

The Vanilla Ice era is marked by its separation of whiteness from hip hop authenticity; after House of Pain in 1992, no *new* white artist made Billboard's Hot 100 chart until Eminem's 1999 debut. Eminem put forth a very different rhetoric of whiteness. Eminem inverts the narratives of black artists to show whiteness hindering his acceptance as a rapper. At the same time, he addresses the marketability of his whiteness as a privilege he would not have if he were black. In the fullest study of Eminem's authenticating strategies, Armstrong showed that music journalists focus heavily on Eminem's whiteness. While Eminem's lyrics often ask his listeners to look past his whiteness, these lines actually serve to reinforce his consciousness of his position as a hip hop minority. Armstrong contends that Eminem writes lyrics to make himself "conspicuously white."[40] I would extend this reading to argue that Eminem not only makes himself conspicuously white, but also shows a critical attention to hip hop's representations of white privilege. Eminem's lower-class background is key to his authentication, and to his refutation of hip hop's representations of wealthy whites rushing to profit from rap. First, he emphasizes his genuine love of hip hop and the adversity he faced on his path to a rap career. His lyrics reflect his actual biography within a poor, urban social location. At the same time, he emphasizes his whiteness to persuade listeners that he does not attempt an imitation of blackness. Then, as the first major white artist to emerge since Vanilla Ice, he writes lyrics in response to Ice's discrediting. He specifically criticizes Vanilla Ice on three songs (Armstrong 355). He works to diffuse his listeners' rejection of a white artist by anticipating their arguments, for example, in his song "Without Me" (2002), he compares himself to Elvis Presley and calls himself selfish for making money from "black music." Eminem goes on to suggest in these lyrics that his success opened the floodgates for "twenty million other white rappers."

In these lyrics, Eminem is critical of the broader racial landscape that frames hip hop, and the structures of racial advantage that historically have seen whites profit from black-created forms of music. Eminem's marketing concept includes his understanding of the history of whiteness in hip hop, and his lyrical attention to the reception of his whiteness. On "The Way I Am" (2000), he complains about interviewers who think he's "some wigger who just tries to be black," and who test the truthfulness of the biography he reports. The questions Eminem says he receives from interviewers match two central contentions of Perkins's article that exposed lies about Vanilla Ice's high school and neighborhood. Similarly, Eminem's comparison of himself to Elvis in "Without Me" recalls specific criticisms of Vanilla Ice.

Ultimately, the marketing and reception of Vanilla Ice made Eminem a more marketing-conscious performer. The content of Eminem's authenticating claims has not been significantly different from that of Vanilla Ice. Both claim to have grown up in predominantly black neighborhoods, and both claim to have earned prestige from their black peers through vocal and lyrical skill. A crucial distinction, however, lies in the press's reception of these claims, and in the fact that Eminem anticipates a hostile reception in his lyrics. Armstrong credits much of Eminem's widespread acceptance to the guidance of Dr. Dre, the black hip hop legend who discovered Eminem and who produces his music and performs with him both onstage and in recordings. According to Armstrong, Dr. Dre maintains some level of control over representations of Eminem, from Eminem's own lyrics to the script of the partly autobiographical film *8 Mile* (2002), in which Eminem stars. With Dre's guidance, Eminem has so carefully established his right to perform hip hop despite his whiteness that his career has survived numerous attacks, particularly from *The Source* magazine, which in 2003 made public an unreleased Eminem recording and accused the rapper of using racist language and promoting racial stereotypes.

The Source won a court decision allowing it to print lyrics from a freestyle vocal session Eminem recorded when he was twenty-one, five years before he released *The Slim Shady LP*. Most importantly, the tape contains the only recording of Eminem's use of the word "nigger," which, Armstrong shows, he consistently avoids in his music. Eminem's taped vocals also characterize black women as gold diggers. While this story generated a few weeks of discussion, it was in no way as extensive or far-reaching as the scandal that surrounded Vanilla Ice's false claims of ghetto credibility.

The Source was unable to initiate a backlash against Eminem. In fact, journalists defend him as performing staunchly within the genre:

> And under what hip hop standard is it appropriate for black rappers to liberally use the N-word and refer to and portray black women in unflattering terms, but the same is off limits to white rappers? (Campbell)

> Considering that Eminem has said little out of the ordinary in a genre in which, to a considerable degree, black women are subject to daily insults, [*The Source's*] indignant stance is confusing. (Kolawole)

Eminem has established himself so firmly within hip hop culture that these lyrics are defended as part of it.

Eminem's lyrics mark a return to earlier narratives of white artist immersion in hip hop culture, but it is a return that remains particularly informed by reactions to Vanilla Ice, and one which often is framed in response to, or in anticipation of, those reactions. Using the rhetorical strategy of anticipation, Eminem calls attention to his own whiteness in the context of complaining about critics' focus on it. Eminem extends this strategy in *8 Mile*, where he counters attacks on his whiteness by beating his opponents to the punch. In a pivotal scene, Eminem's character B. Rabbit wins an MC battle against a black opponent, Papa Doc. He first anticipates attacks on his whiteness, then turns the crowd's attention from race to class as he reveals that Doc attended private school and came from well-off parents and a supportive home. In effect, B. Rabbit silences his critic's attacks on his credibility by acknowledging his own whiteness, then challenging Doc's own performance of a ghetto blackness which does not fit with his biography. In anticipating criticisms of his whiteness, B. Rabbit embraces his trailer park upbringing as part of his credibility and in the same verse discredits Papa Doc's private school education. Eric K. Watts argues that "in terms of both class and race, *8 Mile* portrays Rabbit as an 'oppressed minority.'"[41] Watts identifies the film's message as "while it may be 'easier' for white rappers to have commercial success, it is very difficult for them to get *respect*."[42] This statement echoes Eminem's lyrical commentary about the larger racial structures at work in hip hop. On "White America" (2002), Eminem rhymes, "look at my sales, let's do the math, if I was black, I would've sold half." He acknowledges his marketability to white listeners even as he credits Dre with authenticating him: "Kids flipped when they knew I was produced by Dre, that's all it took, and they were instantly hooked right in, and they connected with me too because I looked like them." Eminem attributes his hip hop credibility to

Dre's sponsorship, and his commercial appeal to his white identity, but if whiteness equals sales, how do African-Americans maintain control of hip hop, and how does hip hop remain a black form of music?

A fear of white people taking over hip hop has long existed. In 1991, black rappers and critics worried that Vanilla Ice's commercial success would compromise hip hop like other forms of black music before it. In a 1991 interview, Havelock Nelson extended a comparison of Ice to Elvis by stating "Rock-and-roll was black back in the days when it began.... I don't know if rap in the year 2050 will be seen as white. But it damn sure could be."[43] The success of Eminem again raised these fears of rap's being taken over by whites. Yet, eight years after his debut, the white artist remains a minority in hip hop, even as the music continues to grow in commercial dominance. Eminem claims on "Without Me" (2002) to have opened the floodgates for white rappers, yet no subsequent white artist has reached Eminem's level of success. White artists such as Bubba Sparxxx, Paul Wall, or Alchemist have seen mainstream airplay since Eminem's debut, yet more white artists record for small, independent rap labels. Outside of mainstream radio and corporate record labels, white artists like Sage Francis, Edan, and Eyedea and Abilities have established themselves as lyrical innovators, and certain underground artists have returned to narratives of cultural immersion, asserting their authenticity through rhyme skill rather than confronting the issue of their race in lyrics. As underground hip hop defines itself as a purer form of hip hop, in opposition to the record industry's pop rap, underground artists emphasize the authenticity of their *music* more than they market the realness of performer identity. This structure has extended to white artists in the underground. Hip hop's current era does include mainstream crossovers, including two artists, Haystak and Bubba Sparxxx, who adapt Eminem's strategy of inversion to play on a white stereotype of the southern redneck. While some of rappers listed here (particularly Paul Wall and Bubba Sparxxx) have seen heavy rotation on MTV, none of these white artists has yet achieved Eminem's level of sales or his staying power across multiple releases.

The Beastie Boys, then Vanilla Ice, then Eminem each broke rap sales records with their debut albums. Even their combined sales, though, are no match for the magnitude of the sales of black artists. These three white breakout artists emerged in 1986, 1990, and 1999. Before, between, and after them, sales records were set or broken by black artists. Run DMC's *Raising Hell* (1986) sold three million copies, and was the first rap album to go multiplatinum. Their sales were topped by the Beastie Boys' *Licensed to Ill* (1986), which sold five million. Then, in 1990, MC Hammer more than doubled the Beasties' sales with *Please Hammer Don't Hurt 'Em*, and Ice knocked Hammer out of the top spot, selling 17 million. More telling, though, is the consistency of album sales over time. The Beastie Boys have seen none of their subsequent five albums outsell *Licensed to Ill*. Vanilla Ice has never produced another album to even break the Top 40. After *To the Extreme*, he released a live album, 1991's *Extremely Live*, and then four studio albums, including 1994's *Mind Blowin'*, which was funk-influenced, and 1998's *Hard to Swallow*, which fit with the rap/metal sound of groups like Limp Bizkit and Korn. Even as he changed his sound, Ice has been unable to live down his earlier image. He most recently resurfaced as a reality television star, appearing on the WB's *The Surreal Life*, a show that groups former celebrities as roommates, and on NBC's *Hit Me Baby One More Time*, on which one-hit wonders compete in performing their old songs. Of these three key white artists, only Eminem has enjoyed continued success across multiple albums. *The Slim Shady LP* (1999) sold over four million copies. *The Marshall Mathers LP* (2000) and *The Eminem Show* (2002) each sold eight million copies and reached number one on the *Billboard* album charts. Eminem is an exception to hip hop marketing patterns that see white rappers' sales decrease after their first releases. Even with the consistency of Eminem's sales, however, Tupac remains the world's biggest-selling rap artist, with sales of his 13 different albums totaling 36 million copies.

(IN)VISIBILITY OF WHITENESS IN HIP HOP

The autobiographical basis of Eminem's lyrics and his attention to his own whiteness have helped him negotiate a new form of white authenticity through his position as a white outsider. Rather than try to hide his whiteness, Eminem inverts black narratives to show how his race held him back in early stages of his career. He describes his whiteness, like his poverty, as an obstacle to overcome on his path to acceptance in hip hop. Yet he avoids a reverse discrimination argument as he is careful also to acknowledge the privilege of his accessibility to white listeners. In addressing his reception as a white rapper from white listeners and black rap stars, Eminem marks not only his whiteness, but also the history of white-black interactions within which he performs. His attention to white listeners is crucial; the multi-platinum sales of Vanilla Ice's *To the Extreme* prompted black rappers to address the position of whites who buy and listen to African-American music. In 1992, Ice-T speculated that more than fifty percent of his sales were from white consumers: "Black kids buy the records, but the white kids buy the cassette, the CD, the album, the tour jacket, the hats, everything."[44] Ice-T acknowledged, as did Rose, that sales do not represent the full spectrum of rap's circulation via bootlegs and DJ mix-tapes. Rose also noted the high "pass-along rate" among young black consumers.[45] As Vanilla Ice made white involvement with hip hop more visible, black artists began to address the role of white listeners in rap's consumption. Earlier in this chapter, I introduced the scholarly discussion about the visibility of whiteness as a racial identity. This discussion is reflected in rap artists' tension between preserving hip hop culture and making money via the record industry, which has led prominent black artists to confront the existence of their white audience. In a 1992 bell hooks interview, Ice Cube claimed that his messages are directed at a black audience, and that he prefers to think of white listeners as "eaves-dropping."[46] Ice Cube's cousin Del the Funky Homosapien revised this statement on his song "Catch a Bad One," where he urges "Please listen to my album, even if you're white like talcum."

If whites eavesdrop on hip hop, they hear messages not intended for them. Yet several rap artists make the white listener visible by addressing this audience in their lyrics. Ice Cube clarified in the hooks interview that "even though they're eavesdropping on our records, they need to hear it."[47] Lyrics addressed to white listeners recognize whites' consumption of hip hop even as they often criticize whites. On De La Soul's "Patti Dooke" (1993), Posdnous rhymes that a white boy can't understand rap, but, even so, he tries to take it over and "steal it, dilute it, pollute it, kill it." The same song features an interlude that depicts a record label executive saying, "We decided to change the cover a little bit because we see the big picture. Negroes and white folks are buyin' this album." De La Soul's attention to producing crossover hits for the white listener, and to ways in which that corporate process often dictates changes in both marketing and content complicate Ice Cube's eavesdropping analogy because the artist often is involved in marketing rap to whites. While the white listener is criticized for diluting hip hop's culture, white consumption becomes more visible to artists who run their own labels, and who see the marketing potential of white MCs. Armstrong cites Dr. Dre's specific intent to sign a white artist, Eminem, in order to sell more records through his own fledging label, Aftermath Records.[48] Like Dre, several other black artists have tried to market white MCs. Ice-T discovered Everlast, who went on to form House of Pain. Eazy-E released albums from a white Jewish group, Blood of Abraham (1994), and a white woman, Tairrie B. (1993). Queen Latifah claimed she would sign a white artist because "white kids want their own hero more than they want ours."[49]

Speaking about Vanilla Ice in 1991, Nelson voiced his fear that blacks would cede rap to whites. He noted black artists' complicity in hip hop's assimilation into white culture (Mills "White Thing"). In opposition to such a reading of black-white interaction, black artist-executives assert their control even as they market a white artist to white listeners. As black artists become record label executives, they extend the concept of authenticity through blackness to the business of selling rap. Hip hop music's attention to its own production complicates the concept of hip hop as a black expressive culture resisting co-optation from a white industry. Throughout hip hop's development, both black *and* white artists have alternatively disguised or exposed the large extent to which whites have been involved in the making of hip hop, and the large extent to which blacks have been involved in its selling. Hip hop's current construction of whiteness is tied closely to this industry structure, and necessitates both visibility (Dr. Dre's marketing of his protégé Eminem to a white audience) and invisibility (Dre's earlier obscuring of his relationship with Jerry Heller, the white man who managed his group Niggaz Wit Attitude). Dre's music didn't acknowledge Heller until after N.W.A's breakup and the release of Dre's solo album *The Chronic* (1992), where Dre parodied Heller on "Dre Day," and characterized Eazy-E as Heller's lackey. Dre's former N.W.A. bandmate Ice Cube employed this same tactic on his first solo release, *AmeriKKKa's Most Wanted* (1989), where Cube's "A Message to the Oreo Cookie" seemed directed at Eazy-E, and used a slang term for a black person who's white at heart. On "No Vaseline" (1991), Cube called out his former group for the hypocrisy of their name (which he had approved), claiming that the Niggaz Wit Attitude had "a white Jew telling [them] what to do." The central difference in Dre's making white-black interaction visible with Eminem, versus invisible with Heller, is the question of artist control. Heller is notorious for having signed N.W.A. to an unfair contract which ultimately broke up the group, while Dre has played a crucial role in managing and marketing Eminem. Dre boasts of his role in Eminem's sales on "Still D.R.E." (1999), a song that persuades the listener that even with all his industry success, particularly as a record label executive, Dre remains true to the same identity he put forth on his early recordings with N.W.A, where he used the group's racially marked name to challenge radio stations to play his music. With Dre's guidance, Eminem established a new form of white authenticity as he narrated his struggle as a white rapper trying to make it in a black hip hop world.

In "Without Me" (2002), Eminem predicted that his success would open the floodgates for new white rappers trying to cash in on hip hop.

Since Eminem's debut, white artists like Paul Wall, Alchemist, and Bubba Sparxxx have emerged on the mainstream hip hop scene in the U.S. White rappers like Necro, Ill Bill, Edan, and Sage Francis emerged earlier as respected underground rappers, but it wasn't until 2004 that several white artists began to release albums on major labels and receive airplay on mainstream radio and MTV. These new white artists represent a range of white identities, from the good ol' Southern boys Paul Wall and Bubba Sparxxx to the British artists The Streets (Mike Skinner) and Lady Sovereign. In contrast to his name, The Streets tells stories about his everyday life in Birmingham, England—from being late for tea with his mother to not getting good reception on his cell phone.

Of the American artists, Paul Wall in particular follows Eminem's career path in gaining part of his credibility from the strength of an association with black artists. With the emergence of the Dirty South as a powerful hip hop scene, and the debut records of Atlanta's OutKast and Goodie Mob in the mid-1990s to the breakout records from Houston's Mike Jones in 2005 and Memphis's Three 6 Mafia in 2006, hip hop has seen a focus on a different type of white identity, the redneck rapper. Georgia's Bubba Sparxxx worked with established black producers Timbaland (who had worked with Missy Elliot) and Organized Noise (who had worked with OutKast) to produce his 2001 album *Dark Days, Bright Nights*. Both this album and Sparxxx's 2003 follow-up, *Deliverance*, center on Southern Gothic motifs and create a mix of Southern rock and hip hop, although generally of a softer, more introspective variety than Kid Rock's similar blending of the two. Sparxxx's lyrics and musical style also saw him labeled "country rap." For his 2006 single, "Ms. New Booty," however, Sparxxx teamed up with fellow Southerners, the Ying Yang Twins, to produce the party rap hit. In the music video, Sparxxx plays an entrepreneur recording an infomercial for a fabulous new product that offers women the chance to enhance their butt-shaking talents. "Ms. New Booty" plays off the title of Mos Def's "Ms. Fat Booty" (1999), and falls into a tradition of rap songs about appreciating big butts, going back to T La Rock's "Tudy Fruity Judy" (1987) and Sir Mix-A-Lot's "Baby Got Back" (1992), which urged black women to appreciate their curves. But where Mix-A-Lot's song opened with dialogue between two white Valley girls complaining about the size of a black woman's ass, Sparxxx's video opens with Sparxxx, a white guy, selling an ass-enhancing product to white and black women alike, and ends with Sparxxx coming home to his African-American wife.

Bubba Sparxxx has worked with black producers and guest stars like the Ying Yang Twins, but Paul Wall, another white Southern rapper, emerged within a collective of Houston, Texas, artists who began to hit the mainstream record charts in 2004–2005. Paul Wall began his career as a promoter in Houston, where he formed relationships with several emerging independent rap labels, in particular Michael "5000" Watts's Swisha House (formerly called Swisha Blast). While he was working as a promoter, Paul began rhyming with a group called The Color Changin' Click with his partner Chamillionaire. Like 3rd Bass, who included two white MCs (Pete Nice and MC Serch) and a black DJ (Richie Rich), The Color Changin' Click included both black and white members. Paul Wall left the group because Chamillionaire did not want to record with Swisha House, the label that would jumpstart Paul's solo career. By 2006, both Chamillionaire and Paul Wall had achieved successful solo careers, with Paul Wall secure in the roster of Swisha House breakout artists, and the music video for Chamillionaire's "Ridin' Dirty" recalling their old group name, The Color Changin' Click, as it depicted Cham changing into a white person to avoid trouble with the cops. Unlike Eminem, who released his first major-label album under the sponsorship of Dr. Dre, Paul Wall made it big in 2004–2005 along with other Swisha House artists Mike Jones and Slim Thug. Paul's Southern drawl and Houston slang fit right in with these other guys on Mike Jones's "Still Tippin'," the song that debuted Paul Wall on MTV. Paul Wall's success without much attention to his white skin seems to indicate that whiteness and rap identity have been reconciled. Although he did attend to his skin color in the name of his first group, his lyrics on his major label solo album don't call attention to his whiteness.

When Eminem emerged onto the hip hop scene in 1997, the Southern hip hop identity had not achieved the status it would have by the time Paul Wall made his MTV debut in 2005. Although No Limit Records and Cash Money Records were based in New Orleans, and OutKast had established Atlanta as a hip hop hotspot, followed by ATL artists Goodie Mob and Ludacris, the South was not fully recognized as a hip hop powerhouse until 2005, when MTV Films released *Hustle and Flow*, a hip hop film set in Memphis, and the Memphis group Three 6 Mafia won an Oscar for the song "It's Hard Out Here for a Pimp," from the *Hustle and Flow* soundtrack. With the Atlanta, New Orleans, Houston, and Memphis scenes, the Dirty South set the stage for Paul Wall's success. Paul's entrepreneurial spirit matched that of many of Houston's artists, who couldn't gain as much nationwide radio play as rappers from New York and Los Angeles, and thus had to hustle and grind to start their own record labels, produce their own mixtapes, and promote their own sound. Paul's other contribution is to fashion. He owns a jewelry shop in Houston and popularized the wearing of diamond grills. Three 6 Mafia guest stars on his album, and he guest stars on Kanye West's "Drive Slow" (2005). Unlike Eminem, Paul doesn't make his white skin a topic of his songs, and he instead returns to the immersion relied on by The Beastie Boys, mainstream rap's first white act. Paul's success may indicate that the rift between white identity and hip hop credibility is lessening, and that Eminem's career has repaired some of the damage done by Vanilla Ice's fake bio.

HIP HOP, WHITENESS, AND PARODY

This book has examined hip hop's emphasis on preserving its original culture while turning that culture into a major industry. Black artists rhyme about wanting to get rich from rap music without giving up control of their music, and black entrepreneurs and label executives—many of them rap artists themselves—fight to keep control in the boardroom. Hip hop has established itself as a form in which black artists assume new roles in producing and distributing the music, and several artists have founded their own labels and sponsored the careers of new stars and brought more young black Americans out of poverty by signing them to their labels or employing them in management, public relations, security, or other positions. Hip hop is black-owned, and black artists have maintained controlling interests in the careers of white stars, from Russell Simmons's management of the Beastie Boys to Dr. Dre's signing Eminem to his Aftermath label.

Because of the involvement of African-Americans in the creation of hip-hip music, hip hop's prevalent image of the black man who rose from crime and poverty to commercial success becomes controversial in that it universalizes African-American experience. Black artists write career narratives that link their struggles to become rap stars to a larger systemic racism, and white artists borrow or adapt these narratives to show that poverty is not racially exclusive. Eminem's success and acceptance hinges on his proof of social struggle, while Vanilla Ice became a target of ridicule after his claims to struggle were found false. Rap's efforts to maintain the core values of its original cultural context of the 1970s South Bronx have led to a standardization of the rap image that often is criticized and parodied by rap artists themselves in songs, videos, and interviews. These critiques and parodies often target the essentialized image of rap artists as aggressive, consumerist, and flashy, and in this way the culture polices itself. Underground artists call out mainstream artists for moving too far away from the communities where hip hop began, and mainstream artists respond by saying that they're making money that flows back into those same communities.

This ongoing dialogue among hip hop artists extends to comedians like Dave Chappelle, whose *Chappelle's Show* featured a sketch in which a racial draft—modeled after the NBA draft—took place. Black people claimed Tiger Woods and tried to steal Eminem from the whites. Asian people claimed Wu-Tang Clan, a black rap group who incorporates martial arts imagery and Eastern religion and philosophy into their music. These parodies use hip hop to target stereotypes at the core of how we look at race and ethnicity in America, and most pointedly what it means to be black in America. But how do white parodies of hip hop culture fare in this tradition? In 2006, Weird Al Yankovic released "White and Nerdy," a parody of Chamillionaire's "Ridin' Dirty (2006)," a song about evading police. In the original music video, Chamillionaire, true to his name, morphs into a middle-aged white businessman when pulled over by police in order to avoid being arrested. The "White and Nerdy" video is seemingly innocuous in that a white comedian, Weird Al, targets white people as uncool. Weird Al's character wears thick glasses and a pocket protector, and is interested in computers and Harry Potter. Although these hobbies are presented as "white and nerdy" instead of "black and cool," the danger is to say that even if whites are not as cool as black people, they are also more industrious and more interested in intellectual pursuits instead of the criminal pursuits depicted in Chamillionaire's original song. In both songs, though, the black figures come out on top.

Hip hop artists themselves have presented whites in a similar fashion, from the white executives at White-Owned Records in the Geto Boys "Do it like a G.O." (1990) to Dr. Dre's parody of his former manager Jerry Heller in the 1993 "Dre Day" video. Hip hop has a long tradition of using parody to target racial identities. In chapter one, I discussed De La Soul's parody of the rap image in such songs and videos as "Me, Myself, and I" (1989) and "Ego Trippin' (Part II)" (1993), where Trugoy, who elsewhere (on 1993's "Fallin'") calls himself a "washed up rapper," singsongs "I'm the greatest MC in the world." A similar parody has been employed by the artists I have discussed throughout this book, from Masta Ace's fictional character "Ace" in chapter two to the personae and costumes of Humpty Hump and MF DOOM in chapter three. These artists respond to the commodification of hip hop by developing a self-criticism through parody. The reflection of characters or personae on the self can form a playful self-criticism, and by extension a criticism of hip hop culture itself. When De

La Soul's Posdnuos politely folds his hands in front of his waist when asked to show his B-boy stance, or when Digital Underground's Humpty Hump looks funny but still makes money, they critique themselves by calling attention to the aspects of hip hop style that they do not exude, and they parody the standardization of hip hop culture as they make evident their lack of these qualities. They step outside rap's standard braggadocio to critique those things they lack that the multiplatinum rappers seem to have.

Turning their backs on the spoils of rap success is a strategy much like Eminem's emphasis on his white skin. By pointing out, then criticizing, the markers of success or authenticity that they don't have, rap artists can anticipate and diffuse arguments against their skill, their style, or their right to belong in the world of rap. When the members of De La Soul rhyme from a mansion, a hot tub, and an expensive car in the 1993 music video for "Ego Trippin' (Part II)," their video looks very much like the Bad Boy Records videos that were popular during the same era, but for the members of one of rap's first bohemian groups, a decade past the height of their success, to adopt these poses creates irony. Parody depends on the imitation, through ironic repetition, of an original.[1] Hip hop parody tends to target the intersections of race and class in the music's representations of racial identity, which is to say images of the ghetto that the typical rap artist claims to have come from, and the mansion he lives in now. Hip hop parody also targets black-white relations in scenes that show artists interacting with record executives.

Because hip hop is so tied to race, a successful white parody needs to be self-aware in confronting issues of racial relations in the music and culture. White parody differs from the imitation or inversion of black narratives (discussed in chapter five) that white stars have used to gain credibility, and instead tends to focus very intently on what it means to be white. MC Paul Barman, a white rapper and Brown University graduate, confronts the issue of parody in his lyrics. Barman intensifies his parody by addressing issues of imperialism, minstrelsy, and assimilation. Dynamite Hack, a white rock group that recorded a cover of N.W.A.'s "Boyz-N-The-Hood" (1987), used the music video for this song to juxtapose images of white economic privilege with N.W.A. lyrics that detail ghetto poverty and black-on-black crime. It can be argued that N.W.A.'s involvement with Hack's cover calls into question their status as the self-proclaimed "world's most dangerous group" ("Always into Somethin," 1991). Dr. Dre, former N.W.A. member, worked closely with Dynamite Hack as they produced the song, and ultimately asked them to censor the word "nigger" that was used in N.W.A.'s original. Dr. Dre's involvement with parody extends to his work with his protégé Eminem: Dre's song "Still D.R.E." (1999) argues his consistency over the years, yet he parodies his N.W.A. image on Eminem's "Guilty Conscience" (1999). Dre has become one of hip hop's most venerable and revered artists, and is considered one of the godfathers of West Coast gangsta rap. Does his career reflect the history of hip hop at large? Is hip hop's impact weakened by parody?

Hip Hop's Parodies of Racial Identity

In chapter five, I introduced the discussion among critics about the visibility of whiteness as a racial position, and I argued that two key developments have shaped the current position of whites in hip hop. Just like Vanilla Ice's imitation of black rap career narratives, Eminem's inversion of these narratives has been said to tread a border with parody. The current state of whiteness for hip hop, in the Eminem era, calls not only for attention to the whiteness of the artist, but to the social privilege associated with whiteness. I showed that Eminem inverts a standard rap narrative to position himself as a racial underdog, but importantly, one who understands the privilege he still carries ("if I was black I would've sold half"). It is by addressing such privilege so directly that Eminem distinguishes his childhood class struggle from his current success as the biggest-selling rapper in the world. Chapter five dealt specifically with white MCs and the ways that they have worked to obscure or emphasize their whiteness. I will now turn to representations of whites in nonperforming roles, as managers, A&R representatives, and record label executives. The invisibility of whiteness in hip hop is invoked in particular for whites in these roles. While artists cannot hide their white skin, hip hop managers, A&R people, and label-owners operate behind the scenes. Speaking to this notion of invisibility, Matthew Cowan examines the history of black-Jewish interaction in the business of hip hop, and finds it more symbiotic than the painful history of music business imperialism in which it is situated. Cowan describes the hidden interaction between black artists and white executives, and Armstrong argues that, "The rap-color issue is so pervasive that it reaches people whom no one ever sees, such as the black manager of the Beastie Boys and the white founder of Priority Records."[2] Yet more cloaking and marking goes on than these representations reveal. The Beastie Boys's video for "No Sleep Til Brooklyn" (1987) featured a shot of their black manager Russell Simmons as the lyrics said "Our manager's crazy, he always smokes dust." Eight years later, after having left Simmons's record label, the Beasties would claim to have "fat bass lines like Russell Simmons steals money." Like Eminem, the Beastie Boys invert narratives of black artists duped by a white record industry.

Hip hop's attention to its own materiality challenges the idea that black-white business deals occur strictly offstage. Throughout hip hop's existence, such interaction has been central to the culture's commercial development, but both black *and* white artists have alternatively disguised or exposed the level to which whites have been involved in the making of hip hop. Yet the representation of corporate whiteness as evil remains. In chapter two, I mentioned the Geto Boys' "Do it Like a G.O." (1990), in which the group receives a phone call from the president of White-Owned Records, who offers to buy out their small, black-owned label, and make them rich. This image of the white man as the embodiment of a corporation resurfaced during and after the break-up of N.W.A., who were managed by a white, Jewish, man, Jerry Heller, whose interaction with the group often is blamed for its break-up. N.W.A. is arguably the most racialized group in hip hop, yet none of their own lyrics addressed the contradictions of a group called Niggaz Wit Attitude managed by a white record executive. After Ice Cube left the group because he wasn't getting a fair cut of N.W.A.'s earnings, he attacked Heller on his 1991 track, "No Vaseline," telling his former bandmates that they were being fucked out of their money "by a white boy with no Vaseline." After the remaining group split up, Dr. Dre also exposed Heller in an attack on Eazy-E, who still worked with him. In the video for his song "Dre Day" (1993), Dre made Heller visible. The video features an Eazy-E impersonator acting as Heller's lackey, repeating "yes boss," and helping Heller lure in two black rappers, who he tells "sign your life, I mean your name, on the X." Dre's parody exposes Heller's manipulation of Eazy-E, and by extension N.W.A., but Dre did not make Heller's role visible until after he left his management company. "Dre Day" was released by the black-owned Death Row Records, yet this label was a subsidiary of Priority Records, operated by Brian Turner, a white man. Even with this connection to Turner, however, Dre's role in Death Row Records marked his emergence as an artist-executive, as the antithesis of the Eazy-E yes-man character he parodied. With *The Chronic* (1992), Dre established his control over his own production, and as impresario for the new black artists he debuted on that album.

Along with such parodies of white privilege for the label executive, artists also have turned their attention to blackness, especially with regard to the aggressive male black image that has dominated television airplay. De La Soul's "Me, Myself, and I" was one of the first releases to challenge mainstream hip hop's primary representation of black identity as aggressive masculinity. De La Soul formed the Native Tongues movement with other groups—Tribe Called Quest, Queen Latifah, Chi Ali, Black Sheep, and the Jungle Brothers—in the early 1990s, and together their music often critiqued hip hop posturing.[3] Black Sheep extend their tradition in "U Mean I'm Not?" (1991), which parodies gangsta violence by taking it to an extreme not reached in the music. Such parodies confront hip hop's representations of racial authenticity as they critique the standardization of the rap image in artist biographies, song lyrics, and music videos.

This standardization is what set the stage for Vanilla Ice's failed attempt to borrow a standard hip hop biography from his black contemporaries. Vanilla Ice adopted black slang and fashion style in order to capitalize on the cultural cache of rap music. Since Vanilla Ice's commercial downfall in 1991, no figure stands as an icon of hip hop scorn more than the wigger. The term is a combination of the words "white" and "nigger," and is used to designate a white person who aspires to African-American coolness and cultural cache by mimicking aspects of the speech and fashion style of black hip hop artists. Norman Mailer's essay, "The White Negro: Superficial Reflections on the Hipster" (1957), described the post-war phenomenon of white Americans who aspired to black cool. Mailer's essay described white hipsters and beatniks who from the 1920s to the 1950s drew much of their cultural cache from the black American cultures of jazz and swing. The "white negroes" of Mailer's study adopted African-American slang and fashion style and surrounded themselves with black friends. Mezz Mezzrow, a white jazz musician from Chicago, married a black woman, moved to Harlem, and declared himself a "voluntary Negro." His 1946 autobiography, *Really the Blues*, describes his aspirations to become a Negro musician.

Just as the African-American music culture of jazz and swing captivated white Americans in the first half of the 20th century, hip hop has caught the attention of white listeners since the early 1970s. *Wild Style* (1982), which is considered the first hip hop film, depicts a graffiti artist's resistance to a white reporter who becomes fascinated with hip hop culture and wants to write a story on it. This tension of whites treading on black turf increased dramatically with Vanilla Ice. In 1991, *Saturday Night Live* aired a sketch in which actor Kevin Bacon played Vanilla Ice as a guest on *The Nat X Show*, a recurring sketch in which Chris Rock played a militant black man with a late-night talk show. Nat X criticized Vanilla Ice's dancing and took him to task for his nickname "The Elvis of Rap," claiming that he likes to call Vanilla Ice "Elvis" only because he wishes that he was dead. The same year, the sketch comedy show *In Living Color* aired a sketch titled, "White, White, Baby," in which Jim Carrey parodied Vanilla

Ice's hit song by singing it with new lyrics that address the lies he told the media. After his back-up dancers ditch him, disappointed with his inferior dance moves, Carrey's Ice turns his back to reveal that his jacket reads "My Grandma Gave Me This Dumb Jacket."

More recently, however, parodies of wiggers have been less directed at one target, and instead more general in addressing black wannabes as a cultural phenomenon. In 2003, Dave Chappelle's *Chappelle's Show* featured a sketch in which Clayton Bigsby, a blind Ku Klux Klan member, discovers that he is actually a black man. Before this revelation, Bigsby yells at three white teenagers to "Turn down that damn nigger music." The white teens stare at the black Mr. Bigsby in disbelief, then reply excitedly, "Dude, he called us niggers!" Also in 2003, Snoop Dogg's MTV comedy show, *Doggy Fizzle Televizzle*, aired a sketch in which distressed white parents called a hotline to help their teen sons who suffered from wigger-itis. Parodying TV docu-dramas such as *Intervention*, Snoop Dogg and company kidnapped and deprogrammed the wiggers, turning them back into stereotypically white teens. These wigger parodies reveal that even as Eminem has reestablished a model of the authentic white rapper, the wigger is still a figure of scorn. In fact, whites who aspire to black coolness are a target for parody from black and white comedians: For whites, wiggers are race traitors who can't accept their white skin, and for black comedians, wiggers are cultural poachers. Hip hop is a rich site for satire of racial identities and the cultural cache of hip hop credibility. In 2000, comedian Sasha Baron Cohen created *Da Ali G Show*, a British comedy series about a white man, Ali G, who aspires to hip hop credibility. The format of the show is a mock talk show in which Ali G interviews various government figures. Rather than just being into hip hop style, Ali G seems to believe that he is black. One of his catchphrases is, "Is it cos I is black?"

WHITE PARODIES OF HIP HOP

The tradition of white parody of hip hop begins with 1980s novelty singles like Rappin' Ronnie's "Presidential Rap" (1986), and Rodney Dangerfield's "Rappin' Rodney" (1984). In these songs, white radio DJs and comedians lampooned hip hop culture to capitalize on rap music's emergence onto mainstream radio. Such parodies, while commercially viable, were ineffective in their limited understanding of hip hop; the success of a parody depends on intimate knowledge of the original. This early white involvement via novelty acts has led critics to see even serious rap efforts as parody. In fact, from the first emergence of a white rap group, visibility of whiteness was linked to parody. Matt Diehl has analyzed the market appeal of the Beastie Boys as a white rap group, describing their appeal to white rock listeners as well as their "stance that didn't make clear where the love of rap and the parody of it began and ended."[4] Similarly, Armstrong contends that as Eminem repeatedly asserts his whiteness, which is obvious to the audience, he comments on traditional assertions of blackness, which is also obvious, from black MCs. "He accomplishes a self-conscious parody of rap's racially based authenticity."[5] Black artists and comedians have parodied hip hop's focus on blackness in such films as *CB4* (1993), a spoof that parodied the black consciousness and black militant rap of groups like N.W.A. and Public Enemy as the character Dead Mike's lyrics consisted of "I'm black, ya'll. I'm black ya'll. I'm bliggity black. I'm black ya'll." Black hip hop artists emphasize their blackness even in their names: Black Rob, Black Moon, Black Sheep, and Niggaz Wit Attitude are examples of this focus on blackness. Vanilla Ice and the Canadian pop-reggae artist Snow created a similar focus on whiteness in their names. Eminem uses his lyrics to remind us that he's white, but instead of reinforcing his whiteness as a way to comment on the emphasis on blackness among African-American artists, I would argue instead that Eminem does not parody rap, but himself in relation to rap. This is another example of Eminem's strategy of anticipation that I discussed in chapter five: If he says he's white first, he lessens the power of the listener pointing it out for himself.

Eminem's emphasis on his own whiteness makes his racial position a hardship that he consistently must overcome in his rap career. Eminem inverts narratives of racial struggle as he asks his listeners to accept that he has been discriminated against in the media, and by fans and fellow artists. Although Eminem inverts this dimension to focus on his whiteness, I disagree with Armstrong's reading of Eminem's lyrics as parody. Armstrong contends that Eminem has been able to assert his authenticity through his lyrical focus on his own whiteness; and through a heightened performance of the misogyny and violence central to gangsta rap. What Armstrong may miss in his reading of Eminem's authenticating strategies is Eminem's prevalent assertion, like Vanilla Ice's, that he is credible *despite* his whiteness. If whiteness is Eminem's defining quality, it is because he argues himself as an exception to the rap communty's concept of whiteness as privilege. In fact, he argues his whiteness as hardship. His career narrative inverts racial struggle to focus on his whiteness as limitation. Eminem shows us first that his whiteness granted him no social privilege, and second that it actually held him back in his career. Haystak also tells us the odds were against him: "I was a big old white boy from Tennessee that wanted to be a rap star. And that was fucking impossible" ("White Boy," 2002). Such inversion differs from parody because it becomes such a central feature of white career narratives. Haystak and Eminem use inversion to reclaim images of whiteness that have been parodied by black artists, and they frame their whiteness as career disadvantage. As Eminem and other white rappers invert black artist's narratives, it can be confused for parody because of class lines. The struggle narrative is a narrative of a racialized underclass.

From his first single, "My Name Is" (1999), Eminem has made comedy a central element of his music. As if to ensure his listeners that, unlike Vanilla Ice, he isn't taking himself too seriously, Eminem introduced himself to MTV viewers with the poppy "My Name Is," which features Eminem dressed as Johnny Carson, Ward Cleaver, and other white television personalities. This same song introduces the darker themes of Eminem's music, such as his mother's drug addiction, but here he presents it as comedy (as opposed to songs like "Stan" (2000) and "Cleaning out my Closet" (2002), in which the topics are treated as tragedy). Eminem's other singles, such as "The Real Slim Shady" (2000), "Just Lose It" (2004), and "Without Me" (2002) have relied on humor and celebrity parody. For Dr. Dre, though, as much as he parodies other forms of music, he never parodies hip hop. But in his appearances in Eminem's music and videos, Dre does parody himself.

So while Eminem may parody his own identity in relation to hip hop, he is careful that he never parodies hip hop culture itself. Parody has been central to white rap, but artists have been careful in their parodying of hip hop culture. 3rd Bass parodied MC Hammer in "The Gas Face" (1989) and Vanilla Ice in "Pop Goes the Weasel" (1991), but they drew a clear line between their parody of "hit pop" versus "hip hop." The Beastie Boys parodied 1970s disco culture in their "Hey Ladies" video (1989), and heavy metal stage antics in their "No Sleep Til Brooklyn" video (1986), yet they did not parody hip hop performance styles. White parody is complicated because white artists perform not only within a history of music industry appropriation, but one of minstrelsy. White parodies of hip hop tend to take one of two general forms, parodying the culture itself (like Rappin' Ronnie) or focusing on a white person's distance from the culture. In this way parody can become a white self-critique, as it does for MC Paul Barman and Dynamite Hack, whose music I'll explore in the next sections.

"YOU PUT ON A MINSTREL SHOW!": MC PAUL BARMAN

One white rapper of the Eminem era, MC Paul Barman, uses parody to confront a history of white involvement in black music cultures. Like

Eminem, Barman positions himself as a racial outsider trying to make it in hip hop, but unlike Eminem, who promotes his rise from poverty as a key aspect of his authenticity, Barman flaunts his Ivy League education, and juxtaposes this culture with his involvement in hip hop. While Barman does parody hip hop in extension of his self-critique, much in the way De La Soul and other black artists have done, he is careful to include in his self-critique an awareness of minstrelsy and white appropriation. Further, he addresses the influence of these histories on his critical reception. In "Anarchist Bookstore Part One" (2002), his friends accuse him of putting on a "minstrel show" when he invites them to a performance. Barman retorts "Someone's psychotic. Someone took too much semiotics." This criticism does not lie solely with Barman's friends. Journalists focus on issues of Barman's "cred" (Patrin, Kois), legitimacy (Sawyer), and "the real" (Nelson). At the same time, they acknowledge that Barman's performance complicates these issues. Alex Pappademas calls him "the first truly post-minstrel rapper, too self-aware to don any kind of lyrical blackface without laughing himself out of the room." Through this self-awareness, Barman addresses the specter of the minstrel show, and on "MTV Get off the Air Part II" (2000), he samples the blackface standard, "Jim Crack Corn." Such direct treatment of racism in his music makes not only whiteness, but white racism visible, and has gained Barman the attention of music critics and hip hop performers alike.

His acceptance within hip hop circles is evident in his connections to the established black artists who produce Barman's albums (MF DOOM and Prince Paul), and invite Barman to collaborate on recordings (Masta Ace, Deltron 3030, Handsome Boy Modeling School, and Mr. Dead). In fact, Barman narrates Masta Ace's *Disposable Arts* (2001), and plays the role of Ace's white roommate. Like Eminem, Barman was introduced to hip hop listeners through his connection to an established black producer. Hip hop eccentric Prince Paul, who produced De La Soul's *3 Feet High and Rising* (1989), also produced Barman's EP *It's Very Stimulating* (2000), as well as tracks on his album *Paullelujah* (2002). Barman's lyrics critique hip hop's values, reclaim parody for the white artist, and assert the value of being true to himself. Like Eminem, Barman addresses his critics in lyrics. "Old Paul" (2002) is narrated from the perspective of a fictional older Barman who reflects on his career and confronts the artists and record executives who challenged his legitimacy and accused him of exploiting and parodying hip hop. Barman claims that he's been charged with using rap as a "stepping stone" to stardom, and that he's disliked "Cause I target the fans that you wish you didn't have."

Like De La Soul, Barman positions himself as a unique personality faced with the standardization of a hip hop image, and develops a self-critical parody to emphasize his distance from traditional rap credibility. First, he incorporates vocabulary from outside hip hop's discourse, using the Yiddish term "schlepping" to parody his position as cultural outsider. In this song and others, Barman establishes his Jewish identity as uber-whiteness, and with this heritage further emphasizes hip hop artists' concerns with exploitation of rap music. Cowan examines the role of Jews in the hip hop industry, and determines that, "The very idea of the machinations of Jews behind the scenes is a topic of historical controversy and itinerant conspiracy theories. There is a well-documented legacy—painful on both sides—of Jewish involvement in black music."[6] Cowan urges his reader not to apply to hip hop the histories of Jewish-black relations in jazz, blues, and rock n' roll. To do so is to "neglect the changing social climate" in which black entrepreneurs and artist-executives have taken on new roles in the realms of production and distribution.[7]

Barman further parodies his own identity as he intellectualizes his relationship with hip hop. When he compares himself to France as a colonizer, he employs academic vocabulary, verbalizing the analogy "Was I colon rap colon colon France colon Morocco?" Through his use of such outside discourse, Barman calls attention to his distance from hip hop credibility. "Old Paul" questions whether critics have discredited Barman's music because he's "not from the ave," and then Barman emphasizes his cultural dissonance on "Excuse You" (2002). The latter song juxtaposes references to hip hop culture with references to visual artists, scholars, and musicians outside that culture, from the sculptor Jeff Koons, to the avant-garde composer John Cage, to the feminist scholar Susan Faludi. This system of citations works to emphasize Barman's position between two worlds and two vocabularies, a parody he extends in "Excuse You," which attacks the hip hop catchphrases that have entered mainstream vocabulary alongside buzz words from the academic and business worlds. Barman's website offers this introduction to the track: "'Excuse You' is pleasurably irony-free. Do you ever feel like you are forced to rhyme pop culture vocab because all the improper nouns have already been used? Do you ever feel like indirectness is as direct as you can get?"[8] "Excuse You" juxtaposes business catchphrases like "push the envelope" and "think outside the box" with hip hop vocabulary like "shoot the gift," "flip the script," and "in the house." Barman uses wordplay to critique each of these vocabularies, and integrates an academic vocabulary as he combines mathematical formulae and literary terminology with hip hop language: "Fibonacci challenge poems, Declarative palindromes." Although Barman's website claims that the song is "pleasurably irony-free," his lyrics take a decidedly parodic approach to rap's braggadocio. Lines like "I'm iller than the *Illiad*," and "I keep it more gully than Jonathan Livingston" combine rap slang with literary references. His combination of these vocabularies critiques hip hop's assimilation with mainstream culture, and by extension, he critiques his own position in relation to hip hop, as a performer who comes from outside the culture that developed the music.

Outside of "Excuse You," Barman refrains from employing much of rap's standard vocabulary. His use of it here emphasizes the disconnect between his personal history and the world of hip hop, and as he combines the two vocabularies, he carves his own spot within the culture through his understanding and critique of it. Barman, like other white MCs, must appeal to an audience's sense of hip hop credibility which has been shaped by performances of blackness. On "Excuse You" he subtly parodies Ice Cube's statement that white listeners are eavesdropping, as he claims to "target the fans that you wish you didn't have." As exemplified in this line, Barman's authenticating strategies center on an informed critique of hip hop culture that can attack basic tenets of, and contradictions within, rap even as Barman performs his own version of the music. As he employs parody and intellectualizes his rhyme structures and lyrics, Barman extends a history of underground hip hop artists who view themselves as an alternative to Top 40 rap music.

Barman's performance does reproduce aspects of rap's vocabulary, yet it lies closer to Bakhtin's hidden polemic in that Barman attacks the assimilation of hip hop's vocabulary, rather than the language itself. In other words, Barman isn't critiquing hip hop slang itself, but the translation of the slang to the popular vocabulary, and to standard American English spoken by whites. Given rap's focus on lyrical inventiveness, Barman's critique is especially meaningful. Nas addresses the issue of "stealing my slang." Raekwon and Ghostface also devote lyrics to this topic. The assimilation of one artist's slang is both a testament to his or her influence, and an encroachment onto his or her territory. The next section will study the encroachment of white rock on hip hop.

ROCK PARODY: DYNAMITE HACK

Barman uses parody to critique both his own distance from hip hop's original culture and the assimilation of that culture's vocabulary. His music remains grounded in hip hop style as he uses wordplay and rhyme to support the identity he puts forth in his lyrics. The question of white parody becomes even more complex when rap lyrics and musical styles are employed by musicians in another genre. The 1990s saw hip hop styles blended with rock, as groups like Sublime and Limp Bizkit incorporated hip hop's slang, vocal style, and the art of sampling into their music. While rap-rock has become a genre unto itself, this same era spawned another distinct trend which saw rock groups cover hip hop songs, reproducing the original lyrics but changing the music and performance style entirely. In the most commercially successful example, Dynamite Hack, a white rock group, covered N.W.A.'s first single, "Boyz-N-The-Hood," in 2000. Dynamite Hack juxtaposes white vocal style and white economic privilege with N.W.A.'s narrative of life in a disadvantaged neighborhood. The cover has raised questions of authenticity, leading one reviewer to describe it as "[N.W.A. member] Dr. Dre's mellow '90s vibe, as fabricated by emaciated college nerds reciting his gang-banging '80s words...."[9] Dynamite Hack delivers N.W.A.'s lyrics, softly, over acoustic guitar, performing "Boyz-N-The-Hood" in a style very different from the original.

The cover song is a late development in hip hop music. In 1995, the *Spin Alternative Record Guide* noted that "When an original [rap] catch phrase is incorporated into the larger audience's vocabulary it signifies the artist's influence on the culture. To have a song covered (it's only happened twice) is hip hop's closest thing to deification."[10] In the ten years since *Spin's* guide was published, however, the hip hop cover has further established itself. Yet while some rap artists have covered older rap songs, rap covers have become most prevalent among rock groups. Along with Dynamite Hack, other white rockers have covered songs from black rappers. Priority released a compilation of rock covers of rap hits, *In tha Beginning ... There was Rap,* in 1997, and in 2000 a collection of rock covers of rap songs, *Take a Bite Outta Rhyme: a Rock Tribute to Rap*, hit shelves. This phenomenon prompts reconsideration of the nature of hip hop music. Deena Weinstein had asserted that "cover songs, in the fullest sense of the term, are peculiar to rock music,"[11] and Keith Negus similarly claimed that rap songs "cannot be covered."[12]

When white rock groups cover hip hop songs, they tread a boundary between tribute and parody. The racist origins of the rock cover in the 1950s—when white rock and roll groups covered songs from black R&B artists who could not achieve the same level of radio exposure—further complicates rockers' covers of rap. Weinstein shows that such appropriation soon gave way to a focus on validation, as British Invasion bands of the 1960s used the rock cover to "validate their own authenticity as musicians," by covering successful American rock songs.[13] And in the 1970s, punk bands used covers to criticize or parody the original. Weinstein illustrates that while 1950s rock and roll bands covered black R & B songs they could assume their own target audience had never heard, punk bands often cover well-known originals with which their audience is familiar.[14] Weinstein argues that "Through parody, the punk cover attacked the conventions of authenticity in rock as pompous, pretentious, and (laughably) lame."[15] Dynamite Hack's cover extends this punk tradition, yet rather than parody the original song or performance, they use parody to critique key representations of race and identity that have developed along with hip hop's success.

Dynamite Hack released "Boyz-N-The-Hood" as the debut single from an album, *Superfast* (2000), which contains no elements of hip hop outside this one single. Hack achieved unprecedented sales for a rock cover of a rap song, yet they were not the first band to produce such a cover. Bands like Phish and Mr. Bungle have covered rap hits in concert, and in the most interesting example, members of Too Much Joy, who recorded a cover of LL Cool J's "That's a Lie (1985)," were arrested for playing a 2 Live Crew song during the 1989-90 controversy surrounding that group's album *As Nasty as They Wanna Be* (1989). Hip hop groups have themselves traditionally relied on rock to connect with the crossover audience. Run DMC, for example, had a radio hit in 1986 with their cover of Aerosmith's "Walk this Way," yet the meeting of rap and rock in the mainstream has never been a great point of authenticity, and has been looked upon as a gimmick, a departure from musical integrity for commercial gain. Diehl argues that "the root of the rap-rock merger's appeal has often stemmed from its novelty status, and the novelty hit has proven to be a pop rap mainstay."[16] The key difference between the novelty aspects of Hack's "Boyz-N-The-Hood" and a single like "Walk this Way" is that Run DMC came into the mainstream with a lot of hip hop credibility. They were a hip hop group taking a step into the mainstream light by way of rock, while Dynamite Hack is a rock group using rap to gain commercial appeal with rock listeners. This is where concerns about exploitation come into play.

Dynamite Hack's Morrison, in discussing popular reaction to the song, has said, "I think it's a pretty emotional track...a lot of people hate it because they think it's blasphemous to Eazy-E."[17] Morrison has acknowledged his respect for the music of Eazy-E and N.W.A., telling one interviewer, "Me and my friends used to drive to and from school listening to nothing but [*Eazy Duz It* 1988] for like three or four months. I still know like every lyric."[18] This respect notwithstanding, some listeners have perceived Hack's juxtaposition of Eazy-E lyrics and indie-rock performance style as a direct parody of hip hop culture. Hack juxtaposes N.W.A.'s narrative with indie-rock vocal and guitar styles, and establishes this meeting of the two cultures as the subject of humor—it is not a parody of N.W.A. or hip hop music. N.W.A.'s original takes the listener on a tour of Compton, California. Coker provides an overview of the song's storyline in saying, "Eazy's character does everything from cruising the street looking for girls...to smacking a girlfriend and knocking out her father...."[19] While this summary identifies the primary action of the song, Coker may oversimplify its narrative, which shows Eazy's character to be trapped in a system of violence—a victim as well as a perpetrator.

Eazy-E's character begins his day with the realization that he has to arm himself before he leaves home. These early lines set up the action to follow, putting the rest of the song's events into perspective. As soon as Eazy retrieves his gun and avoids an altercation with gang members outside his house, the lyrics shift to show him driving in his car, listening to music recorded by him and his group. As Eazy begins to play his own song on his car stereo, the first verse becomes an introduction to the song itself. When N.W.A. first released "Boyz-N-The-Hood" on their 1987 album *N.W.A. and the Posse*, the song did not include this introductory verse. The verse appears in "Boyz-N-The-Hood (Remix)" (the version covered by Dynamite Hack) on Eazy's 1988 album *Eazy Duz It*, and its addition reinforces that the narrator is himself oppressed by the violence of inner-city life, rather than functioning simply as a part of it. As Eazy's character describes ghetto life from the perspective of an insider, the introductory verse makes clear what position this insider holds. The chorus addresses the outside spectator, and at the same time devalues the song's narrative with the warning: "Don't quote me, boy. I ain't said shit."

N.W.A. brought to rap's storytelling a larger struggle between social and commercial construction: "[W]hile their ghetto tales came from the streets of South Central L.A., they were presented in exciting, cinematic narratives that played like blaxploitation action-movie blockbusters, making hard rap that much more accessible to a wider audience."[20] N.W.A.'s stories depicted from the band's perspective the realities of inner city street life, and were at the same time constructed to appeal to the outside spectator. As Dynamite Hack appropriates their narrative, the band devalues this depiction of reality; the "Boyz-N-The-Hood" cover comes to reflect a postmodern view of narrative in that it presents N.W.A.'s original story, delivered by Dynamite Hack, whose reality is outside that which is depicted in the song.

"Boyz-N-The-Hood" became Eazy-E's signature song. He continued to record new versions as a solo artist after N.W.A.'s break-up in 1991. Dynamite Hack covers the only recording of the song to include the introductory verse, yet their cover leaves out the third, fifth, and sixth verses from the original. Along with the obvious commercial implications of shortening the track to single length, it is notable that the three verses Hack chooses to discard would be most uncomfortable for the mainstream listener. In verse three, J. D., a friend of Eazy's character, is compelled by his crack addiction to steal Eazy's prized Alpine car stereo. Eazy catches him in the act and is willing to "call a truce," but J. D. pulls a gun and Eazy is forced to shoot his friend to death in an act of self-preservation. The fifth and sixth verses of N.W.A.'s original portray violence in a similar fashion. Verse five begins with an interaction with police in which a traffic violation quickly escalates into a physical altercation and a resisting arrest charge. The cartoonish violence of the resultant courtroom scene is countered with the fact that the two characters involved are sentenced to prison for attempted murder. Dynamite Hack has avoided the three verses in which N.W.A.'s gangsta violence is shown to have lasting consequences. By omitting these verses, Hack has modified N.W.A.'s original, making it more radio-friendly both in duration and content. Such a modification may echo the 1950s rock and roll cover movement, during which rock bands would record white versions of black R&B songs for white radio.

MAKING THE VIDEO

Members of Dynamite Hack voiced their own reservations about parody in choosing a video for their "Boyz-N-The-Hood" single. The band's strict avoidance of a "stereotypical, gangsta-styled" video speaks for their desire to avoid parody of hip hop performance, and they rejected any script that called for them to present themselves as would-be gangstas:

> ... all the other treatments we got had something to do with us being gangsters, and we were like, "Nope, nope." Anything that had things in quotes, like "gangsta," or "there will be a carload of 'hoochie mamas' that will pull up next to you, who will all be 'getting their groove on,' while Mark, what was it, 'pimps his ride.'"[21]

Reproducing N.W.A.'s original lyrics, Hack avoids parody of the hip hop vernacular. Hack chose a script written by Evan Bernard, whose vision was in line with the band's own: "Don't do anything gangster, at all.

Nothing gangster. It's all as white as you can be. . . ."[22] This choice of video speaks for Hack's desire to avoid a parody of hip hop culture.

The "Boyz-N-The-Hood" video, like the song itself, creates humor through juxtaposition. Instead of presenting themselves as hip hop outsiders in a hip hop world, Hack's video shows the band living a privileged white lifestyle, totally isolated from the black inner-city life associated with N.W.A. Bernard's script juxtaposes this representation with scenes common to many rap videos of the 1990s. In one of his scenes, the camera focuses in on the band gathered in a circle as if they are shooting dice. As the camera's perspective changes, we see Hack's members are instead concentrating on their game of croquet. Presenting the band as it does, the video's humor works through juxtaposition, instead of the parody seen in a video like De La Soul's 1995 "Ego Trippin' (Part Two)." Bernard's video script avoids such a satirical treatment of hip hop culture, and instead presents middle-class white versions of common features of rap's visual representation. Several features are included, such as the community barbecue that became a video standard following Dr. Dre's "Nuthin' but a G Thang," and rap's emphasis on designer fashion (with logos fuzzed out by MTV). In Dynamite Hack's video, these images are accompanied by other commercial rap standards like female dancers and a slow-cruising car, although in this case the women are dressed in country club style and the camera pans back to reveal the car as a police cruiser. Parodying N.W.A.'s conflict with the FBI over their song "Fuck Tha Police" (1988), the white band smiles and waves, and the white officer cheerfully returns their greeting.

This representation, when considered with Hack's omission of N.W.A.'s verse five—in which a black character is involved in an altercation with police—targets race privilege, which is the focus of Hack's "white as you can be" video. Faced with systemic racism, rap lyricists tell us the only way they can break free from poverty is to work outside the system, and outside the law. Many rap artists, especially those who link themselves with gangsta culture, define themselves as businessmen. Eazy-E even claimed to have founded his record label and financed N.W.A.'s "Boyz-N-The-Hood" recording with money he made selling drugs. In light of these considerations, the Hack video's materialist images, such as the huge ice sculpture in the shape of a dollar sign, can be taken as money fetishism by the economically-privileged, instead of desire for money by the disadvantaged. The only scene in Hack's video that approaches parody is a corruption of a well-known scene from N.W.A.'s "Express Yourself" video (1988). In N.W.A.'s original, the group bursts through a paper banner reading, "I have a dream." Hack's video imitates this scene almost

shot-for-shot, but in this one the banner reads, *"American Express* Yourself,"
reinforcing Hack's characters' identities within white economic privilege.

DON'T QUOTE ME, BOY

With "Boyz-N-The-Hood," Hack developed a careful parody of whiteness
as privilege, and confronted the connection of race and class. In doing so,
they avoided parody of hip hop culture, choosing instead to parody whiteness as a racial position. More interesting is what N.W.A. excluded from
the parody. After having approved the cover, Dre later requested that
Dynamite Hack censor the original line "Young niggaz at the pad throwing
up gang signs." Hack guitarist Mike Vlahakis relates Dre's assertion that
"the white boys can't use that word. As soon as they use it, then it's going
to change everything."[23] Dre's request came very late, just before the
Superfast CD was to be pressed, and after a version of Hack's cover was
already available on the Internet. The inclusion and later censoring of the
word "niggaz" sparked debate from Dynamite Hack fans posting to an
online message board on the band's official website. One user, *DON-
MEGA*, complains that, "about 13 seconds into their song Boyz In The
Hood they say the word NIGGER ... which i find really fuckin offensive
coming from a bunch of preppy ass white kids...." A second board user,
calling himself *shut the fuck up*, challenges black ownership of the term:
"... all that rap bullshit is bought by little white suburban kids anyway ...
i say from now on, the word nigger should be used by suburban white
kids, cause if it werent for them, the word nigger would never be on cd."
These two online posts, though certainly abrasive and misguided, offer an
argument about Dynamite Hack's right to use a word which is tied so
directly to N.W.A.'s identity.

N.W.A. had both a commercial and a political agenda for their group
name. Ice Cube has described his reaction to Dre and Eazy's suggested
name, which was to appear on their "Boyz-N-The-Hood" twelve-inch single: "Niggaz Wit Attitude.... Ain't nobody gonna put that out." The
members agreed to list the band by its initials and "wait til people ask."[24]
N.W.A.'s marketing strategy worked, and their group name remains a topic
of debate. Coker argues that the name may have been in part a reaction to
the promotion of black power by New York groups like Public Enemy and
Boogie Down Productions: "When black power and recognizing one's
heritage were all the rage, N.W.A. reveled in their ignorance...pointing
guns at brothers while others were calling for an overthrow of the white
system."[25] Robin D.G. Kelley extends Coker's concept of Niggaz Wit

Attitude as a political statement, and argues that "N.W.A. uses 'Nigga' as a synonym for 'oppressed.'"[26] He links the band's use of the term more to a social than strictly racial identity: "Products of the postindustrial ghetto, the characters in gangsta rap constantly remind listeners that they are still second-class citizens—'Niggaz'—whose collective lived experiences suggest that nothing has changed for them as opposed to the black middle class."[27]

As N.W.A. relate their experience as second-class citizens, they position their white listeners as spectators. This distance for the white listener is what calls into question how close Dynamite Hack can get to gangsta culture. Hack's cover, uncensored, furthers N.W.A.'s commodification of the word "niggaz," and appropriates it for Hack's own commercial success. N.W.A. used the term to draw attention to their lyrics, and the white artist avoids it almost exclusively. The key to the humor in Dynamite Hack's cover is context: The lyrics don't fit with the style in which they are delivered, or the image of the band that delivers them. Hack surprises the listener with its nonchalant delivery of N.W.A.'s verses of crime and violence against women, and before Dre's warning, saw no reason to change the racial language of the original.

STILL D.R.E.?

This final chapter has traced the development of rap's parodies of racial identity as they confront constructions of blackness and whiteness. The chapter also has to a large degree followed the career of Dr. Dre, from his Niggaz Wit Attitude beginnings through his more recent interactions with Dynamite Hack and Eminem. For nearly twenty years, Dre has been one of hip hop's foremost producers, and the history of his career illuminates the history of commercial rap music and the role race plays in its production. As I discussed earlier in this chapter, N.W.A. famously broke up because of disputes over the management of their career, and the relationship between Heller and Eazy-E. The group's members have attacked each other, reconciled, and produced new collaborations. When N.W.A. reunited in 2000, minus Heller (and Eazy-E, who died in 1995), Ice Cube rhymed on "Chin Check": "[F]uck Jerry Heller and the white superpowers." Yet Dre, who had parodied Eazy-E's role as Heller's yes man, has sponsored the career of Eminem, and approved Dynamite Hack's parodic cover of "Boyz-N-The-Hood." Such actions have called into question Dre's credibility and consistency, and he has addressed these concerns in his lyrics.

When Dre released his album *Chronic 2001* (1999), a followup to 1992's *The Chronic*, his first single was "Still D.R.E.," a collaboration with

Snoop Dogg in which Dre confronts his career history and his current place in the hip hop world, both as MC and mogul. In the song, Dre claims his consistency has been called into question by those fans who "wonder if he still got it," and who remind him that rap music has changed dramatically since Dre's heyday. The importance of this song to hip hop's current cultural position? If Dre is still Dre, then hip hop is still powerful. "Still D.R.E." both celebrates Dre's role in making Eminem into the world's biggest rap star, and argues that he "still loves to see young blacks get money." Dre's involvement with whiteness, and the way Eminem's "Guilty Conscience" (1999) challenges Dre's change in position from N.W.A. thug to voice of reason, follows a design I have set up throughout this book. Dre uses anticipation to address criticisms, and to reassert his authenticity through consistency. At the same time, he does not claim not to have changed. In fact, both "Guilty Conscience" and "Still D.R.E." are career narratives that trace Dre's development from his 1980s dance group the World Class Wreckin' Cru, through his current role in Aftermath Records and the career of Eminem. Through these changes and developments, though, he remains Dre, and this is a key feature of autobiography and stories of the self-made man. Once you stop evolving, you are finished. Dre isn't finished yet. While "Still D.R.E." is more straightforward, he parodies his old self on "Guilty Conscience." This is a development, too, from the dead serious N.W.A. days when the group never smiled on album covers and publicity photos.

Dre's development toward self-parody matches hip hop at large. The hip hop community has long feared its eventual assimilation, and I ask whether this has happened. Rap's self-parody is widespread. It is a huge part of what Snoop Dogg does in AOL commercials, and what Lil Jon does in Subway commercials. Ice-T, since 2000, has played a police detective on the television drama *Law and Order: Special Victims Unit.* Has hip hop lost its power to shock, its position as a drug, as a controlled substance? Has it been made friendly through self-conscious parody? Would the cop killer scandal even happen today? Has rap's parody of itself weakened its cultural impact, and is it a symptom of assimilation? Does self-parody make it safe? Dre's career is safe. Realness is an ongoing project, but he has so firmly established his legitimacy that he can afford to laugh at himself. Dre's work with Eminem and The Game emphasize their place in a lineage, and these newer artists discuss their respect for N.W.A. in their lyrics: in fact, to build his own credibility through his association with classic gangsta artists, The Game's 2005 album *The Documentary* mentions Dr. Dre and/or Snoop Dogg thirty-five times.[28] Dre, in his work with these artists, emphasizes their place in a lineage of West Coast gangsta rap that he originated with N.W.A. Reminding us of this lineage in song lyrics serves both to authenticate these new artists and to assert Dre's longevity and his continuing relevance more than twenty years into his music career. Hip hop's notions of authenticity are closely tied to the original culture, yet more than twenty years into his career, Dre narrates his development from those origins, rather than emphasizing that he continues to fit a model of 1980s authenticity.

Unlike N.W.A., Eminem began his rap career with self-parody. He introduced himself to MTV audiences in 1999 with "My Name Is," a song and music video that parodied elements of stereotypically white culture (*Leave it to Beaver*, Johnny Carson, trailer park life) in much the same way that Dynamite Hack did in their video. As a new white rapper, it was important that Eminem not take himself too seriously, even as he argued his credibility by emphasizing his connections with Dre. Nearly ten years into Eminem's career, however, when he has become one of the biggest-selling rap artists of all time, is there still something intrinsically funny about a white person attempting to rap?

BLOWIN' UP: BLURRING THE LINES

In 2006, MTV launched Jamie Kennedy's *Blowin' Up*, a mock-reality show that guest starred several prominent rappers, from Mike Jones and Paul Wall to Three 6 Mafia to Ice-T to Wu-Tang's RZA and Method Man. The willing participation of these rappers in a parody of contemporary rap culture stands in stark contrast to 1990s gangsta rap, where rappers bragged about never cracking a smile. On "Wicked" (1992), Cube bragged that he's "never seen with the happy grin," and on "Insane in the Brain" (1993), Sen Dog says, "happy face nigga never see me smile." In that earlier era, rap parody was reserved for comedians, like Chris Rock in *CB4*, or for an alternative breed of rapper critiquing the culture from within, like De La Soul in "Me, Myself, and I" (1989) or Black Sheep in "U Mean I'm Not" (1991). In 2007, hip hop has become so entrenched in our culture that rappers like Method Man and Ice-T can safely laugh at themselves without losing any of their street cred, but does this new trend of rappers participating in rap parody indicate that hip hop has lost some of its original power?

In the age of Eminem and Paul Wall, the hip hop aspirations of Jamie Kennedy, a thirty-something, white, Jewish comedian would not seem totally out of place, but at every turn, Jamie's career hits a snag: When Method Man refuses to record a guest verse for Jamie's first single, Jamie recruits Bob Saget instead. When Jamie seeks advice from *Saturday Night Live*'s Tracy Morgan, Tracy suggests that he perform in black make-up. *Blowin' Up* is presented in the format of a reality show, but rather than claim to present reality, it instead parodies the format, parodies Jamie Kennedy's own identity (he plays himself up as a spoiled, lazy celebrity), and parodies hip hop's current dominance of pop culture. MTV labels the show "comedic reality," and the show's humor often depends on the question of how seriously to take Jamie and Stu's aspirations to hip hop stardom. This question is complicated in that Stu repeatedly refers to their music as "hip hop comedy," and in that they do seem to earn the respect of major rap artists. The key to *Blowin' Up*'s success lies with the guest appearances from big-name hip hop artists, such as those mentioned earlier. Paul Wall and E-40 guest star on the *Blowin' Up* album that Stone and Kennedy released in conjunction with the series.

The series follows Jamie Kennedy and his partner, Stu Stone (a/k/a Stu the Jew). As they embark on the rap career they've dreamed of since childhood, they seek out advice and direction from hip hop stars. In Episode 1:02, "Law & Disorderlies," Stu sneaks their demo CD to Ice-T, an actor on *Law and Order: Special Victims Unit*, a television drama that has offered a role to Jamie. Ice-T is annoyed with Stu, who seems to be hitting on his wife, but in the end he calls up the duo of aspiring rappers, offering words of encouragement and some advice on dealing with record label executives. In later episodes, Stu and Jamie seek advice from Method Man, Three 6 Mafia, and Russell Simmons, on topics ranging from gaining credibility to getting their music played in clubs. As white Hollywood actors, the duo's main concern is gaining credibility. Importantly, Kennedy addresses his past role as B-Rad, a rich, white, wannabe rapper in the film *Malibu's Most Wanted* (2003) as now holding him back as he sincerely works at a rap career. In a conversation with comedian Tracy Morgan, he describes his desire to shed that image and replace it with a more credible reputation that will help launch his rap career. In this episode, the series' most racially tense, Jamie and Stu ask Three 6 Mafia to let them open for them in concert. On the advice of Tracy Morgan, who urged Stu and Jamie to commit crimes, get girls pregnant, and otherwise build up a more hardcore image, they hire a makeup artist to make them look black. They test out their appearance in a local coffee shop, adopting hip hop slang and an aggressive posture to threaten Jason Biggs, from the film *American Pie* (1999). Then they show up backstage to meet Three 6 Mafia, who are stunned at their costumes. When Jamie explains that Tracy Morgan came up with the plan, Three 6's Juicy J asks "Does he have some kind of beef with y'all?"

As they enter the stage, DJ Paul says "Man, they're gonna get killed." But they don't get killed. They get booed. Then, when they emerge without their costumes, as two white rappers, and launch into their first single, "Circle Circle Dot Dot," the crowd goes wild with applause. Without Three 6 Mafia there to sponsor the comedy, the act would go too far. The rappers who participate in *Blowin' Up* give Kennedy the license he needs to take his parody of race relations in the U.S., as exemplified through rap music, to its fullest extreme.

CONCLUSION

To return to the question I raised in the introduction, is hip hop dead? Is Nas correct, on his 2006 album *Hip Hop is Dead*, that the transition from block parties to big business has killed off the culture? The answer is no.

Hip hop survived its transition to the mainstream because of the attention paid to this transition in lyrics, in the form of warnings about shady record executives, accusations of sell-outs, and criticism of white involvement in the music. A system of checks and balances among rap artists keeps hip hop vital and holds artists accountable to the standards they set forth in lyrics. Even though hip hop has gone commercial, gone mainstream, and gone global, a lively and ongoing debate over these topics in hip hop music indicates that the culture continues to thrive. Nas's *Hip Hop is Dead* is a part of this debate, and so are the responses to it from Southern rappers. Nas's album, even with its contradictions, is an important release. It makes us think about what hip hop was, what it is today, and where it will go in the future. It contributed to the system of checks and balances by which MCs use their music to hold each other accountable to hip hop's original culture. Hip hop became the biggest-selling music in the United States, but this transition to the mainstream did not kill off the culture.

Hip hop artists have long been conscious of threats to their music and its culture. As I showed in chapters 5 and 6 of this book, rap artists, critics, and scholars feared that Vanilla Ice signaled the beginning of the end for hip hop. They worried that he had opened up dangerous floodgates that would allow hip hop to be taken over by white people. As I showed in chapter 5, Havelock Nelson and David Mills, among others, compared Vanilla Ice to Elvis. Nelson voiced his fear that by 2050 rap could be seen as white. Rappers as markedly different in style as De La Soul and Ice Cube argued that rap music is not meant for a white audience. The threat was clear: hip hop music was invented by black people in black neighborhoods, but as it transitioned to the mainstream, would it become another aspect of middle class, white, American culture?

Rap artists were vocal in their criticism of Vanilla Ice, and in that way policed hip hop culture, educating their listeners about the dangers of white rap. In 2007, white rappers are still a minority, and even with Eminem's unprecedented commercial success, he built his credibility through his association with a black artist, and his music deals with the topics of race and being a white rapper in the black world of hip hop. Recent television shows such as *The (White) Rapper Show* and *Blowin' Up* reinforce the fact that the white rapper remains a figure of ridicule. When rappers felt threatened with a takeover by whites, they spoke out, both in their music and in interviews, just as many of them, as I have shown in this book, speak out against record industry business dealings or speak out against their peers who they perceive as fakes or phonies.

Yet many of the rappers, like Nas, who criticize sellouts, are themselves major label recording artists. To make music for a major corporation is not taboo in itself, as long as the artist can prove that he is doing it on his own terms, and has not ceded creative power to the corporation. Further, the mainstream hip hop produced by major labels gives the underground something to which to respond: as yesterday's innovators cross over to MTV and radio, younger MCs create new styles. The wealth of independent rap labels and underground mixtapes proves that hip hop is alive and well. In fact, many major label artists have returned to small, independent labels, or turned to producing their own unofficial mixtapes outside their contractual obligations with the label.

As I discussed in this book, a recent trend sees established, major label MCs returning to the old school promotional technique of producing their own mixtapes and releasing them independently. The war of words between Jay-Z and Nas, two of the biggest-selling MCs in the United States, took place primarily in unofficial releases and mixtapes circulated to New York City radio stations, passed out at clubs, and leaked to Internet file-sharing sites; this technique allowed each MC to deliver a timely response to the other's criticism, without waiting for the lengthy process of producing a major-label album. In 2006, several major-label MCs produced mixtapes. Redman released *Ill at Will Vol. 1 Mixtape* on his own Gilla House label, outside of his commitment to Def Jam Records. That same year, Wu-Tang Clan's Raekwon released three mixtapes: *Vatican, Da*

Vinci Code: Vatican Mixtape V2, and *Heroin Only*. Lil Wayne, as well, released *Dedication 2* (with DJ Drama). This return to mixtape promotion among established mainstream MCs occurred in the wake of the breakout year of 2005 for hip hop in Houston, Texas, where artists like Slim Thug, Mike Jones, and Paul Wall had made their names performing on several mixtapes in circulation in Houston, where the Screwed and Chopped phenomenon made mixtapes a hot commodity, and where few local artists before them had seen MTV airplay or appeared on nationwide radio. This shift between the production and distribution modes of mainstream and underground hip hop indicates that a clear distinction between the two is dissolving. An MC's career may move between the worlds of mainstream and underground, or more accurately, between the realms of corporate and independent recording.

Recording independently, even after signing to a label, allows rap artists to take more control over their music, including what producers they work with, what samples they use, and by what means they promote and distribute their recordings. Many artists release mixtapes via their own labels, like Redman's Gilla House and Raekwon's Ice Water Records, and use them as a forum to showcase new artists who will release future albums. This trend of showcasing a roster of new artists began with Dr. Dre's *The Chronic* (1992), which was Dre's first release outside his contract with Ruthless Records, N.W.A., and that group's manager, Jerry Heller. Dre recorded *The Chronic* for the new label, Death Row Records, that he had founded with Suge Knight. Although Death Row was distributed by Interscope, part of the Universal Music Group (along with Geefen and A&M), running his own label allowed Dre new freedom, since he had moved away from the Ruthless Records contract that he and Ice Cube called unfair. In moving away from Heller's management and forming his own label, Dre took charge of the business side of his career. His experience in the music business provided him with the perspective to mold and shape the new stars he showcased on The Chronic, and on later releases from Death Row, and his latest label, Aftermath Records. Without's Dre's guidance and sponsorship, artists like Snoop Dogg, Lady of Rage, Tha Dogg Pound, Eminem, and 50 Cent, would not have achieved the success that they did.

Dre's story indicates a larger trend across hip hop music since the mid-nineties. Artists have taken a keen interest in making a career of hip hop, and in making sure that they maintain control of their work, both artistically and financially. Monie Love, in voicing her support of Nas's album, criticized the stories of career-building, hustling, and grinding that have become a key feature of recent rap music, but as I have shown in this book, these career stories are a celebration of street smarts and entrepreneurialism. They fit into an American tradition of success stories. No other form of music pays this much attention in lyrics to the business of making music, and these career stories continue to spark debate between hip hop artists and listeners about what hip hop is, and what it should be. These stories and debates are vital to keeping hip hop alive.

At the heart of hip hop's success stories, as they are presented in lyrics, is the artist versus the industry. Even as artists like Dr. Dre and Jay-Z are *becoming* the industry in their new roles as label CEOs and A&R executives, "the industry" remains a villain. In 2007, Nas told *Jet* magazine that the whole industry needs to be destroyed and rebuilt (Christian 55). This impulse to destroy has a history within art—in chapter three I mentioned the connection between MF DOOM's statement that he "came to destroy rap" in 1999 and the Dadaist slogan, "Dada destroys everything," in the years following World War I. Similarly, in the 1970s, the punk group the Sex Pistols sought to bring destruction to British radio, through their crudeness, aggression, and lack of musicianship. By tearing down what came before, artists create space for rejuvenation, even renaissance. So Nas's proclaiming hip hop dead is not an entirely negative statement; arguing that we need to tear down hip hop in order to rebuild it fits into hip hop's ongoing fight to keep hip hop controlled by the artists, instead of the industry.

Hip hop was not killed by going commercial, going mainstream, going global, or even going white, any more than it was killed by censorship. As a testament to hip hop's staying power, we can look at the 1990s, the decade when hip hop faced not only the threat of a white takeover, but a strong political backlash. The FBI issued warnings to N.W.A. after the release of their song "Fuck tha Police," and to Ice-T's group Body Count after their song "Cop Killer" was attacked by a Texas police group. On "Point the Finga" (1994), Tupac samples a soundbite from Vice President Dan Quayle's speech condemning his music: "It has no place in our society." When government officials removed rap music from the boundaries of acceptability, it became a controlled substance, and rap lyrics began to promote trafficking in hip hop. Hip hop faced boycotts and the enforcing of parental advisory stickers and laws that made it illegal for minors to purchase certain rap CDs. Despite, or perhaps because of these efforts, rap sales continued to grow.

As rap grew in commercial dominance, its images of criminality changed. In the late 1980s and early '90s, rap groups like N.W.A. and Public Enemy borrowed images from street gangs and from militant groups such as the Black Panthers. N.W.A.'s Eazy-E bragged about funding his early recordings with drug money. Public Enemy's S1W soldiers marched with fake guns during P.E. performances. By the late 1990s, these images had taken the background to representations of organized crime via rap moguls like Suge Knight, and artists Snoop Dogg, aka "The Doggfather," and Wu-Tang Clan, who took on Italian mafia names on their second album *Wu-Tang Forever* (1997). More recently, rap artists have moved toward images of white-collar or corporate crime. Jay-Z celebrates his role as record label CEO on 2003's *The Black Album*, even as he compares this work to his criminal past. This history of rap's criminal images indicates a shift away from representations of lower-class crime and toward upper-class crime, the corporate or organized crime that often involves greater sums of money. In this sense, rap's representations of criminality have changed along with its market share. As artists sell more records, their crime becomes more white-collar.

Representations of rap moguls and CEOs still are framed within criminal metaphors, and individual artists' achievement of such wealth and status still are tied to narratives that trace their rise from poverty through their rap careers. Although critics are misguided in attributing rap music's invention to the social conditions of the musicians, I would argue that rap lyricists' emphasis on poverty grew with hip-hop's entrance into the mainstream. As rap singles first began to appear on commercial radio, MCs began to tell stories about their neighborhoods, and these stories seemed to be directed to the outside listener. Before rap recordings took hold, the main objective of MCs was to hype the crowd and promote the DJ who kept the music going. Rhymes were improvised, and did not necessarily tell stories. When MCs became the focal element of hip-hop recordings, they began to structure their rhymes into narratives. Grand Master Flash & the Furious Five's 1982 single "The Message" describes lives on the brink of destruction. The song depicted crime, poverty, and failing social programs in New York City, and brought its message to listeners living outside that experience. Flash & the Furious Five narrate their experiences to an MTV audience, and do not distinguish between their lives in the inner city and their careers as popular recording artists. The lyrics do not present a rags-to-riches story of the group's success, the way many current rap songs do with their attention to wealth. Instead, the Furious Five claims to tell their story from *within* the social conditions the song describes. At the end of video for "The Message," Flash & the Furious Five are arrested by white cops who mistake the rap group for a gang, and this scene serves to persuade the viewer that the group's record contract has neither taken them out of their ghetto community nor removed them from racial profiling.

"The Message," which conveyed the hopelessness of ghetto life, rose to number four on the *Billboard* charts, and both the fatalism and commercialism of the song's creation played out in the biographies of the performers. Grandmaster Flash went on to sue Sugarhill Records for $5 million in royalties for the song, while Furious Five member Cowboy fought crack addiction and died at the age of twenty-eight. Such contradictions have existed throughout hip hop's history. Although hip hop was created outside the record industry, early rap's ghetto narratives were sold through the industry to an outside audience, positioning the artists either as cultural emissaries or as sell-outs who translated and diluted the culture for profit. Because of hip hop's commercial success, the threat of industry appropriation inspires nostalgia for an era of pure, "real" hip hop that existed outside of commercial concerns. Essentially, hip hop realness and other forms of popular music authenticity reflect concerns that mainstream assimilation will change the music and its culture. Popular music forms, from country to rock to jazz, have called into question their artists' authenticity as movements that originated as subcultures began to sell records in the mainstream. Standards of authenticity center on the existence of an original, and in the case of popular music, on the notion of an earlier pure and unadulterated form of a music and culture, untouched by the record industry.

This nostalgic view is complicated by commercialism's role in the beginnings of many forms of popular music. Sugarhill Gang, who recorded rap's first hit single, was formed by record company executive Sylvia Robinson. The group did not exist, perform, or record until Robinson recruited them for a band. Nas's argument in *Hip Hop is Dead* is founded on nostalgia, and such nostalgia for a pure origin of the music outside the commercial realm often ignores how early into their histories many popular music forms faced appropriation. Artists themselves often recognize the marketing potential of the subculture's stereotype. In 1920s country music, Gid Tanner promoted his group The Skillet Lickers by playing up the backwoods hick persona and drinking moonshine on stage. In the same era of country music's commercial boom in the mainstream, The Fruit Jar Drinkers took on hillbilly names and dressed for the farm in their performances. In 1970s punk, The Ramones were five grown men dressing like teen thugs, and the Sex Pistols was formed by Malcolm McLaren, a clothing-store owner who envisioned a group that would bring chaos to British radio. Such performances complicate the position of the pioneering artists who often become known as the pure, or the true, form of the music and culture.

These concepts of authenticity contextualized my study of hip hop's own debates about realness. Hip hop's uses of "real" and "true" versus "fake" and "phony" frame hip hop as a culture and industry in which artists struggle to maintain an authenticity of self, community, and culture, while still producing a commercial music. A prevalent argument is that hip hop has lost its relevance, and its realness, because of the hyper-consumerism of its artists, who chronicle their wealth in lyrics, and display their excess in videos. Those representations exist from Top 40 crossover hip hop stars to local, unsigned rap groups, and as I write this introduction, these representations maintain their hold on the charts. Yet criticisms of hip hop excess often neglect how the career and financial agendas are addressed in the lyrics themselves. To write off hip hop excess is to ignore the complex interactions with consumer culture that take place in rap lyrics and in music industry boardrooms as artists negotiate more control in their contracts. I have addressed the mainstream rap star's interactions with wealth, but I also examined those artists who challenge the hyper-consumerist image. These artists share a focus on the material conditions that frame the production of their music. Hip hop addresses its own production more directly and extensively than any other form of music has done, and by this very virtue, lives on.

As hip hop lives on into the future, I end this book with the question of what will happen to hip hop in the years to come. In the introduction, I mentioned the Nielsen Soundscan report that rap sales dropped 20.7% from 2005–2006. As Nas argues that commercialism killed the culture of hip hop, should we take this as a sign of good things to come? Will hip hop return to its roots outside the mainstream—to mixtapes and block parties—or will hip hop music adapt to the changing landscape of mainstream music? In the introduction, I compared Nas's *Hip Hop is Dead* album to "The Day Disco Died," a 1979 promotional effort to drive a nail into the coffin of disco music, which did not survive into the 1980s as a distinct genre or movement. Now, in the conclusion, I extend this comparison to a third popular music genre—punk—which was faced with similar death pronouncements in the early 1980s. In 1981, faced with the emergence of the genres of New Wave, Post-punk, and Hardcore, The Exploited released their debut album, *Punks Not Dead*. The album became that year's number one independent album in the United Kingdom, yet despite the defiance of its title, punk was, in many ways, dead to the mainstream. A number of new musical genres that had grown out of punk replaced much of the punk that had been played on British radio, but punk's spirit lived on in many of these new variants, and punk, in its original form, survived in the underground through a system of independent record labels in the U.K. and U.S.

So if disco died and punk's not dead, where does that leave hip hop? Disco left the airwaves, and while its influence is felt in the contemporary genres of techno, house, and electronica, disco itself disappeared. Punk, on the other hand, went back underground, but continued to thrive via independent labels both before and after it resurfaced on mainstream radio with groups like Green Day in the 1990s. Hip hop has survived in the mainstream much longer than disco or punk. Like punk, it has spawned new subgenres and seen its styles influence rock music, even as many artists still claim to adhere to the original form of hip hop rather than any of its new variants. Punk's history mirrors the developments hip hop saw during 2003–2007, an era in which much of the hip hop on the radio began to fit more into the subgenres of Crunk, Bounce, Snap, Reggaeton, and Hyphy. Yet hip hop, inside and outside these new subgenres, still lives. Commercial success didn't kill hip hop music, and a commercial decline won't either. Despite the waxing and waning of mainstream interest, hip hop will live on.

NOTES

INTRODUCTION

1. When I talk about the music, I'll use hip hop and rap as synonyms, the way they have been used most consistently across the history of the music's lyrics.

2. Critics such as David Toop even attribute the creation of hip hop music to the musicians' lack of resources. Toop claims that hip hop was invented as a way for inner-city youths to make music with limited access to traditional instruments (15). In Joseph G. Schloss's *Making Beats*, however, rap artists Prince Paul and DJ Kool Akiem challenge the notion that rap music was created because of poverty (Schloss 28–30). Paul and Akiem show that not only did most early DJs have access to traditional instruments in their schools, but that hip hop production equipment in fact cost *more* than traditional instruments.

3. Reed, "Airing Dirty Laundry," 181.

4. My use of "self-styled success" develops from Jeffrey Louis Decker's *Made in America: Self-Styled Success from Horatio Alger to Oprah Winfrey.*

CHAPTER 1: THE RAP CAREER

1. Scholars such as Tricia Rose and Russell A. Potter theorized hip hop's resistance, while more recent studies by Krims and Negus challenged earlier theories of hip hop's resistance, and focused on hip hop's growth as an industry.

2. Krims, *Rap Music and the Poetics of Identity*, 1.

3. For further examples of print journalists' criticisms of hip hop excess, see Wedge, E12, and Izrael, B13.

4. For examples in other forms of music, see Graham Parker's "Mercury Poisoning" (1979), The Sex Pistols' "EMI" (1977), and Aimee Mann's "Calling it Quits" (1999).

5. Judy, 216.

6. Negus, in "The Music Business and Rap: Between the Street and the Executive Suite," is skeptical, not recognizing the advances hip hop has made toward

artists' control of their musical production. Negus argues that rap artists seek both autonomy and recognition from corporate labels, and he identifies a hip hop business model that "challenges tales of co-optation, exploitation, and forced compromise" (Negus 492). Yet in the end, he believes that "the making of rap is managed by the music industry," and that "major companies tend to *allow* rap" certain levels of independence because it furthers their own commercial agendas (Negus 503, 500, emphasis in original). Although Negus does acknowledge the efforts hip hop artists make to challenge corporate music, he finds their efforts ineffective, and believes the artists are duped by industry executives who co-opt their work. Dipa Basu, in "What is Real About 'Keeping it Real'?," challenges such a reading in her study of black entrepreneurship within hip hop, where she identifies "entrepreneurial strides, in a context of systematic racism" and argues that, "On an unprecedented level African Americans are making business footholds in the music industry; rappers and black rap entrepreneurs are transgressing cultural boundaries, and the boundaries between business, pleasure and politics" (Basu 372).

7. Negus articulates hip hop's "deliberate attempts to maintain a distance between the corporate world and the genre culture of rap." (Negus 488.)

8. While the Fatback Band's King Tim III (Personality Jock) was released prior to "Rapper's Delight," in 1979, making it the first rap record ever released, its commercial success and cultural impact did not match that of Sugarhill Gang's "Rapper's Delight," which technically is rap's second commercial release.

9. Gilroy, 73.

10. Smith, 348.

11. Neal, 161.

12. Henry Louis Gates defines Signifyin(g) as "the figure of the double-voiced," a process by which texts speak to other texts (Gates xxv). Gates identifies the function of revision in Signifying (Gates 88–94), and argues that a motivated Signifying "functions to redress an imbalance in power, to clear a space, rhetorically" (Gates 124). Kopano, Potter, and Wheeler each connected hip hop rhetoric to the tradition of Signifying. Wheeler uses Gates' reading of Mikhail Bakhtin's dialogism in its connections to African-American rhetoric, yet her study came too early to fully engage the current dialogue over commercialism that I take on as my subject here.

13. Baldwin, 4.

14. See Trilling, *Sincerity and Authenticity: The Charles Eliot Norton Lectures, 1969–1970*, for a detailed history of these terms.

15. Armstrong, 7–8.

16. McLeod, 139.

17. Krims, 95.

18. Frith, 71.

19. Stratton, "Between Two Worlds: Art and Commercialism in the Record Industry," 12.

20. Ano, "Count Bass D: Down for the Count."

21. Because of a conflict with a West Coast reggae group using the same name, Common Sense changed his name to Common on 1997's *One Day It'll All Make*

Sense. Many fans and other artists still refer to him by his original artist name, Common Sense, as Jay-Z does in the lyrics to which I refer in this chapter.

22. See Brian Morrisey, "Coke Adds Interactive Fizz to New Ad Campaign," *Internet News.Com* (January 10, 2003), http://boston.internet.com/news/article.php/1567731.

23. Fricke and Ahearn, 28: "I was giving parties to make money, to better my sound system. I was never a DJ for hire. I was the guy who rent the place. I was the guy who got flyers made. I was the guy who went out there in the streets and promote it. You know? I'm just like a person who bring people together, like an instrument, an agent who bring people together and let 'em have fun. But I was never for hire. I was seeing money that the average DJ never see. They was for hire, I had my own sound system. I was just the guy who played straight-up music that the radio don't play, that they should be playin', and people was havin' fun."

24. Davey D. "March Letters."

25. Merwin, 33.

26. Baudrillard, 12–13.

27. Auslander, 71.

28. Rosaldo, 69.

29. Fernando, "Back in the Day," 21.

30. Gracyk, 75.

31. Auslander, 65 (emphasis in original).

32. Davey D. "An Historical Definition of the Term Rap."

33. Christian, Margena A. "Has Hip Hop Taken a Beating, Or Is It Just Growing Up?" *Jet* 111:14 (2007): 54–59.

CHAPTER 2: THE RAP LIFE

1. bell hooks examines the continuing allure of crime for young black men, and she argues that, "A shift in class values occurs in black life when integration comes and with it the idea that money is the primary marker of individual success, not how one acquires money" (hooks 18).

2. David Buxton traces the roots of the rock star lifestyle and its visibility of wealth to the manufacture of the American dream in the 1930s, and to the star's role in promoting consumption (Buxton 432). Buxton shows that, in the 1960s, stars rejected rock's increasing commercialization as they promoted the "internal convictions of the *artist,*" rather than an outward style that showcased their wealth (Buxton 436).

3. To historicize such a performance, Brent Wood links gangsta rap's "violent and misogynist hyperbole" to a tradition of boasts, toasts, and bad man legends used throughout African-American folklore in stories about fearless men like Stackalee (Wood 134–135).

4. In one theory of how rap artists construct credibility, Adam Krims proposes that hip hop necessitates a "symbolic collapsing" of the artist onto the performer, so that in lyrics the artist must appear to speak "from authentic experience" (Krims 95).

5. Lejeune, 5–6.

6. Allan Moore theorizes a first-person authenticity for popular music through which artists convey to their listeners that they are speaking sincerely and with a personal integrity (Moore 214).

7. De Man, "Autobiography as De-Facement," 920.

8. "Rapper Ice-T Defends Song Against Spreading Boycott," *New York Times* (June 19, 1992): C24.

9. Shank, Notes.

10. Kopano, 211–212. Kopano historicizes the naming of hip hop artists in connection to black radio personalities of the 1950s and '60s, and to traditions of African-American rhetorics. Hip hop artists take on titles like Dr. Dre or Mixmaster Ice to assert their "talents and expertise." Kopano also cites black traditions of semantic inversion by which groups like N.W.A., OutKast, or Black Sheep flip slurs to reclaim the power of the words.

11. Eakin, *Fictions in Autobiography: Studies in the Art of Self-Invention*, 3–4.

12. This metaphor of music as drug fits with Tricia Rose's concept of hip hop's "sociology-based crime discourse," in Rose, 237.

13. Conway, 19–20.

14. Carol Ohmann understands *The Autobiography of Malcolm X* as a "parodic inversion" of the life-as-journey tradition (Ohmann 136), a reading extended by Eakin in his discussion of Malcolm's descent into a life of crime (Eakin 185).

15. Applying such a construct to hip hop, Davarian Baldwin argues that the rap hero seeks to achieve wealth outside the means of the middle class (Baldwin 138).

16. McLeod identifies Will Smith's *Big Willie Style* (1997) as a response to critics that had accused him of selling out (McLeod 144–145), and Krims illustrates that many fans turned against Ice Cube as he started to focus more heavily on his acting career, and as his music moved more into the realm of dance or party rap, rather than the hardcore or gangsta style he became known for in his early recordings. According to Krims, certain fans point to his early work as "the real Ice Cube," and see his later work as something less than authentic (Krims 95).

17. Rosenblatt, 171.

18. Alex Haley and Malcolm X, 381. Rosenblatt identifies this unique phenomenon within the endings of black autobiographies, while other critics also have paid particular attention to the ways autobiographies end. De Man argues that the quality of autobiography lies in its power to shake up how we view plot and endings, because any ending is simply a choice, and the life is still in motion (De Man 922). Eakin reads Malcolm X's anticipation of death as lending to the narrative a finality and "posthumous authority" unavailable to more conventional endings (Eakin 182). Rosenblatt, though, theorizes all autobiography as an "extended suicide note" where authors narrate a life as completed to a certain point, which becomes the end of the narrative (Rosenblatt 178).

19. Rosenblatt, 179.

20. Sway Calloway, "Jay-Z: 99 Problems, Hundreds of Rumors," http://www.mtv.com/bands/j/jay_z/99_problems/.

CHAPTER 3: THE RAP PERSONA

1. Trilling, 8.

2. Ibid., 120.

3. Krims proposes that for the rap listener to accept that a performer is credible, there must be a "symbolic collapsing" of the artist onto the performer (Krim 99).

4. Just as hip hop values a collapsing of performer and artist, Auslander finds that "rock ideology demands parity between the performer's stage and private personae, even if that parity is wholly illusory" (Auslander 89). Auslander finds significant the fact that 1970s rock artists like David Bowie "were more concerned to create spectacular stage personas than images of authenticity" (Auslander 89).

5. Rose applies James Scott's investigation of power relationships through social transcripts to acknowledge rap music's "hidden transcript" of resistance, which plays a key discursive role, outside of the music's direct critique of oppression in the public transcript, in engaging in "symbolic and ideological warfare with institutions and groups that symbolically, ideologically, and materially oppress African Americans" (Rose 100–101). Potter explores rap music as radical postmodernism, and he synthesizes Theresa L. Ebert's dichotomy of ludic versus resistance postmodernism to argue that hip hop culture often stages resistance through play itself. For Potter, rap music's resistance through play can become "the mask for a potent mode of subversion" (Potter 2).

6. Majors and Billson present a history of black masking and black acting, tactics through which "roles, facades, shields, fronts, and gaming helped to ensure survival" (Majors and Billson 60) as African-Americans faced systemic racism in daily life. Majors and Billson cite black authors James Baldwin—who believed whites accepted the mask as an authentic performance—and Richard Wright—who defined masking as a kind of black acting that "entails hiding deepest reactions from those who have the power to punish them" (Majors and Billson 62).

7. See Diehl, 125–127.

8. McLeod, Hip Hop, 140.

9. Peterson, 20.

10. Diehl, 125.

11. Potter views hip hop as a "collective work" comprised of several characters rather than attributed to a single author. For Potter, the costume is central to hip hop's ludic resistance, and performers stage characters through their fashion—for example, in the way gold chains, untied Adidas sneakers, black leather jackets, and fedoras mark Run DMC. Through performed characters, hip hop "*stages* the difference of blackness, and its staging is both the Signifyin(g) of its constructedness *and* the site of its production of the *authentic*" (Potter 121–122).

12. This same issue is addressed in 3rd Bass's "The Gas Face" (1989) and The Pharcyde's "It's Jiggaboo Time" (1992). Marla L. Shelton explores music video representation of the African-American *female* body, yet these artists, along with Digital Underground, show that concerns with black body image in video extend to the male performer as well.

13. Potter, 112.

14. Potter, 113.

15. Lichtman, 16.

16. Recalling Du Bois and Frantz Fanon, Marc Singer theorizes "The idea of the split identity, one of the most definitive and distinctive traits of the superhero, is also one of the most powerful and omnipresent figures used to illustrate the dilemmas and experiences of minority identity" (Singer 113). Singer's study of race in comic books develops the concept of the "costumed identity," in which superheroes (and supervillains) experience "a noticeable and visually characterized division between their private selves and their public, costumed identities" (Singer 113). Singer claims that superhero identities, although not necessarily always secret, must by nature be split in that they cannot reconcile the fantastic with the everyday. Such reasoning for split identity of the comic book character contrasts Krims' idea of a necessary identity-collapsing of the hip hop performer and artist, for whom the everyday is a commodity.

17. Negus has criticized what he calls "fun capitalism" theories of hip hop (Negus 492), as he cites Ann Marlowe's reading of rap as business made to look like fun (Marlowe 223).

18. Rose states, "Commercial marketing of rap music represents a complex and contradictory aspect of the nature of popular expression in a corporation-dominated information society" (Rose 17), yet she and Forman disagree on issues of corporate appropriation and exploitation in the development of rap music into a viable industry. Forman complicates the relationship between hip hop and the market as he challenges Rose's idea of an appropriative, profit-driven media industry rushing to cash in. Although he agrees rap music has been exploited by the corporate music industry, Forman at the same time attributes rap's expansion into an industry to "entrepreneurs...participants and fans" from within hip hop culture itself (Forman 107).

19. Potter sees rap music as a counter-capitalist, rather than anti-capitalist, enterprise. He asserts that "hip hop is not merely a critique of capitalism, it is a counter-formation that takes up capitalism's gaps and contradictions and creates a whole new mode, a whole new economics" (Potter 111).

CHAPTER 4: SAMPLING AND STEALING

1. Foucault, 52.

2. Ibid., 125. Schumacher, 180, and Porcello, 77, each cited Foucault (his name *and* ideas) in their studies of sampling. Schumacher argued that songs built from samples are not granted an author function. Porcello used Foucault's theory to outline the shortcomings of copyright systems; he found sampling to resist capitalist notions of property through its "previously tabooed modes of citation" (Porcello 69).

3. Schloss, 105.

4. Ibid., 120.

5. RZA, *The Wu-Tang Manual*, 191.

6. Connors, 239.

7. Ibid., 219.

8. Ibid., 238.

9. Foucault, 52.

10. Armstrong, at 7-8, describes the importance of Eminem's links to "an original source of rap" through his work with Dr. Dre, who pioneered the West Coast gangsta rap sound in the 1980s. Dre produced Eminem's albums and performs with him on stage. Dre's sponsorship and collaboration authenticate Eminem to listeners who doubt the credibility of white hip hop artists.

11. Gates, 88.

12. Ibid., xiv.

13. Gilroy, 104.

14. Porcello, 69.

15. Rose, 237.

16. Josh Tyrangiel, "In the Doctor's House: A Visit to Dr. Dre's Recording Studio Reveals That He Eats, Drinks and Sleeps Rap—and Rarely Rests," *Time*, http://www.time.com/time/musicgoesglobal/na/mdre.html.

CHAPTER 5: WHITE RAPPERS

1. Krims, 154–57. Krims notes in his discussion of Canadian, Dutch, and French rap that the image of African-American hip hop as "real" hip hop prevails (Krims 154–57).

2. Ibid., 7.

3. Sartwell, 4.

4. Ibid., 7 (emphasis in original).

5. Critics have addressed this racial tension when writing on related subjects. In 1968, for example, Richard Gilman published an article in the *New Republic* which argued that white scholars should not write about black autobiography (Banks 202). Ishmael Reed claims that white jazz critics have misunderstood and misrepresented the music, and that "most jazz criticism is a form of white-collar crime" (Reed xvi). The tension extends to black scholars whose ideas seem to fit too well within the white academy. In the 1980s, Joyce A. Joyce criticized Henry Louis Gates and Houston Baker, whom she accused of writing about black subjects using the theoretical apparatus of the white academy.

6. Ibid., 4.

7. Amanda Lee Myers, "Ariz. Cop Had Black Men Rap Away Ticket," *Associated Press* (December 2, 2006).

8. Jonathan Rowe, "The Greek Chorus, Jimmy the Greek Got It Wrong But So Did His Critics—Jimmy Snyder and His Views on Pro Sports and Race," *Washington Monthly*, April 1988.

9. Perkins, 1A.

10. Ibid., 1A.

11. Saw, 52; Popkin, 33; and Mills, G10.

12. McLeod, 139.

13. Armstrong, 7–8.

14. This construction of the authentic reflects Peterson's definition of country music authenticity as "being believable relative to a more or less explicit model, and at the same time being original, that is not being an imitation of the model. Thus what is taken to be authentic does not remain static but is renewed over the years" (Peterson 220).

15. Even in the Eminem era, Imani Perry argues that "hip hop music is black American music" (Perry 10). Perry acknowledges that her position is unpopular among critics who privilege hip hop's hybridity and recover the histories of multi-cultural involvement in the culture's creation. Counterhistories by Juan Flores and Nancy Guevara, for example, argue for Puerto Ricans' and women's creative roles in the development of hip hop, which has been attributed most widely to African-American males.

16. Deena Weinstein historicizes this tension as she describes white artist covers of black R&B groups in the 1950s in terms of record labels' efforts to modify the original songs to reach a "wider and whiter" (Weinstein 139) audience. Her pairing of the terms wider and whiter speaks for popular music's concept of a white mainstream.

17. The question of whiteness's visibility has sparked scholarly debate. Richard Dyer notes the "invisibility of whiteness as a racial position in white (which is to say dominant) discourse" (Dyer 3). "Whiteness," as Dyer uses it here, refers both to an identity and to a system of advantage based on racial identities. White identity gets erased in white discourse as it becomes the default racial position, and the social privilege which comes with whiteness remains unspoken among whites. Peggy McIntosh investigates the invisibility of white privilege and argued that white people don't see the privilege they carry with them into job interviews, loan applications, etc. (McIntosh 1–2). Ruth Frankenberg, though, has revised her own position now to see whiteness as very visible, and to see its invisibility as a "white delusion" (Frankenberg 73) under which scholars such as herself have operated. Frankenberg now sees whiteness in a continuing state of "marking and cloaking" (Frankenberg 74). Frankenberg's current position fits closest with my own, and her idea of marking and cloaking complicates whiteness as a racial position in hip hop, where artists have obscured their white privilege, made white identity a selling point, and even argued that underneath their white skin they are essentially black. Most importantly, Vanilla Ice's failed cloaking of his "white" background brought the question of white authenticity to the surface.

18. George, 66.

19. George, 57.

20. Rubin, 126.

21. Diehl, 124. Matt Diehl and Crispin Sartwell share Q-Tip's view that the Beasties made no attempt at blackness. Each critic suggests, however, that the Beasties adopted vocal styles to emphasize their whiteness. Diehl cites their "'white' accents" (Diehl 123), and Sartwell argues that "they *try* to sound *extremely* white" as opposed to Vanilla Ice, who attempted to mimic black vocal styles (Sartwell 171).

22. Mike D., 8.

23. Light, "The Story of Yo," 153.

24. Light, "The Story of Yo," 153.

25. Beastie Boys. "Ill Communication." Letters to the Editor. *Spin* 14:10 (October 1998).

26. Brown, N11.

27. Phillip Auslander cites Paul Theberge's theory that Milli Vanilli was scandalous for listeners because music was becoming increasingly digitized and because music's performance culture was giving way to the recorded to such an extent that even live concerts were delivered via recording (Auslander 86).

28. Kennedy, E1.

29. Tricia Rose argues that Vanilla Ice's simulation made the ghetto "a source of fabricated white authenticity," and that his controversy "highlights the significance of 'ghetto blackness' as a model of 'authenticity' and hipness in rap music" (Rose 11). Murray Forman illuminates the important role of the social and geographic location for hip hop artists; the ghetto for Vanilla Ice, however, served as a marketing tool for an outside artist, and this breach spawned a crisis of authenticity for the white rapper. Forman explained that "MC Hammer and Vanilla Ice were more frequently cast as the scapegoats for rap's slide into a commercial morass. In one of the worst imaginable accusations in hip hop, both were regularly accused of selling out the culture and the art form" (Forman 216).

30. Coady, D1.

31. Brown, N11.

32. For example, David Mills's article, "Another Round of White Rappers in Search of 'Black Authenticity'" opens: "Remember that flash flood of white rappers last year? When record companies (and a few black producers), covetous of Vanilla Ice's multi-platinum success, foisted upon the pop market such wannabe mike-wreckers as Jesse Jaymes, Icy Blu, J.T. and Young Black Teenagers? The only one to hit was Marky Mark, whose rhyming skills would've gotten a black man nowhere" (Mills 610).

33. Popkin, 33.

34. Kohan, 38.

35. Harrison, 13.

36. Rogers, 35.

37. Rogers, 32.

38. Duster, 113.

39. Critics disagree on the ways whites confront their own social advantage. George Lipsitz argues that "white Americans are encouraged to invest in whiteness, to remain true to an identity that provides them with resources, power, and opportunity" (Lipsitz vii). Duster, on the other hand, sees white privilege as involuntary, and asserts that "whites who have come to a point where they acknowledge their racial privilege are in a difficult circumstance morally because they cannot just shed that privilege with a simple assertion of denial" (Duster 114).

40. Armstrong, 342.

41. Watts, 5.
42. Watts, 20.
43. Mills, G1.
44. Light, "Ice-T," 31.
45. Rose, 7–8.
46. hooks, *Outlaw Culture: Resisting Representations*, 129.
47. Ibid.
48. Armstrong, 339.
49. White, 198.

CHAPTER 6: HIP HOP, WHITENESS, AND PARODY

1. This definition develops from Henry Louis Gates's theories of Signifying in African-American literature. Gates, along with Geneva Smitherman (118-34), finds parody to be a key part of Signifying, as authors revise and distort other texts. Gates developed his definition of parody from Mikhail Bakhtin's "parodic narration," by which authors repeat the words of another text but use their own voices to oppose the intent of the original, and "hidden polemic," by which authors allude to, rather than repeat, the words of another text (Bakhtin 185–87). Gates acknowledges that "Signifyin(g), of course, is a principle of language use and is not in any way the exclusive province of black people, although blacks named the term and invented its rituals" (Gates 90).

2. Cowan, 339.

3. Baldwin argues that with "Me, Myself, and I," De La Soul "attempted to open a space where blackness could be understood through parody and the interrogation of multiple identities within hip hop" (Baldwin 4). Baldwin further contends that De La Soul introduced a class consciousness to hip hop as the group parodied rap's performance of ghetto authenticity from their "relatively affluent Long Island background" (Baldwin 4).

4. Diehl, 123.
5. Armstrong, 21.
6. Cowan, 41.
7. Ibid., 41.
8. *MC Paul B.,* http://www.mcpaulbarman.com/audio.html.
9. Eddy, http://www.livoice.com/issues/0029/eddy.shtml.
10. Weisbard and Marks, 359.
11. Weinstein, 138.
12. Negus, 498.
13. Weinstein, 141.
14. Ibid., 145–46.
15. Ibid., 144.
16. Diehl, 125.
17. Craine, "Interview: Dynamite Hack."
18. Ibid.
19. Coker, 257.

20. Diehl, 128–29.

21. Basham.

22. Ibid.

23. Davis, "Dre's Advice to Dynamite Hack," http://www.launch.com/music/content/newsDetail/0,2820,true_6696_,00.html.

24. Coker, 257.

25. Ibid., 258.

26. Kelley, 137.

27. Ibid., 137.

28. Diallo, 317.

BIBLIOGRAPHY

Adorno, Theodor, and Max Horkheimer. "The Culture Industry: Enlightenment as Mass Deception." From *Dialectic of Enlightenment*, 1944. Translation by John Cumming. London: Verso, 1979.

ANO. "Count Bass D: Down for the Count." http://www.alphabeats.com/interviews/artists/bassd.htm (February 13, 2005).

Armstrong, Edward G. "Eminem's Construction of Authenticity." *Popular Music and Society* 27:3 (Fall 2004): 335–55.

Auslander, Philip. *Liveness: Performance in a Mediatized Culture.* New York: Routledge, 1999.

Bakhtin, Mikhail. "Discourse Typology in Prose." *Readings in Russian Poetics: Formalist and Structuralist Views.* Edited by L. Matejka and K. Pomorska. Cambridge, Mass.: MIT, 1971: 176–95.

Baldwin, Davarian L. "Black Empires, White Desires: The Spatial Politics of Identity in the Age of Hip-Hop." *Black Renaissance* (July 31, 1999): 138–51.

Banks, William M. *Black Intellectuals: Race and Responsibility in American Life.* New York: W. W. Norton, 1996.

Basham, David. "Dynamite Hack on Avoiding 'Gangsta' Vid for 'Boyz.'" *MTV News Gallery* (June 1, 2000; September 15, 2000). http://www.mtv.com/sendme.tin?page=/news/gallery/d/dynamite000601.html.

Basu, Dipannita. "What is Real About 'Keeping it Real'?" *Postcolonial Studies* 1:3 (1998): 371–87.

Basu, Dipannita and Pnina Werbner. "Bootstrap Capitalism and the Culture Industries: A Critique of Invidious Comparisons in the Study of Ethnic Entrepreneurship." *Ethnic and Racial Studies* 24 (2001): 236–62.

Baudrillard, Jean. *Simulacra and Simulation.* Translation by Sheila Faria Glaser. Ann Arbor: University of Michigan Press, 1994.

Benjamin, Playthell. "Two Funky White Boys." *Village Voice* (January 9, 1990): 32–35.

Beastie Boys. "Ill Communication." Letters to the Editor, *Spin* 14:10 (October 1998).

Beastie Boys. "James Newton vs. Beastie Boys." (September 17, 2002) Available at http://www.beastieboys.com.

Binder, Amy. "Constructing Racial Rhetoric: Media Depictions of Harm in Heavy Metal and Rap Music." *American Sociological Review* 58:6 (1993): 753–67.

Bronson, Fred. *Billboard's Hottest Hot 100 Hits.* New York: Billboard (2003).

Brown, Joe. "Crossing Over and Cashing In." *Washington Post* (January 18, 1991): N11.

Buxton, David. "Rock Music, the Star System, and the Rise of Consumerism," in *On Record: Rock, Pop, & the Written Word*, edited by Simon Frith and Andrew Goodwin, 427–40. New York: Pantheon, 1990.

Campbell, James T. "Hip-Hop Community Can't Have it Both Ways on Rap." *The Houston Chronicle* (October 18, 2004): B9.

Coady, Elizabeth. "Dress Reversal: Some High School Students Defy Class and Clothing Labels in Cross-Cultural Fashion Statements." *Atlanta Journal-Constitution* (February 20, 1992): D1.

Coker, Cheo Hodari. "NWA." *Vibe History of Hip-Hop*, edited by Alan Light. New York: Vibe, 1999: 251–63.

Connors, R. "The Rhetoric of Citation Systems, Part II: Competing Epistemic Values in Citation." *Rhetoric Review* 17(2) (1999): 219–45.

Conway, Jill Ker. *When Memory Speaks: Reflections on Autobiography.* New York: Knopf, 1998.

Count Bass D. Personal communication with the author, March 26, 2004.

Cowan, Matthew. "All About the Benjamins: Some of the Biggest Names in Hip-Hop are Jewish. Just Not the Ones on Stage." *Heeb: The New Jew Review* 4 (Fall 2003): 38–43.

Craine, Charlie. "Interview: Dynamite Hack." *Hip Online* (July 24, 2000; September 20, 2000). http://www.hiponline.com/artist/music/d/dynamite_hack/interview/100143.htm.

Davey D. "March Letters." November 10, 2004. http://www.daveyd.com/marchletters.html.

———. "An Historical Definition of the Term Rap." November 10, 2004. http://www.daveyd.com/whatisrapdav.html.

Davis, Darren. "Dre's Advice to Dynamite Hack." *Launch* (May 22, 2000; August 10, 2000). http://www.launch.com/music/content/newsDetail/0,2820,true_6696_,00.html.

de Certeau, Michel. *The Practice of Everyday Life.* Berkeley: University of California Press, 1984.

Decker, Jeffrey Louis. *Made in America: Self-Styled Success from Horatio Alger to Oprah Winfrey.* Minneapolis: University of Minnesota Press, 1997.

DeCurtis, Anthony. "Word." *Vibe History of Hip-Hop*, edited by Alan Light. New York: Vibe, 1999: 91–99.

de Man, Paul. "Autobiography as De-Facement." *MLN* 94 (1979): 919–30.

Diallo, David. "Dr. Dre & Snoop Dogg." In *Icons of Hip-Hop: An Encyclopedia of the Music, from Kool Herc to Kanye West*, edited by Mickey Hess. Westport, CT: Greenwood, 2007: 317–40.

Diehl, Matt. "Pop Rap." *Vibe History of Hip-Hop*, edited by Alan Light. New York: Vibe, 1999: 121–33.

Dimitriadus, Greg. *Performing Identity/Performing Culture: Hip-Hop as Text, Pedagogy, and Lived Practice*. New York: Peter Lang, 2001.

DONMEGA. "DYNAMITE HACKS ARE RACIST MOTHER FUCKERS!!!!" Dynamite Hack Bulletin Board. July 2, 2000. http://www.dynamitehack.com/bbs.

Drumming, Neil. "The Nerd Behind the Mask." *Village Voice* 46:32 (August 14, 2001).

Du Bois, W. E. B. *The Souls of Black Folk: Essays and Sketches*. 1903. New York: Dodd, Mead, 1961.

Duster, Troy. "The 'Morphing' Properties of Whiteness." In *The Making and Unmaking of Whiteness*, edited by Birgit Brander Rasmussen, et al. Durham: Duke University Press, 2001: 113–37.

Dyer, Richard. *White*. London: Routledge, 1997.

Eakin, Paul John. *Fictions in Autobiography: Studies in the Art of Self-Invention*. Princeton: Princeton University Press, 1985.

———. "Malcolm X and the Limits of Autobiography." In *Autobiography: Essays Theoretical and Critical*, edited by James Olney. Princeton, NJ: Princeton University Press, 1980: 181–93.

Ebert, Theresa L. "Writing the Political: Resistance (Post)modernism." Address delivered at a conference on "Rewriting the Postmodern: (Post)Colonialism/Feminism/Late Capitalism." University of Utah, Salt Lake City. March 30, 1990.

Eddy, Chuck. "Singles Again." *Village Voice* (September 10, 2000; September 27, 2000) http://www.livoice.com/issues/0029/eddy.shtml.

Fanon, Frantz. *Black Skin, White Masks*. Translation by Charles Lam Markmann. New York: Grove, 1967.

Fernando, S.H., Jr. *The New Beats*. New York: Doubleday, 1994.

———. "Back in the Day: 1975–1979." *Vibe History of Hip-Hop*, edited by Alan Light. New York: Vibe, 1999: 13–21.

Fiske, John. *Power Plays, Power Works*. London: Verso, 1993.

Flores, Juan. "Puerto Rocks: New York Ricans Stake Their Claim." In *Droppin' Science: Critical Essays on Rap Music and Hip-Hop Culture*, edited by William Eric Perkins. Philadelphia: Temple University Press, 1996: 85–105.

Forman, Murray. *The 'Hood Comes First: Race, Space, and Place in Rap and Hip-Hop*. Middletown, Conn.: Wesleyan University Press, 2002.

Foucault, Michel. "Prison Talk." *Power/Knowledge: Selected Interviews and Other Writings 1972–1977*, edited by Colin Gordon. Brighton: Harvester, 1980: 37–54.

——— "What is an Author?" *The Essential Foucault*, edited by Paul Rabinow. New York: New Press, 2003: 101–20.

Frankenberg, Ruth. "The Mirage of an Unmarked Whiteness." In *The Making and Unmaking of Whiteness*, edited by Birgit Brander Rasmussen. Durham: Duke University Press, 2001: 72–96.

Fricke, Jim, and Charlie Ahearn, eds. *Yes Yes Y'all: The Experience Music Project Oral History of Hip-Hop's First Decade*. New York: Da Capo Press, 2002.

Frith, Simon. *Performing Rites: On the Value of Popular Music*. Cambridge: Harvard University Press, 1996.

Gates, Henry Louis, Jr. *The Signifying Monkey: A Theory of African-American Literary Criticism*. New York: Oxford University Press, 1988.

George, Nelson. *Hip-Hop America*. New York: Penguin, 1999.

Gilroy, Paul. *The Black Atlantic: Modernity and Double-Consciousness*. Cambridge, Mass.: Harvard University Press, 1993.

Goedde, Brian. "Behind The Iron Mask: MF DOOM Faces Art's Volatility." *The Stranger*, August 16, 2001. http://www.thestranger.com/2001-08-16/music3.html.

Gordon, Colin. "Preface." *Power/Knowledge: Selected Interviews and Other Writings 1972–1977*, edited by Colin Gordon. Brighton: Harvester, 1980: vii–x.

Gracyk, Theodore. *Rhythm and Noise: An Aesthetics of Rock*. Durham, N.C.: Duke University Press, 1996.

Grand Upright vs. Warner. (1991). 780 F. Supp. 182 (S.D.N.Y. 1991).

Guevara, Nancy. "Women Writin' Rappin' Breakin'." In *Droppin' Science: Critical Essays on Rap Music and Hip-Hop Culture*, edited by William Eric Perkins. Philadelphia: Temple University Press, 1996: 49–62.

Harper, Phillip Brian. *Are We Not Men?: Masculine Anxiety and the Problem of African-American Identity*. New York: Oxford University Press, 1996.

Harrison, Nancy. "Unknown Rapper Gets a Shot." *New York Times* (July 28, 1991): 12LI:13.

Hesmondhalgh, David. "Indie: The Institutional Politics and Aesthetics of a Popular Music Genre." *Cultural Studies* 13:1: 34–61.

hooks, bell. *Outlaw Culture: Resisting Representations*. New York: Routledge, 1994.

———. *We Real Cool: Black Men and Masculinity*. New York: Routledge, 2003.

Ignatiev, Noel. *How the Irish Became White*. New York: Routledge, 1996.

Izrael, Jimi. "Hip-Hop Needs More Than a Good Beat to be a Political Force: Bling-Bling and Ching-Ching are No Substitutes for a Civic Education." *Los Angeles Times* (August 27, 2004): B13.

Judy, R.A.T. "On the Question of Nigga Authenticity." *boundary 2* (1994): 211–31.

Kelley, Robin D. G. "Kickin' Reality, Kickin' Ballistics." *Dropping Science*, edited by William Eric Perkins. Philadelphia: Temple University Press, 1996.

Kelly, Katy. "Marky Regrets Remarks." *USA Today* (February 19, 1993): 2D.

Kennedy, Bud. "The Ice Man Cometh Clean: Vanilla Ice Says He's Not Another Milli Vanilli." *San Francisco Chronicle* (November 22, 1990): E1.

Kloer, Phil. "25 Years of Hip-Hop: For Many, Hip-Hop's Excess is Too Much of a Good Thing." *Atlanta Journal-Constitution* (September 27, 2004): Living, 1E.

Kohan, Te. "Icy Rapper Fears Black Backlash." *Miami Herald Sun* (September 5, 1991): 38.

Kolawole, Helen. "Comment & Analysis: Keeping it in the Family: Eminem is Under Fire for Denigrating Black Women. That's the Job of Black Rappers." *The Guardian* (November 24, 2003): http://arts.guardian.co.uk/features/story/0,11710,1091934,00.html.

Kopano, Baruti N. "Rap as an Extension of the Black Rhetorical Tradition: 'Keepin it Real.'" *Western Journal of Black Studies* 26 (2002): 204–15.

Krims, Adam. *Rap Music and the Poetics of Identity.* Cambridge: Cambridge University Press, 2000.

Lejeune, Phillipe. *On Autobiography.* Minneapolis: University of Minnesota Press, 1989.

Lemke, Thomas. "Foucault, Governmentality, and Critique." Paper presented at the Rethinking Marxism Conference, University of Amherst (Mass.), September 21–24, 2000.

Lichtman, Irv. "Elektra Pulls KMD Disc." *Billboard* 106:16 (April 16, 1994).

Light, Alan. "Introduction." In *Vibe History of Hip-Hop*, edited by Alan Light. New York: Vibe, 1999.

———. "The Story of Yo." *Spin* 14:9 (September 1998): 146–61.

———. "Ice-T." *Rolling Stone* 20 (August 20, 1992): 31–32, 60.

Lipsitz, George. *The Possessive Investment in Whiteness: How White People Profit from Identity Politics.* Philadelphia: Temple University Press, 1998.

Majors, Richard and Janet Mancini Billson. *Cool Pose: The Dilemma of Black Manhood In America.* New York: Touchstone, 1993.

Malcolm X and Alex Haley. *The Autobiography of Malcolm X.* New York: 1973.

Marlowe, Ann. "The Hermeneutics of Rap." In *Rap on Rap: Straight-Up Talk on Hip-Hop Culture*, edited by Adam Sexton. New York: Delta, 1995.

McIntosh, Peggy. "White Privilege: Unpacking the Invisible Knapsack." *Peace and Freedom* (July and August 1989): 10–12.

McLeod, Kembrew. "Authenticity Within Hip-Hop and other Cultures Threatened with Assimilation." *Journal of Communications* 49 (1999): 134–50.

MC Paul B. http://www.mcpaulbarman.com/audio.html.

Merwin, Scott. "From Kool Herc to 50 Cent, the Story of Rap, So Far (Bustin' Rhymes/First in a Three Part Series)." *Pittsburgh Post-Gazette* (February 15, 2004). http://www.post-gazette.com/ae/20040215rap0215aep1.asp.

Mike D. "A Quick Talk With Q-Tip from A Tribe Called Quest." *Grand Royal* 1 (Fall/Winter 1993): 8.

Mills, David. "Another Round of White Rappers in Search of 'Black Authenticity.'" *Washington Post* (August 30, 1992): G10.

———. "It's a White Thing; Is It Serious Hip-Hop or a Pale Imitation?" *Washington Post* (July 14, 1991): G1.

Moore, Allan. "Authenticity as Authentication." *Popular Music* 21.2 (2002): 209–23.

Neal, Mark Anthony. "Sold Out on Soul: The Corporate Annexation of Black Popular Music." *Popular Music and Society* 21.3 (1997): 117–36.

Negus, Keith. "The Music Business and Rap: Between the Street and the Executive Suite." *Cultural Studies* 13:3, 1997: 488–508.

Ohmann, Carol. "The Autobiography of Malcolm X: A Revolutionary Use of the Franklin Tradition." *American Quarterly* 22 (1970): 131–49.

Paniccioli, Ernie and Kevin Powell, eds. *Who Shot Ya? Three Decades of Hip-Hop Photography.* New York: Amistad, 2002.

Perkins, Ken Parish. "Under Raps: Hot Pop Vocalist Vanilla Ice Shrugs Off Conflicting Versions of His Background." *Dallas Morning News* (November 18, 1990): 1A.

Perry, Imani. *Prophets of the Hood: Politics and Poetics in Hip-Hop.* Durham: Duke University Press, 2004.

Peterson, Richard A. *Creating Country Music: Fabricating Authenticity.* Chicago: University of Chicago Press, 1997.

Popkin, Helen. "Beating the Rap on Style." *St. Petersburg Times* (February 14, 1992): 33.

Porcello, Thomas. "The Ethics of Digital Audio Sampling: Engineer's Discourse." *Popular Music* 10(1) 1991: 69–84.

Potter, Russell A. *Spectacular Vernaculars: Hip-Hop and the Politics of Postmodernism.* Albany: SUNY Press, 1995.

Pough, Gwendolyn. *Check It While I Wreck It: Black Womanhood, Hip-Hop, and the Public Sphere.* Boston: Northeastern University Press, 2004.

Powers, Ann. "Rap and Rock's Bad Date." *Rolling Stone* (September 2000): 172.

"Rapper Ice-T Defends Song Against Spreading Boycott," *New York Times* (June 19, 1992): C24.

Reed, Ishmael. "Introduction." *The Reed Reader.* New York: Basic, 2000.

———. "Airing Dirty Laundry." *The Reed Reader.* New York: Basic, 2000.

Rice, Jeff. "The 1963 Hip-Hop Machine: Hip-Hop Pedagogy as Composition." *College Composition and Communication* 54(3) 2003: 453–71.

Rogers, Ian. "What's My Name? Yo! Kid! Rock!" *Grand Royal* 4, 1999: 30–35.

Rosaldo, Renato. "Imperialist Nostalgia." In *Culture and Truth.* Boston: Beacon, 1989: 68–87.

Rose, Tricia. *Black Noise: Rap Music and Black Culture in Contemporary America.* Middletown, Conn.: Wesleyan University Press, 1994.

Rosenblatt, Roger. "Black Autobiography: Life as Death Weapon." In *Autobiography: Essays Theoretical and Critical*, edited by James Olney. Princeton, NJ: Princeton University Press, 1980: 169–80.

Royster, Jacqueline Jones. *Traces of a Stream: Literacy and Social Change Among African American Women.* Pittsburgh: University of Pittsburgh Press, 2000.

Rubin, Mike. "Beastie Boys." In *Vibe History of Hip-Hop*, edited by Alan Light. New York: Vibe, 1999: 126–27.

RZA. *The Wu-Tang Manual.* New York: Penguin, 2004.

Sanford, Jason. "Support for Brad Vice and a Few Words on Sampling." *Story South.* November 6, 2005. Available at http://www.storysouth.com/comment/2005/11/support_for_brad_vice_and_a_fe_1.html.

Sartwell, Crispin. *Act Like You Know: African-American Autobiography & White Identity.* Chicago: University of Chicago Press, 1998.

Saw, T. "Beasties Rap It Up in Rhythm." *Miami Herald Sun* (August 13, 1992): 52.

Schloss, Joseph G. *Making Beats: The Art of Sample-Based Hip-Hop.* Middletown, Conn.: Wesleyan University Press, 2004.

Schumaker, Thomas. "'This is a Sampling Sport': Digital Sampling, Rap Music, and the Law in Cultural Production." *Media, Culture, and Society* 17(2) 1995: 253–73.

Scott, James C. *Domination and the Arts of Resistance: Hidden Transcripts.* New Haven: Yale University Press, 1990.

Second Hand Songs: A Cover Songs Database. "Nautilus, by Bob James." Available at http://www.secondhandsongs.com/song/5463.html.

Shank, Barry. "Fears of the White Unconscious: Music, Race, and Identification in the Censorship of 'Cop Killer.'" *Radical History Review* 66 (1996): 124–45.

Shelton, Marla L. "Can't Touch This! Representations of the African-American Female Body in Urban Rap Videos." *Popular Music and Society* 21 (Fall 1997): 107–16.

Singer, Marc. "'Black Skins and White Masks: Comic Books and the Secret of Race." *African American Review* 36.1, 2002: 107–19.

Sirc, Geoffrey. "Stagolee as Writing Instructor." *Enculturation* 4:2 (Fall 2002). Available at http://enculturation.gmu.edu/4_2/sirc/.

Smith, Christopher Holmes. "Method in the Madness: Exploring the Boundaries of Identity in Hip-Hop Performativity." *Social Identities* 3.3, 1997: 345–75.

Stone, Albert E. "Patterns in Recent Black Autobiography." *African American Autobiography: A Collection of Critical Essays,* edited by William L. Andrews. Englewood Cliffs, N.J.: Prentice Hall, 1993.

Stratton, Jon. "Between Two Worlds: Art and Commercialism in the Record Industry." In *Popular Music: Critical Concepts in Media and Cultural Studies,* edited by Simon Frith. New York: Routledge, 2003.

Terrell, Tom. "The Second Wave: 1980–1983." *Vibe History of Hip-Hop,* edited by Alan Light. New York: Vibe, 1999: 43–51.

Theberge, Paul. *Any Sound You Can Imagine: Making Music/Consuming Technology.* Hanover, N.H.: Wesleyan University Press, 1997.

Trilling, Lionel. *Sincerity and Authenticity: The Charles Eliot Norton Lectures, 1969–1970.* Cambridge, Mass.: Harvard University Press, 1972.

Vineyard, Jennifer. "N.W.A.'s MC Ren Disses Dynamite Hack." *S.V.P. News Archives* (May 2000; September 9, 2000) http://www.svprecords.homestead.com/may.html.

Wahl, Greg. "'I Fought the Law (and I Cold Won!)': Hip-Hop in the Mainstream." *College Literature* 26.1, 1999: 98–112.

Watts, Eric. "Border Patrolling and 'Passing' in Eminem's 8 Mile." *Critical Studies in Media Communication* 22.3 (2005): 187–206.

Wedge, Dave. "Gangsta Clichés Reign on 'R.U.L.E.'" *Boston Herald* (December 10, 2004): E12.

Weinstein, Deena. "The History of Rock's Pasts Through Rock Covers." *Mapping the Beat,* edited by Thomas Swiss, John Sloop, and Andrew Herman. Oxford: Blackwell, 1998: 137–51.

Weisbard, Eric and Craig Marks, eds. *Spin Alternative Record Guide*. New York: Vintage, 1995.

Wheeler, Elizabeth. "Most of My Heroes Don't Appear on No Stamps: The Dialogics of Rap Music." *Black Music Research Journal* 11:2 (1991): 193–216.

White, Evelyn C. "The Poet and the Rapper." *Essence* 1 (May 1, 1999): 122–24, 194–200.

Wood, Brent. "Understanding Rap as Rhetorical Folk Poetry." *Mosaic: A Journal for the Interdisciplinary Study of Literature* 32:4 (1999): 129–46.

Wright, Richard. "Blueprint for Negro Writing." *New Challenge* 2 (Fall 1937): 53–65.

Young, R. C. "A Charming Plagiarist: The Downfall of Brad Vice." *New York Press* 19:2 (January 11–17, 2006). Available at http://www.nypress.com/18/48/news&columns/RobertClarkYoung.cfm.

INDEX

About the Author

MICKEY HESS is Assistant Professor of English at Rider University, and the editor of Greenwood Press's *Icons of Hip Hop: An Encyclopedia of the Movement, Music, and Culture.*